ALSO BY CLAUDIA ROTH PIERPONT

Passionate Minds: Women Rewriting the World

Roth Unbound: A Writer and His Books

AMERICAN RHAPSODY

AMERICAN RHAPSODY

WRITERS, MUSICIANS, MOVIE STARS, AND ONE GREAT BUILDING

CLAUDIA ROTH PIERPONT

FARRAR, STRAUS AND GIROUX   NEW YORK

Farrar, Straus and Giroux
18 West 18th Street, New York 10011

Published in 2016 by Farrar, Straus and Giroux
First paperback edition, 2017

Many of these essays were previously published,
in slightly different form, in *The New Yorker.*

The Library of Congress has cataloged the hardcover edition as follows:
Pierpont, Claudia Roth.
    [Essays. Selections]
    American rhapsody : writers, musicians, movie stars, and one great
building / Claudia Roth Pierpont.
        pages   cm
    Includes index.
    ISBN 978-0-374-10440-5 (hardback) — ISBN 978-0-374-70877-1 (e-book)
    1. Authors, American—20th century—Biography.   2. Performing arts—
20th century—Biography.   3. Popular culture—United States—20th century.
I. New Yorker.   II. Title.

PS129 .P53 2016
810.9'005—dc23
[B]
                                                        2015036371

Paperback ISBN: 978-0-374-53694-7

Designed by Jonathan D. Lippincott

Our books may be purchased in bulk for promotional, educational, or business use.
Please contact your local bookseller or the Macmillan Corporate and Premium
Sales Department at 1-800-221-7945, extension 5442, or by e-mail at
MacmillanSpecialMarkets@macmillan.com.

www.fsgbooks.com
www.twitter.com/fsgbooks • www.facebook.com/fsgbooks

For Etta and William,
Lena and Albert,
and for Lucy,
who became Americans

CONTENTS

AMERICAN
RHAPSODY

INTRODUCTION

American Rhapsody was George Gershwin's original title for the revolutionary work that his brother Ira persuaded him to name, instead, *Rhapsody in Blue*. Gershwin wanted to call his jazzy masterpiece "American" because he'd conceived it as "a musical kaleidoscope of America—of our vast melting pot, of our unduplicated national pep, of our blues, our metropolitan madness." And, musically speaking, a "rhapsody" is a sequence of distinctive parts, not as formally structured as a symphony but held together, in Gershwin's case, by recurring themes; it was a form that left the composer room for spontaneity and digression within the story he had to tell. Gershwin's work also fulfills the celebratory promise that the nonmusical idea of rhapsodizing holds for us. His kaleidoscopic America reflects all the romance and bright innocence that the young musical genius could summon in 1924, when both he and the country were coming into their own. A true melting-pot portrait, the *Rhapsody* mixes jazz and Rachmaninoff and Tin Pan Alley with unself-conscious freedom. It's the creation of an American as proud and grateful and ecstatically wondering as only a child of immigrants could be.

The immigrant's exaltation of America is a well-known, even common component of our national story (quite apart from the genius that Gershwin brought to it). My grandmother, a Polish Jewish immigrant, used to tell of the journey she made across Europe, from Krakow to Cherbourg, alone, in the early 1920s. Her train arrived late at the French port city, and, in a panic, without a word of French, all she could do in the hope of finding the ship on which she had booked passage was to run through the streets near the port, shouting, "America?!" For the rest of her life, she spoke in a way that could undoubtedly be called rhapsodic about the country that had saved her. Gershwin's father, a penniless immigrant from St. Petersburg, began his American life in the 1890s, working in a shoe factory in New York City. He had gone through a number of occupations—the alternatives seemed endless—by the time that, in 1910, he and his wife bought a piano for the family's Lower East Side apartment. More than a musical instrument, it was a symbol of the opportunities they had made possible for their sons.

But there are, of course, very different kinds of American stories. James Baldwin's stepfather, the son of a slave, came north from New Orleans in the 1920s, another sort of immigrant. The Harlem community into which Baldwin was born, in the year of *Rhapsody in Blue*, was a haven only when compared with the violent racial nightmare of the "old country" his stepfather had escaped. There has never been any doubt that it is possible for two people of different races or conditions to live in the same time and more or less the same place and yet inhabit two different Americas. It is possible even for one person to inhabit two Americas: Peggy Guggenheim grew up on New York's wealthy Upper East Side, but her family was turned out of a hotel in Vermont for being Jewish no less firmly than Baldwin was turned away from a New Jersey diner for being black. Guggenheim eventually helped establish the canon of modern American art, and Baldwin, with his vision of a shared and mutually beneficial future, helped sustain a belief in the country through the racial traumas of the sixties. Yet both Guggenheim and Baldwin ultimately left America for good, as did several others whose stories constitute the cultural history chronicled in this book.

It came as a surprise, when I surveyed the completed book, that figures who emerged from backgrounds of immigrant success (including F. Scott Fitzgerald, on his Irish Catholic mother's side; and Guggenheim, through both of her German Jewish grandfathers) contrasted not only with long-settled Yankees and Midwesterners (Katharine

Hepburn, Orson Welles, Marlon Brando) but with Americans who fled the country with something like the desperation of those who had traveled half the world to get here and then stayed away for the rest of their lives. Edith Wharton and Nina Simone, this collection's chronological bookends, were as different as two women could be, and so were their reasons for leaving. Setting off for France in 1906, Wharton, a wealthy novelist from East Coast aristocracy, was escaping the social and cultural backwardness of American society. Simone, a Southern-born black musician, moved to France some seventy years later to escape the racial prejudice of the country that she called "the United Snakes of America." And there are others, temporary exiles, for whom leaving the country was the only way to see it clearly or to do the kind of work that seemed prohibited by American provincialism or economics. Fitzgerald also fled to France, on the counsel of his friend Edmund Wilson, to write the serious book he could never manage on these shores—it turned out to be *The Great Gatsby*, the ultimate portrait of the American dream gone awry—and Orson Welles, drummed out of Hollywood, made his two greatest Shakespeare films overseas. Considering the number of figures here who fled or did their finest work elsewhere, this collection might have been named not for Gershwin's *Rhapsody* but for one of Baldwin's novels, *Another Country*.

And yet *this* country is the place where these individuals became who they were. And they reflected this country in so much of what they did: its optimism, its energy, its ruthlessness. If this book is not always a celebration, it is nevertheless a rhapsody in the sense that its stories are linked by recurring themes and problems, forming sequences and cycles and sometimes even marking progress. Not that I began with any master plan, beyond the exercise of certain interests and instincts in the choice of subjects—subjects that, as the book progressed, came to seem like individual plants connected by systems of underground roots. The shattered gentility of so many of Edith Wharton's early twentieth-century heroines, for example, caught between familiar if confining customs and the rising demands for personal happiness and sexual freedom, leads within a generation to the flapper hedonism of Zelda Fitzgerald, and is transformed further, in the thirties and forties, into the movie-screen-sized command of Hepburn and the dangerous dames of Dashiell Hammett's hard-boiled world—where women are wholly free and wholly terrifying. The process then starts all over with the domestic absolutes of the 1950s, which made even Hepburn into a timorous spinster, in *Summertime*, released in 1955, by which time Hepburn herself could not find any Hepburn roles to play.

Other sequences: the changes in American language as the home-grown novel took up new spheres of experience, from Fitzgerald to Hammett to Baldwin; the first modern American school of painting coming into focus at the same time as the first-ever American school of acting—Jackson Pollock, Marlon Brando—and together producing a new style of artistic masculinity; the recurring hope for an American classical theater, and how its failure may relate to this new style of acting. There is also sustained and undeniable progress from the segregated turn-of-the-twentieth-century theater in which Bert Williams began his career and the humiliating screen roles, decades later, that made Stepin Fetchit a byword for racial pandering, to the civil rights legislation of the 1960s and the outspokenness of Baldwin and Simone. The essays about these four figures inevitably deal with the growth of the civil rights movement. A related historical thread runs through them, too, about the race riots that have plagued the country, including the widespread attacks by white mobs during the early decades of the century—in New York City, in 1900, Bert Williams's theatrical partner, George Walker, was dragged off a streetcar and beaten—through what Baldwin called the "slave rebellions" of the sixties, when Nina Simone stood on a stage in Detroit, just two weeks after a five-day riot had left the city in ruins, and told an enthusiastic concert crowd, "Detroit, you did it . . . I love you, Detroit—you did it!"

All these pieces were published in *The New Yorker*, although many have been subject to considerable revision, updating, and amplification; the piece on Bert Williams is almost entirely new. Williams, the first black American celebrity entertainer, is the least known figure in the book. He has received a great deal of scholarly attention since I first wrote about him, in 2005, and an important early film of his has been discovered. His life seems to me revelatory in terms of the ways that African Americans moved onto the national stage—literally and metaphorically—in the years when the country was becoming recognizably modern, and his career laid the groundwork for those of Baldwin and Simone. By happenstance, this book contains a larger number of male subjects than female, one Englishman—Laurence Olivier—allowed in for comparative purposes on the subject of acting and directing Shakespeare, and one essay about an enormous inanimate object, the Chrysler Building. The only skyscraper ever to be viewed as distinctly female, the Chrysler may somewhat redress the gender imbalance, and also add to the book's series of paradigmatic American couples: Scott and Zelda, Tracy and Hepburn, Hammett and Lillian Hellman, the Chrysler and the Empire State Building.

Writing about the Chrysler Building was an extraordinary experience. At the time, in 2002, there was not a single book available on the world-famous building aside from the volume of photographs that was the occasion for this essay, and no book or any serious work on its architect, William Van Alen. (There was a fine biography of its patron, Walter Chrysler.) This mysterious neglect became part of the story, for which my primary sources were contemporary accounts in newspapers and architectural journals. But this is not what made the experience unique. At a fairly late point in my research, I found myself caught between countering claims: the Art Deco Society of New York announced that the building's owner, Tishman Speyer, had destroyed the once-glorious triplex Cloud Club on floors sixty-six through sixty-eight, within the Chrysler's silvered crown; Tishman Speyer claimed that the space was untouched but closed to the press, and a leading architectural critic claimed it "partly survived." Whom to believe?

In *The New Yorker*'s traditional division of forces, I am a critic rather than a reporter, but here I was compelled to change hats, because I couldn't bear to tell readers that I'd heard contradictory reports and didn't know the truth. Security in the building that fall was high. Pretending to myself that I was some mixture of Brenda Starr and Janet Malcolm, I interviewed building tenants and learned of a single place where it might be possible to gain access to the fire stairs. Loitering discreetly until I was alone; pushing a door and being suddenly inside; climbing madly, fueled by so much adrenaline that at first I went right past my goal; and then pushing another couple of doors . . . The answer to what I found is contained in the essay. But, as many mountain climbers say, by the time I came down I felt I had been transformed. Unlike most mountain climbers, however, I was also grateful not to have been arrested.

I received some informative responses to these pieces when they first appeared. A whiskey-voiced woman who'd been "Dash's secretary" called to let me know that "Lillian" hadn't lifted a finger to get Hammett out of jail and that, in her experience, she was even worse than people said. I heard from Shirin Devrim, the Turkish actress who had met James Baldwin at a party in Istanbul, on the first weary night of his arrival, in 1961, and in whose lap he had fallen asleep. Devrim was ninety-three when she wrote to me and was living on Beekman Place, in New York City, where I was lucky to have tea with her and hear her memories of Baldwin and Istanbul. On the other hand, a number of surprisingly angry letters arrived when I identified Nick and Nora's dog Asta, in *The Thin Man*, as a schnauzer. Here, at last, I get to present the evidence in the opening of Hammett's chapter 4: "This afternoon I took Asta for a walk," Nick relates, and "explained to two people that she was a Schnauzer and not a cross between a Scottie and an Irish terrier." It is not entirely clear what deep-seated Hollywood prejudice led to the role of Asta being played on the screen by a wire fox terrier, but what is clear is that Americans are crazy about their dogs. Nothing else I've written has come close to earning me such scorn.

In sum, this book is about ideals and ambition and alcohol and heartbreak and hard work and a great open expanse of country that promised everything even when delivering bloody intolerance. Orson Welles believed, not unreasonably, that Shakespeare was, in his soul, an American; Baldwin wondered if the red earth of Georgia was produced by the blood of the bodies of the black men hanged there. These essays are inevitably about the joy and profit of being an invented and a heterogeneous people, and the immense difficulty of this human experiment, too. The subjects of race and ethnicity kept surfacing while I was writing, in often unexpected and involuted ways: Virgil Thomson accuses *Porgy and Bess* of being racially offensive while employing anti-Semitic insults about Gershwin; Nina Simone's most innocent hit, the joyous "My Baby Just Cares for Me"—surely, I thought, no racial issues here—turns out to have been introduced by Eddie Cantor wearing blackface in the 1930 movie *Whoopee!*, a cowboy musical about a forbidden romance between a white girl and an Indian (who turns out really to be white); Olivier's heavily blacked-up performance as Othello, released on film in 1965, the year of the Selma-to-Montgomery march, was almost unwatchable to a number of people because Olivier so resembled what *The New York Times* called "an end man in an American minstrel show." There is no way of getting around our history.

But this book is also about individuals who overcame tremendous odds, many of them internal, to create works that have lasted: books and songs and films and architecture that have become the common air we breathe and that we call a culture. There is genius here but also failure, and plenty of it. These figures are embedded, as we are, in the continuing struggle to live up to our ideals and failing and beginning again and again from a position just a little closer to the American rhapsody that Gershwin imagined.

CRIES AND WHISPERS
EDITH WHARTON

Edith Wharton, 1905

W riting a story called "Beatrice Palmato," Edith Wharton got no further than an outline and a single two-page scene, exquisitely detailed and explicitly pornographic, in which a father lovingly completes the sexual initiation of his daughter. The date of composition is uncertain, and has been almost as hotly debated as the significance of the story since it was discovered among Wharton's papers more than forty years ago. R.W.B. Lewis first published the fragments in his Pulitzer Prize–winning biography, in 1975, along with newfound evidence that Wharton, in middle age, had carried on a wildly passionate, adulterous love affair—from 1908 to 1910, or, roughly, between *The House of Mirth* and *Ethan Frome*—and the paired disclosures revolutionized the image of America's literary dowager queen. Wharton was suddenly up-to-date: familiar, approachable, a woman with her hair coming undone and her priorities in equally fetching disarray. Even feminist critics claimed that the sexual revelations made her "more intriguing and more likable" and allowed us to view her "with new compassion and increased respect." One could reasonably fear for Wharton's new likability when Shari Benstock's 1994 biography, a work of careful if killjoy revisionism, argued that the notorious affair had been more talk than action and the action confined to just a few nights. Wharton would have understood all too well the threat of inverted scandal, the implicit diminution. As a prophet of the female condition, she had noted wearily, back in 1915, "What a woman was criticized for doing yesterday she is ridiculed for not doing today."

There has been no place for "Beatrice Palmato" in the various collections of Wharton's stories that have appeared since its discovery; it is hardly more than a sketch, after all, the most famous story that she never wrote. But, like E. M. Forster's openly homosexual novel, *Maurice*, or the swooningly homoerotic letters of Henry James, or Virginia Woolf's memoir of childhood sexual abuse—all posthumously published, for good and ill—its existence has inevitably cast a lurid glare across the rigorously controlled and nuanced works that define the writer's achievement. Wharton's eighty-five published stories reflect a lifetime's occupation, extending from her first story to appear in print, in 1891, to one that she sent to her agent just before her death, in 1937. Aside from the sheer pleasure she took in their creation, they served their author at various times as a workshop for her novels, or as a means of earning quick money—Wharton was one of the highest-paid short-story writers in America—or as an emotional release that was unavailable to her in any other way. Far more than her novels, the stories are rooted in the fluctuations of her life; the longer, richer works, though unquestionably her greater accomplishment, stand at a magisterial remove. In the wake of "Beatrice Palmato," scholars have scoured the stories for telltale signs of father-daughter incest. But readers are apt to be struck with the exposure of far-more-everyday varieties of horror: moral cowardice; being unloved or unloving; making rational compromises in order to live and discovering that one has reasoned one's life away; and enduring unendurable loneliness, which Wharton seems to have done from 1891 to 1937.

Her life was, to all appearances, brilliantly social and successful—hardly a writer's life at all. Born into the commercial aristocracy of New York City in 1862, Edith Newbold Jones was the only daughter of a woman so fashionable that she was rumored to have made "keeping up with the Joneses" a proverbial necessity. Edith's father was a being of a different order: a devourer of books on exotic travel, deeply moved by Tennyson, a man who taught his small daughter to read and who might have embraced a literary life if his wife had not been closed to all it represented. At least this was how their daughter depicted the mismatched pair, in a memoir written during the last years of her life. There is some evidence that Lucretia Rhinelander Jones was not entirely indifferent to her daughter's literary calling; she did, for example, have a volume of Edith's adolescent *Verses* privately printed. What Wharton best remembered, though, was her mother's stern discouragement. Edith's father, the tall and blue-eyed George Frederic Jones, has left few records. Anything beyond what his daughter intended to reveal must be sought in what she may have revealed without intention.

The unearthing of "Beatrice Palmato" did not bring biographers to believe, en masse, that Edith Wharton had been the victim of her father's sexual advances. Lewis was quick to assert that the incest motif was "pure and utter fantasy." Cynthia Griffin Wolff, who discovered the fragment, wrote that, biographically, it provided no more than "an aperçu into the wellsprings of the girl's fantasy life," and Wharton's most recent biographer, Hermione Lee, takes a similar position. But some scholars have gone a more literal route. The legitimate desire to redress long-held, Freud-sanctioned doubts about women's reports of early abuse has led, alas, to the wresting of sexual "facts" from the haziest of fictions. Barbara A. White, the author of the only book-length study of Wharton's stories, strenuously argues for linking Wharton's identity with the ravished Beatrice, on the basis of evidence that becomes less convincing with every stretch on the rack of interpretation. Dead husbands, claustrophobic wives, anything remotely resembling a secret, even a voice speaking a foreign language on a radio: all become "a perfect paradigm for child sexual abuse." One cannot state with certainty that White is wrong, but with a different selection of plot details, one could as easily "prove" that Wharton had borne an illegitimate child or committed a murder.

Still, might there be something more to those dead husbands and claustrophobic wives? Edith Jones was twenty-three when, abandoned by two earlier suitors, she married the guileless and hapless Edward Wharton, a decision that Henry James would later call the "inconceivable thing." The marriage was a disaster: intellectually, emotionally, and, above all, sexually. Setting down the particulars forty-nine years later, Wharton reserved all blame for her mother, writing that Lucretia's refusal to answer her desperate questions, on the eve of her wedding, about what happened between married men and women "did more than anything else to falsify and misdirect my whole life." After what seems to have been one or two attempts at grappling with their mysterious bodies, Teddy and Edith lived together in celibacy for twenty-eight years.

Perhaps the only thing more difficult to conceive is how all this may apply to literature. And yet it is undeniably striking that among the four major female writers in the English language of this period—Virginia Woolf, Willa Cather, Gertrude Stein, and Wharton—there was so astoundingly little practicing of heterosexuality, so much aversion to the male. If one accepts Woolf's account of her early abuse by her stepbrothers, and the intimations of abuse by an uncle to be found in Stein, it is Wharton's two-year affair with a man rather than the possibility of incest in her childhood that is the truly anomalous part of her experience. The causes of these sexual unorthodoxies may be a matter for psychologists, but the results are a matter for us all. It seems fair to say that, in the generation that made the dangerous crossing from the nineteenth century into modernity, an ambitious woman who wanted to write could choose any but the traditional feminine role, and suffer anything but thralldom to a man. Lesbianism, celibacy, repression, suppression, stepbrothers, uncles, trauma: How many books do we owe them?

"The marriage law of the new dispensation will be: *Thou shalt not be unfaithful—to thyself.*" So concludes the speech of a powerful drawing-room orator on the subject of "the new ethics" in a story called "The Reckoning," which Wharton published in 1902, when she was forty and had been married for seventeen years. Divorce was in many quarters still a scandal but no longer an impossibility. The quest for personal fulfillment—even, in some ways, the sexual revolution—had begun. Divorce in all its ramifications is one of the constant themes of Wharton's fiction, and, even at her most satiric, she gives it something of the anguished moral weight that abortion has for us today. Obviously, it was a matter of much personal relevance. In her earliest stories, a weak husband is compared to a grandmother and a poodle before he turns up as a corpse, stiffening in an upper berth while accompanying his wife on a train home to New York. Wharton declined to include these stories in her first collection because she found them so emotionally overwrought. From the time of her marriage, in 1885, through nearly the turn of the century, she wrote stories and poetry only sporadically—when she needed to, it might be said. This lack of steady focus was partly due to the social schedule of a wealthy young lady of good family, and partly due to the fact that the young lady kept breaking down.

Throughout this period, Wharton suffered the classic symptoms of hysteria: asthma—literally, she could not breathe—an inability to eat, and a depression so increasingly dire that, in 1898, she underwent a version of the standard "cure" (Woolf was given much the same treatment), consisting of isolation, bed rest, no writing, and much food. This happened on the brink of the publication of her first collection of stories, which doubtless added to the state of her nerves, since she was convinced that "there isn't a single sentence in the book with natural magic in it." As it happened, the reviews were so radiantly encouraging that she set to work at last on a long-delayed novel and was, basically, as strong as a horse for the rest of her life. Not so Teddy, who began to crumble almost as soon as his wife started thriving. Over the next decade, she published some thirty stories and three novels, while he acquired a full complement of the symptoms she had overcome.

Her first collection is, in fact, one of the best she ever published and contains several indisputable marvels. "The Pelican," "Souls Belated," and "The Muse's Tragedy" are enormously varied in color and tone, and yield an equally varied series of insights into women's hearts and strategies. The first is a character portrait, as startlingly fresh as a Sargent watercolor, of a doting mother who turns to public speaking in order to support her son, and who cannot admit that she comes to love the work rather more than she does him. The second, a socially inflected romance of the kind that Wharton was to make her own, tells of a married woman who runs away with her lover and discovers what Anna Karenina could not bear to know—that love feeds on the duties and distractions of a shared society ("those common obligations which make the most imperfect marriage in some sort a centre of gravity"). The third is a rich reimagining of a genre belonging to James, in which a poet's muse, looking back, rues the inspiration she has given.

Wharton was not by any standard measure a feminist. The muse's tragedy is not the fact that she is not a poet herself but that the poet never loved her as a woman. The public speaker is ridiculously bad at the work she can't bear to give up. But no one between Nietzsche and Simone de Beauvoir was so ruthlessly clear in depicting the deforming effects of social history on the human female, in examining the dreadful methods she has been constrained to use to obtain the trivial things she has been taught to want. And no one has given us so many ways to love and to hate, often simultaneously, the weak, manipulative, pitiful, dangerous, and beautiful creatures this history produced.

The great women writers of the English tradition have always been eager to express their disdain for the conventionally desirable, professionally feminine women of their day. This less than sororal attitude goes back at least to Jane Eyre's contempt for the meretricious arts and curls of the undeniably magnificent Blanche Ingram ("Miss Ingram," thanks to her moral faults, "was a mark beneath jealousy") and to George Eliot's poisonous Rosamond Vincy in *Middlemarch*, patting her fair hair and despoiling her husband's soul. A secondary character by necessity, the conniving woman is the one sitting across the room, batting her eyes at the hero while the far more worthy authoress watches and writhes and plots her revenge in print. Wharton has often been criticized for a lack of sympathy for her characters. But, in daring to place the fashionable beauty at the center of her story, she was offering a glimpse into a rarely visited consciousness, far more complex, if not assuredly more noble, than it had ever been taken to be.

Wharton's most forthright statement about this woman is contained in a buoyant little satire titled "The Other Two," of 1904. The story traces a man's growing awareness that his beloved wife has not only climbed her way to wealth, husband by husband, but easily adapted herself to be a perfectly fitting mate to each. "Her elasticity was the result of tension in too many different directions. Alice Haskett—Alice Varick—Alice Waythorn—she had been each in turn, and had left hanging to each name a little of her privacy, a little of her personality, a little of the inmost self where the unknown god abides." In Wharton's strongest novel, *The House of Mirth*, published just a year after this story, the heroine, Lily Bart, similarly "disciplined by years of enforced compliance," pretends not to smoke or gamble or think in order to catch a rich and priggish bore. ("We could none of us imagine your putting up with him for a moment," a friend remarks, "unless you meant to marry him.") But Lily, Wharton's most profound and subtle portrait of a lady, is as repulsed by her slavish tactics as she is dependent on their results. And in Wharton's world, the conflict ensures that she will not survive.

But, then, in Wharton's world, all the alternatives are bleak. The essential experience behind every choice is loneliness. Wharton's first published story, "Mrs. Manstey's View," written when she was twenty-eight, is about an old lady so alone that her nearest connections are with the magnolia and the caged parrot that she sees from the window of her New York rooming house. Marriage possibly makes things worse. Wharton was an admirer of George Eliot's observation that "marriage is so unlike anything else. There is something even awful in the nearness it brings." Yet she added to this her own belief that love outside a marriage-like union simply made for a different sort of misery, characterized by a starved inadequacy of common bonds. In her work, the explicit unhappiness of a marriage often forms a major premise of the action. And yet divorce, for all of Wharton's brooding on it as a subject and her tacit support of it as a right, is possibly the most fearsome enterprise of all.

Wharton concludes "The Reckoning" with a stunning social prophecy, delivered by the drawing-room orator's wife, a woman who left her own boring husband years before to marry this ardent freethinker, and who is devastated now at being left, in her turn, for a more exciting, younger woman. "The law represents material rights," she begins, threading her way hesitantly through her thoughts. "It can't go beyond. If we don't recognize an inner law . . . the obligation that love creates . . . being loved as well as loving . . . there is nothing to prevent our spreading ruin unhindered . . . is there?"

Edmund Wilson observed, rather testily, just a few years after Wharton's death, that "there are no first-rate men" in her novels.

No heroes: no Mr. Darcy, no Mr. Rochester, no Will Ladislaw or Tom Outland, no one even to offer a hand and help the lady out. In *The House of Mirth*, Lily Bart is badly damaged by the man who, in the work of another novelist, might have carried her away. Lawrence Selden, Lily's companion, offers her the regard of a connoisseur admiring an exquisite bit of animated porcelain, a regard that he nevertheless encourages her to confuse with love. It is Selden's peculiar function to draw out Lily's feelings and to continually subvert her marital plans, while refusing to make any claim on her himself. Instead, he presents her with sublime, if hypocritical, ideals—indifference to money, to society—which serve only to mock the realities that she confronts. ("Why do you make the things I have chosen seem hateful to me," Lily cries, "if you have nothing to give me instead?") Whether Selden is cruel or a coward or simply unable to love the heroine as she might wish—or, perhaps, as he might wish—is left to the reader to decide. Wharton herself vacillates; as much as Lily and Selden, she seems uncertain about what this character intends by his soul-shattering advances and retreats.

There are several versions of this "negative hero," as Wharton referred to Selden, in her early stories, in which he may be said to form an equally sorry counterpart to the marital corpse. The muse of "The Muse's Tragedy" seeks to forgive the poet: "He had never made love to me; it was no fault of his if I wanted more than he could give me." In "The Touchstone," published in 1900, a great woman novelist also suffers the pain that such a negative hero inflicts: "the physical reluctance"—on his part—"had, inexplicably, so overborne the intellectual attraction, that the last years had been, to both of them, an agony of conflicting impulses." When Wharton attempts the man's point of view—as late as 1912, in "The Long Run"—there is no further enlightenment. All he recalls of fleeing an ideal romance at its sexual threshold is panic, numbness, and loss. Of course, this lack of comprehension must be qualified: this is all that Wharton allows him to recall. The confusion remains very much her own.

What is this man afraid of? What is it that he, or Wharton, cannot express? It is odd that critics and biographers, who have made so much of Wharton's dependence on James, have failed to fix on the crucial similarity between her "negative hero" and the emotionally deadlocked, sexually barricaded heroes of the Master—heroes whose homosexual desires, like James's, are concealed within a jungle of verbal circumlocution. Wharton has no such verbal screens in her stylistic repertoire. But the logical inconsistencies and emotional riddles of *The House of Mirth*, and of several early stories, become equally understandable if seen in the light of the unadmitted homosexuality of her leading man. Diana Trilling, writing half a century ago, in a social climate that accepted James as celibate for the sake of his art—rather than, as he is seen today, sexually suppressed for the sake of his culture—viewed Lawrence Selden as a portrait of James himself, in all his moral elevation and aesthetic piety. This cannot be accurate: the type occurs in Wharton's stories well before she became a friend of James's, in 1904. Yet there is a larger accuracy in the notion that Wharton was caught up with a Jamesian hero in the flesh.

Wharton's friend and first biographer, Percy Lubbock, identified "the dry and narrow and supercilious" Walter Berry (himself a friend of James's and of Proust's) as the invariable model for Wharton's misbegotten hero. Berry was the first man Wharton loved. In 1883, she had waited in vain for him to propose; instead, he'd fled without a word and kept away for fourteen years. By the time he returned, she was long married, he was a "confirmed bachelor," and their friendship resumed the overtones, if not the substance, of romance. She considered him her best literary adviser, but whatever comments he may have made about his baleful appearance in her work went up in smoke; Wharton burned all but the most innocuous of their letters. (The heroine of "The Muse's Tragedy," publishing her letters from the poet, fills them with phony ellipses to suggest intimacies that never existed; one cannot help wondering whether Wharton burned Berry's letters for what they didn't say.) On Berry's death, in 1927, Wharton requested that his ashes be scattered over the garden of her home in France. His funeral wreath, however, was placed by his executor and loving cousin, the bohemian expatriate Harry Crosby, on the grave of Oscar Wilde.

Wharton did not burn her so-called love diary—a little volume begun in 1907, filled with dizzyingly joyous and tortured entries addressed to an anonymous man—but left it among her papers, clearly marked: "The Life Apart." Because Wharton had written extensively and adoringly of Berry in her memoirs, several scholars assumed, after the diary's discovery, that he was the lover who had brought her to this frenzied state. It is even possible that Wharton intended the misidentification, as a sort of posthumous bibliographic consummation. But the distinction of breaking the pattern of sexual thwartedness and giving Wharton her first experience of a "positive hero" actually belonged to a man she did not mention at all.

W harton tried to get Morton Fullerton to return her letters, but he had, apparently, too much pride and too much of a sense of history (and perhaps its dollar value) to do it; more than three hundred of them can now be read in university collections. He also preserved the private, often frankly sexual poems that she wrote for him, carefully copying them out and annotating the date and sometimes the occasion before returning them to her as she had requested. Fullerton, like Berry, was an American and a friend of Henry James's, but there the resemblance ends. Wharton's biographers tend to refer to him as a Lothario or a Don Juan, and a biography of Fullerton himself, by Marion Mainwaring, labels him a lifelong "victim of devotion." Lanky, fair, and psychologically canny, Fullerton seems to have known how to make himself irresistible to everyone, male and female. He often juggled two or three affairs at a time, and his range extended from Oscar Wilde's friend Lord Ronald Gower (the reputed model for Wilde's Lord Henry Wotton, who lures Dorian Gray to "what the world calls sin") to an older woman with the splendid title of Ranee of Sarawak (Fullerton lived in fear of reprisal from her husband, the Rajah). He was also involved with his considerably younger cousin, to whom he was in fact engaged during much of the time he was making love to Wharton. An aspiring littérateur and a professional Francophile, Fullerton worked as the Paris correspondent for the London *Times*; he is said to have turned out his dispatches in a peculiarly ornate, Jamesian style.

James himself fell in love with Fullerton in about 1900, although he had known him by then for nearly a decade. Around the turn of the century, James, facing advancing age and immense loneliness, seems to have begun to confront his sexual desires, however teasingly and allusively, in doting letters to several younger men. First among these was Fullerton, twenty-two years James's junior and the object of his most histrionic praise and fervent expressions of longing. "You do with me what you will," James wrote to him in September 1900. "You are dazzling, my dear Fullerton; you are beautiful; you are more than tactful, you are tenderly, magically *tactile*." In December 1905, he wrote to Fullerton in terms that James's biographers have long been at pains to call metaphorical: "I can't keep my hands off you."

Fullerton, seeking full muse status, claimed to be James's model for the "longish, leanish, fairish" journalist Merton Densher of *The Wings of the Dove*—arguably the most sexually forthright male in James's work—which was completed in 1902, and was the first of his novels that James sent to Edith Wharton. She had previously sent him several gifts of her own stories, already categorized by the critics as "Jamesian." (One critic went so far as to call her "a masculine Henry James.") James, who had been living in England since 1876, had not responded with great interest to her earlier overtures. But now, in August 1902, he had both carefully measured praise and an urgent message for her: "Don't pass it by—the immediate, the real, the ours, the yours . . . DO NEW YORK!" he virtually bellowed, entreating her to ignore his own example "of exile and ignorance." This was, ironically, the precise moment in James's career—the emergence of his late style, with its combined monumentalism and microscopy—when Wharton lost all desire to emulate his increasingly difficult art. "Don't ask me what I think of *The Wings of the Dove*," she appended to a letter proudly informing her publisher of James's praise and advice. About her very real delight in finally meeting James himself, in December 1903, she confided that he "talks, thank heaven, more lucidly than he writes."

In counseling Wharton to "do" New York, James was warning her against the mode of her first novel, a pseudo-Italian historical hodge-podge titled *The Valley of Decision*, which was having a big commercial and even a critical success. Wharton informed James that, with her proceeds, she had purchased a fancy new motorcar. (Motoring together, with Wharton's chauffeur at the wheel, was to become one of the great shared pleasures of their friendship.) To which James replied, "With the proceeds of my last novel"—*The Wings of the Dove*—"I purchased a small go-cart . . . It needs a coat of paint. With the proceeds of my next novel I shall have it painted." The joke must have seemed less funny when the actual proceeds of his next two novels—*The Ambassadors* and *The Golden Bowl*—were not sufficient to paint a go-cart, since the publisher's advance, of six hundred pounds, totaled more than they earned in sum. In 1904, James wrote to William Dean Howells that "the Golden Dream was as broken outside, as the Golden Bowl within."

The following year, Wharton did New York in *The House of Mirth*, writing at top speed to make the monthly serialization deadlines of *Scribner's Magazine*. The book went on to become the fastest-selling novel in Scribner's history, selling more than a hundred thousand copies in its first two months. James sent her his warm congratulations and assured her that the novel was *"extremely* well written" if not quite so well composed, that Lily was "very big & true" even if Selden was "too *absent*," and that the best way to say all that he wished would be to return to the United States to deliver a lecture on "The question of the *roman de mœurs* in America—its deadly difficulty."

In this period, James was increasingly depressed. Isolated at his home in Sussex through long seasons of bad English weather, he had begun almost to beg his young and lively friends to visit. In the fall of 1907, he asked Fullerton to spend a few days there on his way from Paris back to America. "My difficulty is that I love you too fantastically much," he wrote. "You touch and penetrate me to the quick, and I can only stretch out my hand to draw you closer." Fullerton did not stop to see James. Once in America, however, he did go to visit the Whartons (only recently introduced to him by James) at The Mount, the great neoclassical villa that Edith had built in Massachusetts. ("Mrs. W. is planning to put her hand on you," James had forewarned.) There, Fullerton and Mrs. W. took long walks together in the countryside; she began writing her "love diary" three days after he left. There followed several months of moral and emotional anguish, after which, as the same document reveals, they became lovers, in Paris, the following spring. She was forty-five; Fullerton, forty-two. "I have known what happy women feel," Wharton wrote exultantly in April 1908. "For the first time in my life *I can't read*."

She couldn't write terribly well, either. During the period of roughly two years that the affair went on, she produced no novels, and her stories display a marked falling off from earlier standards, suggesting an argument if not for celibacy then for a basis of emotional stability in a certain kind of writer's life. To be sure, she had written lesser stories before, botched through overemphasis and heavy-handed plot reversals, but nothing quite so deadeningly formulaic as "The Daunt Diana," "The Debt," and "Full Circle," which stand in the chronological sequence of her stories like a row of tombstones. Reasonably better, and enlivened with a charge of psychological tension, are two that clearly reflect aspects of the affair: "The Pretext," of 1908, in which a dully married middle-aged woman is caught up in an excruciatingly ardent if unspoken love, and "The Letters," of 1910, in which a rich young woman marries an amoral but extremely sexy dilettante and lives happily ever after with her eyes determinedly half shut. The portrait of Fullerton in the latter, in all his dreamy golden lassitude, seems historically exact, as does the state of continual emotional turmoil into which he had plunged the author. And to whom, besides her diary and the occasional short story, could the proper Mrs. W. confide this turmoil? To one person only, it seemed: her dear and understanding friend Henry James.

By the autumn of 1908, James was writing Wharton calming letters about Fullerton's tendency to disappear without explanation and assuring her of his own "aboundingly tender friendship." James himself hardly saw Fullerton anymore, but he seemed to participate vicariously in the affair, writing to Wharton in January 1909, "Glad as I am that we 'care' for him, you & I; for verily I think I do as much as you, & that you do as much as I." And then, in March 1909, James published a story in *The English Review* titled "The Velvet Glove," in which a magnificently rich, domineering, motorcar-owning authoress of tawdry popular romances corners a fine-grained man of letters at a soirée and, taking him for a spin, crudely exhorts him to write a preface for her new novel. He is revolted. Not only is she guilty of the "dreadful amateurish dance of ungrammatically scribbling" her far-too-popular books; she is secretly embroiled with a spoiled and dazzling youth, over whom our fine-grained fellow admits that he "in fact imaginatively, intellectually, so to speak, quite yearned."

The letter Wharton wrote to James in immediate response no

longer exists; he burned almost all her letters, along with others that he received in these years. But we know, from his reply, that she had pronounced the story "really good" and offered nothing but lavish and apparently innocent praise. In response, James grew a bit sheepish. He volunteered that the story had been rejected by two American "high-class" periodicals, which was, he told her, a good deal like "declining *you* since *bien assurément* the whole thing *reeks* with you," as well as with her car and her chauffeur—no mention of her novels—and he thanked her, finally, for renewing his confidence in his work. As for Wharton, she blithely recommended "The Velvet Glove" to a friend and singled it out in her memoirs as "perhaps the most beautiful" of James's later stories, casually adding that it was based on his experience with a "young Englishwoman of great position" who had sought from James a literary "boost." Her various ploys seem to have worked. Even readers who have observed "something deeply mocking and hostile" in the story—these are the words of James's biographer Leon Edel—concluded that Wharton herself perceived nothing seriously amiss.

True, nothing in her letters to anyone betrayed hurt or rancor. But she channeled these feelings into one breathtakingly rancorous work of fiction: "The Eyes," published a little more than a year after "The Velvet Glove," in June 1910, a story bilious and insinuating and spiked with revenge—and one of the best she ever wrote. Although the plot involves ghostly apparitions, this is an emotional horror story, much in the mode of James's "The Beast in the Jungle," in that it tells of a haunted man who does not understand the meaning of the thing that haunts him. As it opens, a circle of friends, all male, has gathered in the home of their oldest and most admired member, Andrew Culwin. Highly discriminating, self-preoccupied, unmarried, and undisturbed by common human experience, Culwin is a detached observer of other people's lives. He habitually clings to his guests late into the night, and on this evening only two remain—the narrator and the latest in a series of Culwin's young protégés—when he relates the story of a ghost that used to visit him in the disembodied form of a pair of eyes, hideously old and red-rimmed and corrupt, glaring out of the dark at the foot of his bed. "They seemed to belong to a man who had done a lot of harm in his life, but had always kept just inside the danger lines. They were not the eyes of a coward, but of someone much too clever to take risks . . . Their look left a smear like a snail's."

The inexplicable thing to Culwin is that these demonic accusers appeared on the two occasions in his life when he had acted most selflessly. On the first, he had proposed marriage to a dull but amiable girl whose affections he had half-wittingly aroused (and from whom, compelled by the eyes, he finally fled). On the second, he had offered literary encouragement to a "slender and smooth and hyacinthine" young man who was entirely devoid of talent. The result, Culwin points out, was no great tragedy—the boy had merely become a laughingstock and, finally disabused of his illusions, a drunk. "Put two and two together if you can," Culwin remarks. "For my part I haven't found the link." His protégé, however, is overcome and buries his head in his arms. Laying a gouty hand on the young man's shoulder, Culwin looks up into a mirror and confronts himself "with a glare of slowly gathering hate."

James does not appear to have commented on the story. The resemblance between him and Andrew Culwin, suggested by Adeline R. Tintner in an article in 1971, is convincing—it is hardly possible to read parts of the story without seeing James's image—but the identification has not been widely accepted. Others have preferred to see Culwin as a portrait of Fullerton, or Berry, or, more recently and inevitably, Wharton's father. Whoever he is, he is attacked in overtly sexual terms not seen in Wharton's prose before. Of Culwin's taste for young male protégés, one of his friends asserts that he "liked 'em juicy," and Culwin, who speaks of "the complete impossibility of my marrying" the amiable girl, dotes openly on the young would-be writer's physical charms. ("His stupidity was a natural grace," he tells his listeners. "It was as beautiful, really, as his eyelashes.") His comparison of the youth's beauty to an antique statue of Antinoüs amounts to the use of a homosexual code.

This is one of Wharton's least constrained and most powerful works, as fully mocking and hostile as anything James had dished out. Anger and injury, possibly exacerbated by the pain of feeling Fullerton irrevocably slipping away—the affair ended in June 1910, the month of the story's publication—seem to have swept her past her usual limits. The sexual and financial jealousy boiling beneath James's literary attack in "The Velvet Glove" becomes, in Wharton's story, a sexual fury mercilessly directed at James—or, more precisely, at the hero she had long ago assembled out of Jamesian intellectual charms and sexual evasions, and had never squarely faced. One wonders if she knew exactly what she had done. Stripping her "negative hero" of the protective veils of her own carefully maintained confusion, she exposed not only his sexuality but his consuming selfishness, and delivered him among the damned.

W harton rarely gave her best efforts to her stories after this, although some of her finest work in other forms was still to come. In 1911, she published the novella *Ethan Frome*, which she believed marked her coming-of-age as a craftsman. Completed in the bleak aftermath of the affair, this most pathologically hopeless and wintry of tragedies may bear some relation to Wharton's fear of being buried alive, in the snows of Massachusetts, with a husband to whom her only remaining emotional tie was pity and whose behavior was increasingly unbalanced. She had been spending at least half of every year in Paris, mostly with Teddy, since 1906. Now, in the fall of 1911, the Whartons sold their American home and she moved, alone, to Paris, for good. She obtained a divorce in 1913, the year she published *The Custom of the Country*, a novel so acerbic in its treatment of Americans that she seems to have wished to divorce the entire population.

The war years further overturned her life by impelling her to action. She established refugee hostels and a children's-rescue committee and, under the auspices of the French Red Cross, visited military hospitals at the front to report on their needs. In 1915, the cover of the magazine *Le rire* featured a cartoon of an immensely imposing Wharton, accompanied by Walter Berry and her chauffeur, inspecting war damage through a lorgnette. In truth, she worked tremendously hard to alleviate the suffering that war had brought, when she could have used her wealth to block it out. And through it all, despite her clear disdain for the vast majority of her fellow citizens, she never thought of herself as anything but American. She was appalled when, in the summer of 1915, James gave up his citizenship to become a British subject. "We don't care much for defections," she wrote to a friend, although, after cooling down, she added that James could do nothing that would alter her devotion to him. Indeed, that fall, when he was seriously ill, she traveled to London (not an easy trip in wartime) to see him. His death the following year left her with a feeling of profound loss, which she expressed, in somewhat Jamesian terms, as "this *immense absence.*"

In the remaining years of her life, Wharton returned to the United States only once. In 1917 she published *Summer,* a novella as emotionally bleak as anything she'd written—she called it "the Hot Ethan"—which she set in a New England of numbing hypocrisy and brutalizing squalor. When, in 1919, she decided once again to "do" New York, in *The Age of Innocence,* she paid open tribute to James, naming her hero Newland Archer after James's Isabel Archer in *The Portrait of a Lady.* In her "Portrait of a Gentleman"—the phrase is applied to Newland in the book—Wharton looks back at the provincially righteous New York of her youth, in the 1870s, with a complex mixture of warmth and loathing.

It was Willa Cather who observed that the world broke in two in 1922 or thereabouts; this was the year of *Ulysses, The Waste Land,* and Virginia Woolf's *Jacob's Room.* Just the year before, Wharton had won a Pulitzer Prize for *The Age of Innocence,* albeit by default. (The Columbia University administrators of the award had refused to bestow it on the judges' first choice, Sinclair Lewis's *Main Street,* complaining that it did not sufficiently exhibit "the wholesome atmosphere of American life." Wharton felt insulted that her book was considered sufficiently wholesome.) In 1922, Wharton's new novel, *The Glimpses of the Moon,* was a runaway bestseller, but its story of money and marriage was wearily familiar. This was the sort of book that led people to suppose, as Rebecca West wrote in her review, that "there must be something wrong with the novel as an art-form." Wharton continued to receive critical praise for this and later books—in 1924, reviewing *Old New York,* Edmund Wilson pronounced her an "absolutely first-rate literary artist"—but she found herself suddenly on the dark side of the broken literary planet. In both subject and form, she was old-fashioned, straightforward, unexperimental, unpoetic, and chronically popular with readers.

In 1925, thanking F. Scott Fitzgerald for having sent her *The Great Gatsby,* which she admired, Wharton referred to herself ruefully as "the literary equivalent of tufted furniture and gas chandeliers." She was, nevertheless, not pleased to hear this opinion from others. In an essay on American fiction written the same year, Virginia Woolf dismissed "the Henry Jameses, the Hergesheimers, the Edith Whartons"

as mere imitators of British conventions and, therefore, as incapable
of contributing anything truly American or new; reading the essay,
Wharton is said to have let out an angry cry. (Small wonder. The
Hergesheimers?) In a series of essays of her own, Wharton denounced
such fashionable contemporary trends as "the tedious 'stream of
consciousness,'" and such achievements as the "laborious monuments
of schoolboy pornography" that "are now mistaken for works of genius."
For Wharton, the boundary lines were clear: novels were about
character, stories were about plot, and questions about form were for
amateurs and frauds. Woolf, Lawrence, Eliot, and, above all, Joyce: she
deplored the lot, and, in steady opposition to their explorations, she
entrenched herself in literary practices that seemed lifeless even to
supporters of a more traditional style. (Fitzgerald thought her newest
production, *The Mother's Recompense*, which Wharton sent him by
return mail, "just *lousy*.")

It was not long before her reputation plummeted. By the time of
her death, in 1937, Wharton was a largely disregarded figure, and
Edmund Wilson resolutely chiseled her name out of the pantheon of
first-rate literary artists. Her later stories contain just a few sterling
examples, including the aptly titled "Atrophy," of 1927, which put the
contracted dryness of her writing to expressive use in a tight-lipped
dialogue between a married woman and her lover's spinster sister,
during which nothing meant is said; and a delightful throwback titled
"A Glimpse," of 1932, a Venetian masquerade detailed in all her early,
glowing Sargent colors. Five years later, just before her death, she
completed the oddly powerful "All Souls," which, like "The Eyes," relies on ghosts to get at the fiercer feelings she kept locked away—
here, the terror of absolute loneliness, made all the more chilling for
so perfectly closing the circle of her work.

But the great majority of these later efforts resemble a series of
elaborately staged and stiffly posed *tableaux vivants*, like the frozen
theatrical scenes put on at society parties in *The House of Mirth*. Even
in "Roman Fever," written in 1934 and possibly her most popular story,
the steady grinding of authorial machinery finally overwhelms her
characters' voices and the warm Roman breeze. These stories suggest
that Wharton's fierce opposition to the modern literary era was
more than a resentment of her fading power or passing glory. One

might say that modernism challenged the limitations that had always existed in her work, although they had been polished to the sheen of virtues. The new demands for inward scrutiny and sensory immediacy were a direct assault on her hard and brilliant surfaces; the new delight in exposed mental processes defied the tight control that had helped her become such an astonishingly good writer, but that had also, as much as anything, kept her from becoming the great writer she might have been.

It is particularly strange to think of Wharton turning out her pat and brittle stories for *The Saturday Evening Post* and the *Ladies' Home Journal* while she contemplated writing "Beatrice Palmato," or kept the completed portion—of which the following is a fair example—stashed inside a drawer:

> She hardly heard him, for the old swooning sweetness was creeping over her. As his hand stole higher she felt the secret bud of her body swelling, yearning, quivering hotly to burst into bloom. Ah, here was his subtle fore-finger pressing it, forcing its tight petals softly apart, and laying on their sensitive edges a circular touch so soft and yet so fiery that already lightnings of heat shot from that palpitating centre all over her surrendered body, to the tips of her fingers, and the ends of her loosened hair.
>
> The sensation was so exquisite that she could have asked to have it indefinitely prolonged; but suddenly his head bent lower, and with a deeper thrill she felt his lips pressed upon that quivering invisible bud, and then the delicate firm thrust of his tongue, so full and yet so infinitely subtle, pressing apart the close petals, and forcing itself in deeper and deeper through the passage that glowed and seemed to become illuminated at its approach . . .
>
> "My little girl," he breathed, sinking down beside her.

Wharton was probably referring to this little piece of deviltry when, in a letter of 1935, to her friend Bernard Berenson, she disparaged a story by Alberto Moravia and some "nastier" works by Faulkner and Céline, with the boast "I've got an incest donnée up my sleeve that would make them all look like nursery rhymes." R.W.B. Lewis, who noted that Wharton had also outmatched Joyce and Lawrence on the subject of female sexuality, believed that she set out to write "Beatrice Palmato" at this time—in her seventies, approximately two years before her death. It isn't Wharton's age that makes Cynthia Griffin Wolff's suggestion of an earlier date for the story more appealing, nor is it Wolff's belief that Wharton was reacting to a sexually eye-opening trip to Morocco (harems, child brides, etc.) that she made in 1917. It is, rather, the thought of Wharton angrily picking up her pen just a few years later—say, about 1922—after having forced her way through the "schoolboy pornography" of *Ulysses*, and deciding to show Molly Bloom a thing or two about saying yes.

She might well have kept the story up her sleeve all those years. She knew that she couldn't publish it, and, in the form she'd planned, she couldn't finish it, either. It has been pointed out that the single scene Wharton wrote does not fit anywhere in her outline, which details how Beatrice's older sister mysteriously commits suicide, and how her mother then mysteriously goes mad, and how, at the climax, Beatrice commits suicide, too. It was to be only then, in a sort of dramatic coda, that the terrible secret of Mr. Palmato and his daughters was revealed. Wharton was planning a horror story—like "The Eyes," like "All Souls"—that would have brought together the usual dark thrill and the usual moral price of incest. And, like these other stories, which drew on deeper levels of feeling than she cared to admit or perhaps even knew, "Beatrice Palmato" seems to have run away with her.

Of course, the scene she wrote would have rather spoiled the surprise of her ending. But, even more interesting, it entirely fails to suggest the outline's menacing tone. Ostensibly writing about incest, Wharton rhapsodized about specific and luxuriant pleasures, which sound nothing like childhood abuse and everything like the erotic poems of her Fullerton years. Perhaps most interesting of all, she didn't throw it on the fire. "Beatrice Palmato" remained among her papers, along with her "love diary" and a separate packet she marked "For My Biographer," which contained letters clearly meant to justify her tortured decision to divorce, and documents showing that she had secretly, through her publisher, provided money to the unsuspecting Henry

James. Those who have made public Wharton's most private concerns have not betrayed their subject but, rather, have collaborated with her. We now know what she wanted us to know about her life, and her story has come down to us as she would have written it: a strong plot, a brilliant but self-divided heroine, a full supply of negative heroes, and a smash surprise at the end.

FOR LOVE AND MONEY

F. SCOTT FITZGERALD

Zelda Sayre and F. Scott Fitzgerald in the Sayres's yard
in Montgomery, Alabama, 1919

"I think my novel is about the best American novel ever written," F. Scott Fitzgerald wrote to Max Perkins, his editor at Scribner's, in August 1924. Perkins had to take the appraisal on faith. It would be at least a month, Fitzgerald warned, before his new manuscript could be completed and revised and shipped off to New York from his home on the French Riviera. The book was still a little rough in places, and Fitzgerald worried, too, that it might not be long enough to receive the serious consideration it deserved. But when, three months later, Perkins read the manuscript—the title was to be either *Trimalchio in West Egg* or *The Great Gatsby*—he came close to agreeing with the young author's assessment. He wrote back at once that "the novel is a wonder," possessed of vitality and glamour but also of "a kind of mystic atmosphere." He recommended only a few changes, mostly along the lines of providing more background for the story's rich and enigmatic hero. Fitzgerald, eager to make the best even better, happily set to work again: "If it's as good as you say, when I finish with the proof it'll be perfect."

Fitzgerald was twenty-eight when *The Great Gatsby* was published, in the spring of 1925. He was already a celebrity, as the author of two immensely popular Jazz Age novels—*This Side of Paradise* and *The Beautiful and Damned*—but their commercial success had not earned him the literary standing he desired. ("I believe you might become a very popular trashy novelist without much difficulty," his Princeton friend and mentor Edmund Wilson volunteered, on reading *Paradise*.) What his writing had earned him, instead, was a great deal of money—by the mid-twenties he could count on twenty-five hundred dollars per story—an achievement that reversed all his prospects, allowed him to marry the expensive girl of his formerly anguished dreams, and allowed them together to live a life that exemplified the wildness of the age. Scott and Zelda had been jumping into fountains and getting into drunken brawls (FITZGERALD KNOCKS OFFICER THIS SIDE OF PARADISE) for several years before they fled to France. They went, in part, to escape their exhausting roles as America's favorite models of postwar, post-moral effervescence, but mostly so that Scott could write a more serious book. Wilson had prescribed an expatriate bout in France as a kind of school for style, urging Fitzgerald to leave behind the ideals and plumbing and prosperity that so tightly bound him to America: "Your novels would never be the same afterward."

The Great Gatsby was very consciously a novel about American prosperity and ideals; Fitzgerald did not so much leave the country as back away from it far enough to broaden his view. Wilson was right, of course, in predicting the novel's extraordinary difference from Fitzgerald's earlier work, but the fact that the facile and fizzy author produced what may be the century's most widely read and admired American novel was a mystery that not even Wilson was prepared to explain. A reconstruction of the manuscript that Fitzgerald so excitedly sent to Perkins, titled *Trimalchio* and published in 2002, offers some possible insights into the young writer's transformation. This is the manuscript as it existed before Fitzgerald made what he called the "1000 minor corrections" and "several more large ones" on the galleys, the resetting of which he predicted would be "one of the most expensive affairs since Madame Bovary"—a fair indication of the standards he intended to meet. *Trimalchio*, in other words, is *The Great Gatsby* before Fitzgerald made it "perfect."

The title (which Fitzgerald himself shortened) attests to the scope of his ambitions. The character to which it refers is a filthy-rich ex-slave and extravagant party host in *The Satyricon*, the notorious Roman first-century satire by Petronius, who was the arbiter of elegance at the Emperor Nero's decadent court. Blithely obscene, mocking everything from *The Odyssey* to table manners, the work in modern times was inspirational to Wilde, was quoted by both Yeats and Joyce, and—thanks to a 1922 attempt to suppress a new translation, during which the New York publisher was taken to court by the Society for the Suppression of Vice—was very much in vogue during the Neronian age in which Fitzgerald was writing. For Fitzgerald, the comparison of Gatsby with this Roman counterpart served to magnify his all-American hero through the lens of classical allusion. The overarching significance of the title was not far from that of *Ulysses*, also published in 1922 and immediately prescribed for Fitzgerald's further stylistic development by Wilson, to whom the budding genius responded glumly, "I wish it was layed [*sic*] in America."

Fitzgerald's bid for literary posterity escaped the notice of contemporary readers and reviewers almost entirely. Although some important critics—H. L. Mencken, for one—recognized what Fitzgerald had achieved, *Gatsby* was his first commercial failure. Most copies of the second printing were still in Scribner's warehouse when he died, broke and all but forgotten, in 1940. The revival began almost immediately thereafter. *Gatsby* was republished in 1941, and its enshrinement steadily assumed proportions as astounding as they are, even today, painfully ironic. The book now sells more copies in a month than it sold in Fitzgerald's lifetime; Baz Luhrmann's wildly lavish 3-D film of 2013 is the fifth filmed version to be made since Fitzgerald's death, at a time when he was struggling to earn a living in Hollywood writing screenplays.

Fitzgerald himself has been as mythologized as his hero. Aside from the predictable groaning shelf of biographies, past years have seen the publication of his letters to his editor and his agent, his notebooks, a deluxe facsimile edition of a handwritten early manuscript of *Gatsby*, a deluxe facsimile of his business ledger, and a reader's companion to *Tender Is the Night* that compares, in table form, sentences Fitzgerald "stripped" from thirty-seven of his stories with their slightly reworked versions in the novel. And then there are the *F. Scott Fitzgerald Manuscripts*, in eighteen volumes. Given the depletion of unexploited source material, it is no surprise that the *Trimalchio* manuscript was resurrected. Its publication, however, raises distinctive moral questions.

Smaller questions first: the manuscript as presented is actually something of a fudge, since Fitzgerald's typescript has been lost. To reconstruct this phantom document, *Trimalchio*'s dauntless editor, James L. W. West III, began by examining two copies of the typeset galleys that Scribner's had made from it. (In a footnote that all too clearly illuminates the perils of modern scholarship, he reports that his task was jealously impeded by the University of South Carolina's library, which owns one set of the galleys and allowed him to inspect it "only for two days." The University of South Carolina Press, it turns out, has published its own version of Fitzgerald's proofs, in a near-sacramental facsimile edition of five hundred numbered copies.) Next, West removed an overlay of copyediting that Scribner's automatically supplied. However, since there was no way to know just what the copy editors had changed, the author's wayward patterns of spelling and punctuation were adapted from the earlier, handwritten manuscript—itself a different version of the novel but offering "the original texture of Fitzgerald's accidentals." Even Fitzgerald, who as early as 1922 happily anticipated a professorial analysis of "my 'second' or 'neoflapper' manner," might have boggled at a scrutiny of comma placement once reserved for Shakespeare's Second Folio.

Yet, however we allow for the continuing deification and cannibalization of a writer whom Cyril Connolly once called "an American version of the Dying God," the publication of *Trimalchio*, which its editor claims is "a separate and distinct work of art," poses questions of a larger order. Should this literary artifact be available in bookstores, alongside *Gatsby* and *Tender Is the Night*? How do we justify the marketing of a work that the author never intended us to see? The greatest shame for a writer like Fitzgerald was to write badly, or even at a level below his best. It is true that he did both throughout his life, for money, or because of alcohol, or Zelda, or whatever it was that made him place such needs and demands above his talent. But not in *Gatsby*, his only mature yet uncorrupted book. Although there is nothing embarrassingly "bad" in this earlier version, the revelation of even minor deformations evokes a peculiar sense of violation. For *The*

Great Gatsby is a book that owes much of its aura to our inescapable knowledge that it, like Gatsby's dream, is a manufacture of extreme purity wrested from a life of tragedy and waste, and charged, by the author as much as by anyone else, with that life's redemption.

What *Trimalchio* offers, and what gives it value, is a view of Fitzgerald not as a brief-lived poet-god—our link between Keats and James Dean—but as a writer at work, subject to a word-by-word perfectionism that he claimed to derive from Conrad (who derived it from Flaubert) and resulting in a book so tightly crafted that much of it seems as inevitable as unrhymed writing gets. Fitzgerald's lyric incisiveness isn't every reader's ideal, since it leaves out many things—psychology, detail, the messiness of life—yet it makes for a tautness of line and a verbal iridescence that few techniques can match. When, in 1950, Edmund Wilson examined an early text of *Madame Bovary*, he claimed to be excited by its very flatness, and said that it gave him a higher opinion of Flaubert "to see him bringing these paragraphs to life, turning on the music and color." Perhaps this is just the eager scholar's way out of the moral dilemma: satisfying one's curiosity about a work one was never intended to read. But then it was Fitzgerald who suggested (adapting his beloved Keats) that the mark of a first-rate mind is to be able to contain two conflicting ideas at once—to condemn the idle rich, say, yet bask in realms of gold—and live with them both.

Daisy cries into Jay Gatsby's beautiful pile of colored shirts, and her voice is, as ever, a deathless song, low and thrilling, full of money. Gatsby, however, has not yet acquired his dazzling smile. The yellow cocktail music played by an orchestra as the earth lurches away from the sun is as implausibly and marvelously yellow as we remember, but the afternoon sky outside the Buchanans' home is fairy blue, not blue honey. It is Vladimir Epstien who composes the *Jazz History of the World* in *Trimalchio*, not Vladimir Tostoff, an abstrusely obscene name that Fitzgerald lifted from Joyce's Toby Tostoff, in *Ulysses*, a mythic masturbator who "tossed off" his sexual organ so often that he destroyed it; *Trimalchio* also offers a description of Epstien's spectacular score, a somewhat leaden passage that Fitzgerald was wise to cut. (Changing the evidently Jewish name of the composer, however—and however

Fitzgerald managed to misspell it—left *The Great Gatsby* with just one notable Jewish figure, the repellent gangster Meyer Wolfsheim, who wears cuff links made of human molars. Edith Wharton, writing to Fitzgerald about *Gatsby*—in a letter mentioned in the previous chapter of this book—commended Wolfsheim as "your *perfect* Jew.") Perhaps the most touching earlier detail, testimony to the youth and grasp of the author of "The Diamond as Big as the Ritz," is the price of the wedding necklace that Tom Buchanan gives to Daisy: in *Gatsby*, it is—quite ridiculously enough—three hundred and fifty thousand dollars; in *Trimalchio*, the string of pearls that Daisy flings into the wastebasket set Tom back seven hundred and fifty thousand dollars.

But then, in America, such things were suddenly possible, and Fitzgerald gave us a country reeling with unloosed possibilities: a brand-new America where the national conscience has been doused with gin, and where pop tunes describe the deepest human feelings. In both versions of the book, Gatsby hauls an ever-lurking pianist from a cranny of his mansion to serenade Daisy with love's anthem, "Ain't We Got Fun." Far more is made of Gatsby's devotion to pop tunes in *Trimalchio*, where the works of Tin Pan Alley are revealed to have had a transforming effect in his adolescence, their routine messages converted by his colossal innocence into a guide for living, akin to the cheap romances that inflamed Emma Bovary and the novels of chivalry that set Don Quixote on his path. Fitzgerald liked to say that his own lyric gift might have gone the way of Cole Porter, except that he wanted to "preach at people" rather than merely entertain them. Gatsby's musical debt presents, in neat and vivid form, the classic Fitzgerald contradiction, in which he preaches against the things he most hopelessly loves: the tawdry products of a base society that cast a false yet indispensable enchantment.

But the truly stunning difference that distinguishes *Trimalchio* from Fitzgerald's familiar fairy tale is that Daisy comes to Gatsby's house with her suitcases packed, ready to run away with him, and he sends her home. "In other words you've got her—and now you don't want her," Nick, our narrator and Gatsby's Sancho Panza, reasonably observes. Despite Gatsby's protests—"Of course I want her"—this turn of events does give a seasoned *Gatsby* reader pause. It seems to violate all we know about these characters: Gatsby the obsessed lover, erecting an empire and stringing it with lights to impress a girl; careless, thoughtless Daisy, too languid and desireless to lift a lovely arm during the novel's long summer heat. If Fitzgerald's original impulse was to fashion Daisy with the will and courage to follow Gatsby into his dream, even momentarily, what does it say about the dream at the heart of the book that Gatsby turns her down?

Once the shock of reading this episode subsides, one realizes that it only emphasizes what we've always really known. For the determined dreamer, it isn't the object of the dream that counts; it's the dream itself. Gatsby and Daisy couldn't face each other across a breakfast table every day without destroying his ideal as surely, if not as poetically, as they do through betrayal and death. And Gatsby, for whom disillusion was a form of death, knew this better than anyone—except, of course, Fitzgerald.

In *Trimalchio*, Fitzgerald plays a peculiar variation on this basic tenet of romance. When Gatsby sends Daisy home, it is to "go to her husband and tell him that she never loved him"—a desire he expresses, in passing, in the completed book, but as just one more fantastic element of his plan rather than as a cold condition for its execution. But here it isn't Tom on whom Gatsby wants revenge. Nor is he primarily seeking to eradicate the time that Daisy spent with someone else, as he is in *Gatsby*, where he seems to believe that by sheer force of will he can undo the past. At this point, *Trimalchio* is, briefly, a truly different book: less awash in the golden light of quixotry, more literal and harsh. For the most startling revelation in Fitzgerald's manuscript is that Gatsby wants revenge on Daisy, and not for leaving him but for having ruined his life by loving him in the first place.

The regret embedded in a long-anticipated kiss is a subject with some literary pedigree. Most famously, there is Proust's enamored hero Charles Swann, pausing, as he lowers his lips to his beloved Odette, to study her face as it will appear to him for the last time unpossessed. What Swann is giving up is his own anticipation and his lover's mystery. What Jay Gatsby gave up as he lowered his lips to Daisy Fay's, in the distant Louisville autumn when they first met, is a part of himself that—as *Gatsby* barely whispers, as *Trimalchio* swears out loud—he has fiercely regretted losing ever since. In the famously heightened poetics of Gatsby's record of that kiss, it is hard to know exactly what the loss entails: "His heart beat faster and faster as Daisy's white face came up to his own. He knew that when he kissed this girl, and forever wed his unutterable visions to her perishable breath, his mind would never romp again like the mind of God."

Here the earlier manuscript, far less oracular, is almost alarmingly clear. *Trimalchio's* Nick, on being told what Gatsby has sent Daisy home to do, sees the task not only as a redress of time but as "some sort of atonement" for Daisy herself, a rite of purification, and he warns Gatsby not to ask too much of her. "Daisy's a person," Nick tells him. "She's not just a figure in your dream." And, he adds, she probably doesn't feel that she owes him anything at all.

"She does, though," this Gatsby responds, expressing an opinion that Fitzgerald may have cut, as he cut the entire incident of Daisy's capitulation, to make his hero more sympathetic, and less autobiographical. "Why—I'm only thirty-two. I might be a great man if I could forget that once I lost Daisy." The petulance is unsettling. (There is, fortunately, nothing left of it in the grandly deluded knight of the book we know.) Yet Gatsby goes even further in his explanation of what he is owed and exactly when the debt began: "I used to think that wonderful things were going to happen to me, before I met her. And I knew it was a great mistake for a man like me to fall in love—and then one night I let myself go, and it was too late."

What on earth does Gatsby think he might have become without Daisy, the lure and goal for all he has achieved? Might he have been an honest businessman? Might he really have gone to Oxford, or read some of the books in his library? Is it possible that he could care for any of these things? If Gatsby's voice here is almost intolerably jarring, perhaps that is because it is not Gatsby's voice we are hearing but Fitzgerald's, helplessly intruding—Gatsby "started out as one man I knew and then changed into myself," he wrote to a friend in 1925—at the very moment when he stood at the brink both of his full creative powers and of the catastrophe that would permanently deprive him of their use.

The resentment Fitzgerald came to feel about his own catastrophic love is evident in one of the few truly bitter letters he wrote, in his later years, to his daughter, Scottie. "When I was your age I lived with a great dream," he informed her in 1938, when she was sixteen and away at school, "then the dream divided one day when I decided to marry your mother after all, even though I knew she was spoiled and meant no good to me. I was sorry immediately I had married her." Fitzgerald surely set the date of his awful revelation back in time somewhat, for dramatic effect. The Fitzgeralds married in 1920, and it was not until four years later, while Scott was working all out to complete *Gatsby*, that he seems to have fully grasped what a mistake it had been for a man like him to fall in love.

And yet to suggest that the events of any single year were responsible for the disillusion of the Great American Dreamer threatens to reduce Fitzgerald's dominant subject to what Gatsby might call the merely personal. Fitzgerald's imagination frequently anticipated, and shaped, his life's tragedies. As he saw it, these tragedies were less a result of his choices or decisions than they were a destiny, and one that had its beginnings even before he was born, in September 1896, to Irish Catholic parents in St. Paul, Minnesota. Three months before he was born, to be exact, when the family's two other children, little girls just one and three years old, died in a local epidemic. "I think I started then to be a writer," Fitzgerald surmised. His mother lost another infant four years later, and although she eventually gave birth to a healthy girl, Scott's sister Annabel, her son was the focus of her life.

Mollie McQuillan was from a family that her famous son once called "straight 1850 potato famine Irish," but they were not poor; her immigrant father had made good in the wholesale grocery business in St. Paul. An extremely plain and pious woman, Mollie was thirty years old when she married a dapper and deeply loyal Southerner, Edward Fitzgerald, who had guided Confederate spies while growing up in Maryland, and who charmed his son with stories of a lost and glorious world. Edward had gone west to St. Paul to earn a living, but his talents were for other things. After his furniture company in St. Paul failed, the family moved to upstate New York, living in Syracuse and then Buffalo, when Edward took a job with Procter & Gamble. The second great tragedy of young Scott's life, as he recalled it, was the day his father was fired. Scott was twelve years old, and as soon as he heard his mother on the telephone, he knew that disaster had struck. He returned a quarter that she had given him, assuming that the family would need it. And he began right then to pray: "Please don't let us go to the poorhouse." He said that he saw his father leave the house that morning a relatively young man and come back an old man, completely broken.

The family returned to St. Paul that summer and lived off his mother's inheritance. His father never worked again, except for a futile and humiliating job selling groceries from the back room of his brother-in-law's office. Scott's mother's disappointment in her husband only further concentrated her energies on her beautiful blond and blue-eyed boy. Mollie had immense social aspirations for him, reminding people that he had been christened Francis Scott Key Fitzgerald, after an illustrious ancestor on his father's side. Although the family was merely middle class, and Molly herself was so notoriously dowdy and ill-kempt that neighbors mocked her, she spent everything she could to establish Scott among the snobbish rich of old St. Paul. His suits were purchased from New York; he took dancing classes and was the only boy in the class with evening pumps; he had silk bow ties in every color to complement his Eton collars. He was indulged, cosseted, worshipped. And he did not like his mother the better for it. She was even more embarrassing to him than his father was, and less sympathetic. He was a young man with shining plans, which did not include or even allow for the proximity of two such dull and defeated people. Very much like Gatsby, F. Scott Fitzgerald sprang from a Platonic conception of himself.

He said that he grew up feeling like an aspiring poor boy among the rich, especially at the Catholic boarding school he attended for his last two years of high school, and at Princeton, where he was accepted, despite inferior grades, as a result of the sheer charm and promise of his interview. His primary plan at Princeton was to be a football hero but, at five foot eight and one hundred and thirty-eight pounds, even his best powers of persuasion couldn't get him on the team. Instead, he contributed snappy lyrics to the Triangle Club musicals, wrote short stories, and failed to pay much attention to his classes. He took the opportunity to leave school because of an illness in his junior year, just ahead of flunking out. Overall, he was learning that the world did not take him at his (or his mother's) valuation. As part of this process, it seems, he'd started drinking, hard and steadily enough to be known as "a man who drank" at age fifteen.

There was also the problem of love, specifically his rejection by the first girl he fell for, a wealthy sixteen-year-old Chicago beauty whom he met during his sophomore year at Princeton, when he was home on holiday and she was visiting St. Paul. She was what he admiringly called a "top girl," and she seemed mad about him, too. They exchanged hundreds of letters during the next two years, until she dropped him, as he recalled, "with the most supreme boredom and indifference." It wasn't long before he received news of her marriage to the son of a rich Chicago businessman. He was hurt, but he seemed to know even then that his loss had given him something he could use. He typed up and bound her giddy, flirty letters, which became both an inspiration and a resource as he worked on his first novel, mostly during the year and a half that he spent in the army, often when he should have been performing other tasks. He was reportedly an "unusually dispensable" second lieutenant, and it was considered fortunate that the armistice occurred before he could be sent to fight. But it was the army that brought him to Camp Sheridan, near Montgomery, Alabama—"a languid paradise of dreamy skies and firefly evenings," as he described it in a story two years later—where, at a country club dance one dreamy evening, in the summer of 1918, he met Zelda Sayre.

Not quite eighteen years old, and just a month out of high school, Zelda had a boldness and an unconventionality that were apparent even in the guise of a frilly provincial ingénue. The youngest child of a respected local lawyer, she was very beautiful; the veranda of her parents' home had already become something of an extension of Camp Sheridan, with groups of soldiers continually mooning around. Zelda smoked, she drank, and she loved to shock. As a child, she had once called the fire department and then climbed up to the roof to be rescued. She had a lot in common with Scott—they even looked alike, fair and delicately featured—and she led him on the kind of tortured, jealous chase that made him absolutely certain that he could not live without her.

To earn enough money to marry Zelda, he went to New York upon being discharged from the army, under the assumption that he could write his way into solvency. His novel had been rejected by Scribner's, although with a good deal of encouraging advice, and he believed he could sell his stories to the popular magazines. Edmund Wilson, who'd been just ahead of him at Princeton, had established a flourishing literary career in the city, and Fitzgerald saw no reason he couldn't do the same. Instead, in just a few months, he accumulated one hundred and twenty-two rejection slips, which he used to decorate his room. The little money that he had went for trips to Montgomery, where, at last, he managed to talk Zelda into getting engaged. There followed a miserable period when he worked in advertising ("We keep you clean in Muscatine"), made even more miserable when Zelda, giving up on his prospects, broke off the engagement. With nothing to fall back on, he went on a spectacular bender and then returned to his parents' home in St. Paul, where he holed up through the summer of 1919, rewriting his novel and filling it with Zelda—her words, her terrific modernity, her "eternally kissable mouth, small, slightly sensual, and utterly disturbing"—in a last-ditch attempt to prove his love and win her back. Scribner's was thrilled with the manuscript, which became *This Side of Paradise*, and so was the rest of the country. Scott and Zelda were married eight days after its publication, in April 1920, in the rectory of St. Patrick's Cathedral in New York. A few months later, he told the reporters who now continually hounded him, "I married the heroine of my stories."

Contrary to what Fitzgerald later claimed, the couple seem to have enjoyed a dizzying early happiness. But it is true that from the start Scott's friends worried that Zelda would ruin him, because of her extravagance, because of her evident jealousy of his work, and—perhaps as a result of that jealousy—because he was unable to write when she was present, yet was terrified of what she might do when out of his sight. ("He is going to leave Zelda at the Commodore," Edmund Wilson informed a mutual friend in the spring of 1920, when the Fitzgeralds had been married about three weeks. "I trust that she will seize the opportunity to run away with the elevator boy or something.") Scott does not seem to have known the more troubling aspects of Zelda's family background: both her mother's mother and her mother's sister had committed suicide; in later years, her brother would commit suicide, too. Yet presentiments of ruin ran all through Fitzgerald's work. Planning his second novel, in August 1920, when he was still only twenty-three years old, he assured Charles Scribner II that both the hero and his beautiful wife were to be "wrecked on the shoals of dissipation." There were also times when he seemed to have an appetite for doom, as when, the following year, he wrote to Perkins, "I should like to sit down with ½ dozen chosen companions and drink myself to death."

The immediate problem, though, was that Zelda, however smart and exuberant and talented—Scott sometimes incorporated her diary entries into his work—had been bred to be a decorative accessory to a man. She had hardly any discipline, and no purpose of her own. The situation improved for a while with the birth of their daughter, Frances Scott Fitzgerald, known throughout her life as Scottie, in October 1921, in St. Paul. Zelda's brightly ironic words about her newborn daughter—"I hope it's beautiful and a fool—a beautiful little fool"— are famous because Scott gave them to Daisy Buchanan, but they reflect Zelda's acid view of female possibilities. She had begun to work on stories of her own by the time the couple moved to Great Neck, the Long Island town of rolling lawns and vast estates that, as "West Egg," became the site of Gatsby's lavish parties. The Fitzgeralds' own rather lavish household, complete with a nurse for Scottie, a pair of caretakers, and a laundress who came twice a week, not to mention their brand-new secondhand Rolls, cost a good deal more than Scott made. Even the publication of *The Beautiful and Damned* and a collection of stories, *Tales of the Jazz Age*, in 1922, did not yield enough, and a play he was hoping would make a fortune on Broadway went bust. Earning more money than had seemed conceivable two years earlier, Fitzgerald was pumping out stories as fast as he could, just to pay the bills.

Their move to France, in May 1924, was meant to provide Scott with the time to work on the novel he had begun the previous spring, without the distractions and expenses of home, and in the refining atmosphere that Wilson had prescribed for more serious work. The Riviera was then a relatively undiscovered paradise, and at first things seemed to be going smoothly, even though the irresistible villa they rented in St. Raphaël cost far more than they'd intended to pay, and the staff they hired was also something of a burden. Still, Scott worked steadily every day. Zelda, however, had given up on her writing, and, with a nanny taking care of Scottie, had little to do except walk the beach alone. Of course, she was not alone for long. That summer, her romance with a French aviator was the talk of the *plage* by the time her husband learned about it. Judging from accounts that both spouses have left, it is possible that she asked for a divorce; it is also possible that he planned a confrontation with the man, and even that he locked her in her room to put an end to it. In any case, the aviator quickly flew away. And it seemed as though calm had been restored.

"I've been unhappy," Fitzgerald wrote to Perkins that August, in the same letter in which he crowed over the new novel, "but my work hasn't suffered from it. I am grown at last." A few weeks later, Zelda, in despair over her lost romance, took an overdose of sleeping pills. In time, as the drinking and the drama worsened, she required shots of morphine to treat attacks of "nervous hysteria." The marriage turned into a desperate round of illnesses, battles, accusations, and, most painfully, earnest attempts at mutual salvation, after which the entire round began again. Years later, when Zelda had long ceased to be able to survive outside a mental hospital—she was first confined in 1930—and Fitzgerald's life and career were in pieces, he recalled that it was in September 1924 that "I knew something had happened that could never be repaired."

It is true that Fitzgerald's work did not immediately suffer from his unhappiness. In the course of turning *Trimalchio* into *The Great Gatsby*, he managed to excise the personal intrusions of anger and resentment and reality, purifying both his hero and the myth that he embodied. Only a few traces remain. In *Trimalchio*, Gatsby's point-blank statement that he was ruined by falling in love leads to a passage that remains unchanged in *Gatsby*, and is one of the book's most untethered flights of fancy: Gatsby's recollection of a walk with Daisy on the night of the kiss, when he saw out of the corner of his eye "a secret place above the trees—he could climb to it, if he climbed alone, and once there he could suck on the pap of life, gulp down the incomparable milk of wonder." Of course, he did not climb alone, and the resulting loss, curiously obscure but somehow related to life itself, seems immense.

How odd that this image of the freedom he gives up is so much more sensuously female than the woman who takes its place. Daisy is a girl, not a woman—just eighteen when Gatsby meets her—and we aren't told a thing about how she looks, how she feels to the touch. What color is her hair? Fitzgerald generally suggests that she is fair but once, surprisingly, that she is dark. Her eyes, her mouth? She is lovely; it doesn't matter how. On one occasion, a tiny gust of powder rises from her bosom when she laughs, but this only makes her seem more fairylike, insubstantial; her voice is all the physical substance that she needs. Daisy's far more voluptuous foil is her husband's cheap and flashy mistress, Myrtle, whom Daisy brutally strikes down in Gatsby's car; the only emphatically female flesh in the book, in fact, is Myrtle's torn and bleeding breast, hanging open over her heart like a flap. "I want Myrtle Wilson's breast ripped off—it's exactly the thing," Fitzgerald enthused to a somewhat queasy Perkins. It seems a terrible revenge upon the "pap of life" that another woman had kept him from reaching.

It has long been noted that Fitzgerald, despite his sexually adventurous public stands on flappers and freedom, was a modest and even a prudish man. Both Zelda and his later paramour, Sheilah Graham, attest to a relationship to women that was far more spiritual, even Quixote-like, than passionate. Judging by the young age at which he seriously began to drink, it seems possible that it was his dawning sexuality, so at odds with the Catholic pieties of his upbringing, that he initially meant to drown. In his writing, there is a formal reticence about such matters that easily veers from the chivalrous to the preposterous. We are told that Gatsby once long ago "took" Daisy, and ever after has felt married to her. The blushing verb recurs as the basis of a joke in *Tender Is the Night*: "She came close up against him with a forlorn whisper. 'Take me.' 'Take you where?' Astonishment froze him rigid." Fitzgerald's genteel awkwardness seems to get the best of him when, in a passionate climax in the same book, we learn that the heroine's about-to-be lover has finally "kissed her hardy knees."

Far more convincingly erotic are Fitzgerald's nearly Marxian descriptions of the vast system of production that ultimately begets the vain, proud, childlike girls he worships, girls who convey all the strength of that system in the confidence that animates their slender frames. "For her sake trains began their run at Chicago and traversed the round belly of the continent to California," he writes of his heroine in *Tender Is the Night*. "Chicle factories fumed and link belts grew link by link in factories" until, finally, "as the whole system swayed and thundered onward it lent a feverish bloom to such processes of hers as wholesale buying" (not to be confused with buying wholesale). The mating of this heavily masculinized capitalism with a feminine eros of exquisite consumption yields Fitzgerald's America, thrillingly corrupt and perversely beautiful, as only a true innocent—economic, sexual, moral—would imagine it to be. And *Gatsby*, more than any other of Fitzgerald's works, glorifies the country with this sexualized innocence, which is lavished, like his poetry, on our giant cars and our tinny music and our ruthless economics, and transforms them into elements of romance and literary gold.

When a third, rather abstract breast appears, on the last page of *The Great Gatsby*—"a fresh, green breast of the new world"—any college-trained literary-symbol finder may react with a satisfaction nearly equal to that of the man who conceives of suckling there. The man this time is Nick, not Gatsby, but no matter. Gatsby is dead, and Nick, his champion, is caught up in his own quest. In this geographical breast, he sees the same chance that Gatsby glimpsed in the "pap of life" hidden above the treetops: the chance of finding "something commensurate to his capacity for wonder," a divinity large enough to accommodate his need to believe. Alas, this part of the world was long ago covered with houses, and Nick—as unfit as Gatsby, now, for mere reality—has to head to the West in hope of finding a place unspoiled and new.

Here the teacher's chalk can hardly be restrained from dashing a few equations on the blackboard: East to West = escape from civilization, lighting out for the territory, etc. This is a great American fiction, and a great American reality. That *Gatsby* strikes the epochal theme so efficiently is part of its brilliance, and exemplary of the methods that have brought it so close to being the official great American novel. Short, easy to read, filled with symbols and subtexts and allusions, and also beautiful, *Gatsby* is a supremely teachable novel. Given our age of brief attention spans and broad literary indifference, this is a useful attribute.

In a letter that Fitzgerald treasured all his life, T. S. Eliot wrote to him, in 1925, that he believed *Gatsby* to be the first advance in American fiction since Henry James. Eliot promised to write again to explain what he meant, but he never did. One can only assume that he had in mind Fitzgerald's easy mixture of naturalism and what Perkins called the book's "mystic atmosphere," the often pervading unreality of what a reader nevertheless accepts: the grim Valley of Ashes where poor Myrtle lives above her husband's auto-repair shop, or the moment when a billboard advertisement for an oculist is mistaken for the eyes of God. Eliot may also have admired the smoothly modern handling of a theme particularly meaningful to him, the pursuit of the Grail.

There has been a great deal of interest through the years in whether Fitzgerald was indebted for any of this to *The Waste Land*, which was published in 1922. Given the avidity of his reading and his literary hero worship, it may be so. (Eliot was responding to a copy of *Gatsby* that Fitzgerald had sent to him, inscribed to the "Greatest of Living Poets from his enthusiastic [*sic*] worshipper." Eliot claimed not to have been prejudiced by the tribute, nor, apparently, was he prejudiced by the spelling.) On the other hand, several of Fitzgerald's earliest stories display a surreal bleakness of empty landscapes and shriveled souls, which seems entirely native; his American dream was always shadowed by the soul-destroying failure and fear he had seen, as a boy, so close at hand.

One undoubted intersection with Eliot's poem is the character of Trimalchio. In late 1922, Eliot's publisher, Boni and Liveright, was vindicated in court and brought out the almost suppressed *Satyricon*; shortly afterward, Eliot added a Trimalchian quotation, printed in the original Latin and Greek, as an epigraph to *The Waste Land*. He took the quotation from an uncommonly decorous and disquieting episode, in which Trimalchio tells his guests how he once saw with his own eyes the Cumaean Sibyl, to whom the god Apollo had granted eternal life. She had neglected to ask for eternal youth, however, and by the time Trimalchio came upon her, she had shrunk so horribly that she lived inside a bottle. When local children asked her what she wanted, she replied, "I want to die."

Fitzgerald was never entirely comfortable with the title he finally agreed to for his book. "My heart tells me I should have named it *Trimalchio*," he wrote to Perkins in January 1925; and again the following March, just weeks before its publication, "I feel *Trimalchio* might have been best after all." This persistent impulse hardly seems tied to matters of literary vogue or prestige. Rather, for a man who spent so much of his life in open fear of age and in steady flirtation with death— "You remember I used to say I wanted to die at thirty," he wrote to Perkins that December; "Well I'm twenty-nine and the prospect is still welcome"—it seems an understandable desire to name his book for the witness to the most extraordinary tragedy of living on after youth has gone.

"Scott died inside himself at around the age of thirty to thirty-five," Hemingway wrote to Perkins about a year after Fitzgerald's death, in December 1940, at forty-four; "and his creative powers died somewhat later." Hemingway was trying to account for the "deadness" of Fitzgerald's final, incomplete, and posthumously published novel, *The Last Tycoon*, written when "all the dust was off the butterfly's wing for a long time." Fitzgerald himself had written an only somewhat gentler elegy to his creative powers, in a letter to Scottie in the last month of his life, explaining that it is usually "the poetic" talent that matures early, "which mine was in large part." The past tense must have cost him dear. Fitzgerald was then living in Hollywood, where he had been writing a screenplay for Shirley Temple, and where he had suffered his first heart attack—at Schwab's drugstore, on Sunset Boulevard. It does sometimes seem that the life was as tellingly constructed as the book.

Fitzgerald was laboring at the studios to scrape money together for Scottie's tuition at Vassar, and his last years of letters to her, filled with worry and advice, are among the most moving parental letters ever written, far truer and more substantive than anything in his later "creative" work. Although he struggled continuously with debts (his bank account, he reports one week, is down to twelve dollars), and he had to beg for magazine advances on fees a tenth of what he once earned, he begrudged her money only for taking a course called "English Prose Since 1800": "Anybody that can't read modern English prose by themselves is subnormal—and you know it." Instead, to improve her writing style, he advised her to study great poetry, and his letters are filled with rhapsodies on the subject, above all on Keats. He tells her that he has read the "Ode on a Grecian Urn" a hundred times: "About the tenth time I began to know what it was about, and caught the chime in it and the exquisite inner mechanics."

This must be excellent advice, even if we don't know how Scottie fared with it. We know how Fitzgerald fared: one could not better explain *Gatsby*'s magic than to point to "the chime in it and the exquisite inner mechanics." As for what the poem is about, Fitzgerald caught, perhaps as well as anyone ever has, the hovering threat of time and the decline inherent in consummation, even of a kiss. Yet Romantic poetry's most famous message, the identity of truth and beauty, is something Fitzgerald effectively rewrote for a new national culture: beauty is youth, he told us, youth beauty, and the only way to happiness is through illusion. The cold unbearableness of truth is the final message of his one great book.

Gatsby dies of truth. Nick imagines him, in the hours before his death, realizing that Daisy will not call and will not come, looking out at a world stripped down to ugliness and terror. It is a world he has never seen before, and in which he cannot live. Don Quixote died of such truth, as did Emma Bovary—and there are those who think Fitzgerald died of it, too. Edmund Wilson writes of seeing him in his last years, trying to live without liquor, appearing strangely mild and banal and seeming to look around him with grown-up eyes for the first time. He was grown-up enough by then to try to make sure that Scottie would not be so disabled. "For premature adventure one pays an atrocious price," he warned her, in one of his typical lectures from the heart concerning discipline, work, sobriety, driving in the rain, refusing to get in a car with a drunk, prose style, fame, self-honesty, just rewards, duty, honor, and moral courage. "It's the logic of life that no young person ever gets away with anything."

BEHIND THE MASK

BERT WILLIAMS
AND
STEPIN FETCHIT

Bert Williams, circa 1905

B ackstage in a Detroit vaudeville house during the mid-1890s, a mild-mannered West Indian gentleman named Egbert Williams dipped his hands into a supply of oily black burnt cork and rubbed it over his face until his features all but disappeared. These gestures marked the end of a private moral battle and the beginning of a great career. Williams and his partner, George Walker, had been knocking about the minstrel circuit for a few years, playing medicine shows and hootchy-kootchy joints and, most memorably, a rough Colorado mining camp where, accused of being better dressed than Negroes ought to be, they had been stripped of their clothes and were lucky to exit with their lives. Williams—tall, relatively fair-skinned, a child of the Bahamas—claimed that he learned about racism on these tours. Walker—small, very dark, Kansas-born—already knew everything about it. During these years, Williams had carefully coached himself in "stage Negro" dialect ("To me," he later wrote, "it was just as much a foreign dialect as that of the Italian") and the shambling mannerisms that regularly accompanied it. There was no getting around audience expectations. But both partners seemed to agree that degradation had its limits: they did not use blackface makeup in their act. White minstrel performers used it, black minstrel performers used it, but Bert Williams and George Walker did not. Until the night in Detroit when, "just for a lark," as he later claimed—although it seems more an act of professional desperation—Williams, the straight man of the team, blacked up. To his surprise, he found himself suddenly free to play the clown, and the act got laughs as never before. In no time, Williams and Walker were headed for New York.

Bert Williams went on to become the first African American celebrity: the most famous "colored man" in America during the early decades of the twentieth century. He was a Broadway star, a *Ziegfeld Follies* star, and a leading artist at Columbia Records, where his recordings sold hundreds of thousands of copies. He was also among the first black men to appear in motion pictures, although film stardom eluded him. At the height of Williams's career, Booker T. Washington remarked, "Bert Williams has done more for the race than I have." W.E.B. Du Bois proudly called him "the leading comedian of the American stage." Yet during the decades after Williams's death, in 1922, he was not merely forgotten but determinedly erased from history, precisely because of his success in playing the role of what he himself called "the shiftless darkey."

In recent years, there have been many attempts to reevaluate Williams's life and art, and to come to terms with the racial history he represents. Nevertheless, it was a shock when, in the fall of 2014, the Museum of Modern Art in New York presented the debut of a film that Williams had made just over a century earlier, a film that had never been completed or shown publicly before. That evening, nervous questions about what to expect were heard throughout the jam-packed crowd of people, black and white, waiting for the show to begin. Once the film began to unroll, however, after a couple of brief speeches, anxiety gave way to bursts of startled laughter and occasional cheers. The audience responded to Williams's performance with audible excitement, no small amount of relief, and an ovation. A new cultural hero had been discovered. And he was still wearing blackface.

Williams worked squarely in the tradition of the racial clowns who first set foot on the American stage decades before the Civil War, when blacked-up white performers made the caricature of a plantation slave a national entertainment. Jim Crow, as the caricature was called, was a major element of the traveling minstrel shows that were our first homegrown popular art. It did not take long, however, for imitation and exaggeration to turn to grotesquerie, as the shows became insidiously jaunty arguments in support of slavery and, eventually, of the racist Jim Crow policies so aptly named for the character himself. This grim history was given a further twist when, after the war, aspiring black performers who joined the shows began mimicking the whites who were caricaturing them. There were no other roles they could play. The only major alternative to Jim Crow was his city-slicker counterpart, Zip Coon, a boastful dandy with a mouthful of malapropisms. This was the role that George Walker took on for himself. The reinvented pair billed themselves as the "Two Real Coons," a commercially minded claim of their superior authenticity over so many white "coon" acts. The gambit seems to have worked, at least in the sense of bringing attention to their talents, whatever it did to their souls.

Williams and Walker arrived in New York in 1896, during the long racial twilight between the failure of Reconstruction and the rise of the national movement for civil rights. That spring, the Supreme Court delivered its landmark decision in the case of *Plessy v. Ferguson*, making segregated facilities—"separate but equal"—the law of the land. In this debilitating climate, "coon songs" were the rage, and it shouldn't be entirely strange to learn that some of the most offensive examples were written and performed by blacks: a runaway hit of 1896, "All Coons Look Alike to Me," was by the black comedian Ernest Hogan, and Williams and Walker eventually contributed their share. This was a time when every ethnic group was subject to comic (and not so comic) battering: "When Tony Macaroni Marries Chinky Chanky Lee" was a roughly contemporary song that did double duty on immigrant-bashing. And much of the battering, especially in the case of Jewish and black entertainers, was by their own efforts, as they struggled with the particularly hateful images that America had of Jews and blacks. Turning these images into jokes, and being in on the jokes, or at least making a profit from the jokes, was a not inconsiderable survival strategy and perhaps the most American thing they could do. This is not to say that performers lacked awareness of the damage that even jokes can cause and how easily they perpetuate those hateful images. Hogan later expressed deep regret over his song. But what other sort of songs could they sing? What theatrical forms would contain them? In New York, Williams and Walker, with a close circle of friends and colleagues, determined to bring new possibilities for black performers to the stage.

It's been called "Black Bohemia": a community that existed some three decades before the Harlem Renaissance, before the great migration from the South, even a few years before the population shift to Harlem. The center of black life was the West Twenties and Thirties and, increasingly, streets directly northward—the area then known as the Tenderloin—but black artistic life coalesced around West Fifty-third Street, where Williams and Walker settled in the black-owned Marshall Hotel, off Sixth Avenue. Really more of a rooming house, with a restaurant attached, the Marshall was a gathering place for an immensely gifted if inevitably troubled group of writers, composers, and performers who were eager to break out of the minstrel trap. Among them were Bob Cole, who wrote the first musical comedy to be created and produced by African Americans, in 1897, with the title (here the source of the trouble comes in) *A Trip to Coontown*; the composer Will Marion Cook, a virtuoso violinist who had studied at Berlin's prestigious Hochschule für Musik with a student of a student of Mendelssohn's, and then with Antonín Dvořák in New York, but who chose to focus on "Negro song," by which he meant not spirituals but the ragtime syncopations that were shaking up the staid musical scene; and the poet Paul Laurence Dunbar, who teamed up with Cook in 1898 to write an epochal show called *Clorindy, or The Origins of the Cakewalk*, about the dance craze that accompanied ragtime from the slave quarters to the New York stage. Arriving just a little later was James Weldon Johnson, whose career as head of the NAACP was still far off but whose poem "Lift Every Voice and Sing" had recently been set to music by his younger brother, J. Rosamond Johnson, with whom he shared rooms on the Marshall's second floor. These artists were lifting their voices just as black music was beginning to exert a hold on white America, a deeper and more defining hold than any of them could know.

That all these men were inspired by Williams and Walker suggests the great if subtle changes that the pair were bringing to vaudeville, where their success—they were soon earning five hundred dollars a week—created a new demand for "colored" acts on every bill. (Not more than one act per show, however; vaudeville audiences were racially mixed if generally segregated, and theater owners didn't want too many black patrons to perturb the whites in the higher-priced seats.) Contemporary accounts of Williams's performances, in particular, convey a humanity and pathos well beyond the usual bounds of racial caricature. He was the perpetual loser and the comic dupe, yet he projected a confiding warmth that aroused sympathy and even empathy in his audience; his range of facial expressions belied the flat coal mask. Cook and Dunbar worked tirelessly to find a way to showcase his gifts, producing a series of long-forgotten post-*Clorindy* shows near the century's end. But even their most ambitiously conceived works appeared less than groundbreaking when they reached the stage, where they turned out to be frustratingly tied to the minstrel tradition—the only tradition these artists had to draw on.

They were struggling to escape their era by means of the corrupted elements that the era itself provided; it would take the genius of the blues, rising up from the South, to break through to something wholly new. And yet the artists of Black Bohemia had a vision; they were moving forward. In the political debates that often took place at the Marshall, some in the group even proposed that things were getting better.

Then came the New York riot of August 15, 1900, set off by the death of a white plainclothes policeman at the hands of a black man during a fight. Late that night, angry white mobs tore through the streets of the Tenderloin, beating every black male in sight. According to newspaper reports, the police did little to stop the mobs and at times egged them on, although by one account the police stopped a lynching that was under way, with a clothesline for a noose, from a streetlamp on Thirty-fourth Street and Eighth Avenue. James Weldon Johnson later recalled that the crowds had issued a cry to "get Ernest Hogan and Williams and Walker and Cole and Johnson," the best-known black names in the city. Williams and Walker were performing that night and didn't hear the news; they left a vaudeville theater on West Fifty-eighth Street after the show. Williams made his way home, just a few blocks away, but Walker, going downtown to meet Hogan for a drink, was dragged from a Broadway streetcar and beaten. Reports differ on what happened to Hogan; he either remained for safety all night in the Times Square theater where he was performing, or he was hurt so badly that he had to withdraw from the show. One of the newspapers added insult to injury by adapting Hogan's wretched song title as a heading in its report on the mob's behavior: ALL COONS LOOKED ALIKE.

In the riot's aftermath, outrage in the black community led to some useful lessons in political organizing and to the winning of an investigation into police tactics. (The police were ultimately exonerated of all wrongdoing, a verdict that does not come as a surprise more than a century later.) Privately, Williams—a quiet man, never one to grandstand—is said to have retreated further into himself. Walker—extroverted and politically outspoken—became even more determined to establish "an Ethiopian theater where the plays produced by black men may be staged, and the songs of black people may be sung." At the time, "Ethiopian" stood for black, and stories of Africa were essential to Walker's vision of a "national theater" that would represent the "Afro-American people." It was much easier to imagine telling African stories, though, than to know what stories to tell. Just weeks after the riot, Williams and Walker opened in a new show, *Sons of Ham*, a vaudeville potpourri that had a great success. Hit songs from the show included not only "Miss Hannah from Savannah" (performed by Walker's new wife, Ada Overton Walker) but "My Little Zulu Babe," which Walker proudly cited as an example of the duo's "purely African" themes. Given the song's lyrics and general tone—"She is my little Zulu baby / A perfect lady / Although she's shady"—it is clear he had little notion of what an African theme might be.

Their next show was in many ways a breakthrough. *In Dahomey* was not set entirely in Africa, as the pair had initially planned—it might more truthfully have been titled *In Boston, in Florida, and Finally a Scene in Dahomey*—but it nevertheless changed the theatrical game in the United States in terms of race. A full-length black musical comedy with a cast of fifty, the show toured in tryouts for several months and then, in February 1903, it became the first black show ever to play in a major Broadway theater. Williams revealed that he'd done a private little buck and wing backstage, and announced, more to himself than to anyone else, "We're here!" They had indeed arrived: the New York Theater, on West Forty-fifth Street, was extremely large—twenty-eight hundred seats—and ornate, decorated in good-old American Louis XIV style, with tiers of boxes and a mural depicting the goddess Fame crowning Poetry and Prose. On opening night, however, with Fame about to crown a cast of black performers, black patrons were outraged to find themselves directed around the corner to a separate entrance and then seated in what the *Times* called a "bleak and inhospitable gallery."

Segregation in New York theaters was both illegal and commonplace. The unusual aspect of this evening was the expectation, by the black audience, that the advent on Broadway of Williams and Walker—"the pioneers of all Colored Organizations," as their advertisements billed them—would undo the generations-old pernicious custom at a stroke. There were apparently complaints and even feuds in the house that night, although nothing like the "race war" that the *Times* claimed had been predicted by "trouble breeders" ever since the show was announced. The theater's manager bluntly told the papers that he was prepared to be sued to ensure that "the orchestra and boxes of this theater are for our white patrons and no others." (Previous lawsuits had resulted in a fifty-dollar judgment here, two hundred there—hardly an onerous price to pay.) If the black audience had expected their heroes to stand up for them, they were disappointed; the power and the leverage just weren't there. For the rest of the run, as the papers also reported, the only black people allowed on the orchestra level were the musical conductor and the "boys" peddling water in the aisles.

Yet it seems that once the lights went down and the music started up—and particularly once Bert Williams took the stage—complaints and arguments ceased. The applause, described as "on a Maxim gun scale," went on past midnight. The next day, *The Mail and Express* concluded that "the race problem was most successfully handled at the New York last night," by which it meant that the black members of the audience had stopped demanding an end to discrimination in its most immediate manifestation and had settled down to enjoy themselves as best they could. And their best was very good. For if Williams and Walker had failed to carry them along into their promised land that night, they provided more than a little onstage compensation. And the white audience, carefully provided with its own rewards, didn't notice anything at all.

On its surface, *In Dahomey* was just another genially self-mocking mix of song and dance, hardly distinguishable from earlier shows. The curtain opened on a respectably dressed black crowd in a public square, clustered around a huckster selling hair-straightening tonic and skin-lightening bleach: "the greatest boon that mankind has ever known." (As proof of his skills, he has turned half of one man's face chalk-white, with a vertical line right down the middle.) A rare skeptic breaks through the commotion to announce, "I do think the colored race is the biggest set of fools I ever cast my optics against." It's a standard laugh line with a pointed meaning in the circumstances: these blacks are fools because they are trying to be white. The plot kicks in when the skeptic is revealed to be the president of the Dahomey Colonization Society, an organization designed to lead African Americans back to Africa. (The onetime kingdom of Dahomey is part of modern-day Benin.) And why would African Americans want to leave America? Jokes about finding gold and raising watermelons seem to have provided enough of the expected laughs to cover for a more startling observation: "They ain't satisfied" one straight-talker sums it up. "They figure this country's a dead one."

Plans for American blacks to return to Africa in a kind of mass repatriation had been on the agenda of whites and blacks, racists and abolitionists, since the founding of Liberia as a home for that purpose in the 1820s. For a time, even Abraham Lincoln had championed the idea. But such movements didn't belong just to history. George Walker's father had left his wife and children to go to Denver, where he became president of the Colorado Colonization Society of Liberia, Africa. By 1903, the year *In Dahomey* opened, the unrelenting pressures of Jim Crow had put such schemes back in the news. And Williams and Walker had some personal history with Dahomeyans, widely believed in the United States to be a particularly savage people, even rumored to be cannibals. A group of Dahomeyan warriors had been presented in a kind of living ethnic display at the 1893 Chicago World's Fair, in no small part to bolster theories of the natural inferiority of blacks and to justify the American social order. One year later, when the Dahomeyans were late in arriving at the San Francisco reprise of the fair, Williams and Walker were among the locals hired to fill in until they got there, exhibiting themselves as fearsome, half-naked savages without arousing the least suspicion. It was this event that sparked their interest in depicting Africans onstage, along with the American Negroes more traditionally seen there. In both cases, they'd had experience in acting out fantastical ideas of race.

In Dahomey inevitably reflected the love-hate relationship that so many African Americans had with the only homeland they'd ever known, a conflict clearly expressed by the show's creators: Will Marion Cook (music), Paul Laurence Dunbar (lyrics), and another Marshall Hotel regular, Jesse Shipp (book). The show's would-be colonists are so thoroughly American that they plan to bring "civilization" along with them to Africa, in the form of streetcars, electric lights, and saloons. When asked what they will do if the Africans make war on them instead of welcoming them and their improvements, they reply that they will do exactly what Uncle Sam did with the Indians: "Kick the stuffin' out of dem and put them on a reservation." Near the end of the show, when the colonists have finally reached Dahomey, the plot goes off in two directions. On the one hand, a stately African chorus (chiefs, soldiers, dancing girls) offers a spectacular image of a society unlike anything suggested at the Chicago fair. On the other, a series of cultural misadventures—the plot was always something of a muddle— lead the colonists to decide they must return immediately to America. No matter their devotion to an Africa they'd never seen, or the depths of their complaints about their own country, the Americans who made the show really couldn't imagine any other ending.

In Dahomey went through considerable changes when it moved to London in the spring of 1903, and was altered still further—new songs in, old songs out—when it returned to tour the United States. All along, the star performers were continually interpolating their own material. The result was an ever-changing production, yet one that never lost its tone of pride and strength. One big ragtime number that was always performed was "On Emancipation Day," a celebration of the annual holiday held in Cook's native Washington, D.C., ever since the end of the Civil War: "the grandest day of the year," according to the script and, in the even bolder lyrics, a day when "All you white folks clear de way." The brassy Ada Overton Walker gave off plenty of attitude in an added

number by Clare Kummer—the great-niece of Harriet Beecher Stowe—
called "A Rich Coon's Babe": "Fo' as I told de rest, / I'se accustomed to
de best, / De Waldorf ain't a bit too good fo' me." Mrs. Walker later
replaced this number with an aria from Meyerbeer's *L'Africaine*, which
says something about the range of the show's material. Whether you
got the coon song or the aria depended on when you came.

Quieter yet even more radical was the ballad "Brown-Skin Baby
Mine" (music by Cook, lyrics by Cook and Cecil Mack), which revels
in a black woman's beauty—"Browner den de huckleberries, / Ripenin'
on de vine"—in a manner seldom heard again until the recordings of
Abbey Lincoln and Nina Simone, half a century later. What allowed
for such confidence in 1903? The song was performed by another of
the show's stars, Abbie Mitchell, who may herself have been its inspiration: Mitchell was nineteen years old and married to Cook when
she turned "Brown-Skin Baby Mine" into one of the show's hits. Was
this nearly forgotten singer a precursor of Lincoln and Simone? There
are no recordings of Mitchell from this time, but her classically trained
soprano was still ravishingly pure more than thirty years later, when
George Gershwin chose her to introduce "Summertime" in *Porgy
and Bess*.

But Williams was the biggest star of *In Dahomey*, the indisputable
heart of the show; despite the obscuring makeup, his humanity was
fully evident. He made his entrance bringing up the rear of a Salvation
Army band, wearily beating an enormous drum. The slow-moving, dole-
ful, extremely ponderous but far-from-stupid character he portrayed
became his signature persona from then on. He had a smooth baritone
voice, although he tended to speak his songs as much as sing them.
Above all, he was a brilliant mime and elicited a mixture of emotions
even without the use of words. He was known to bring on shouts of
laughter and then, in the next instant, "with a few peering glances, an
intent attitude, and a wonderful manipulation of the lips, he almost
made you want to cry," one critic wrote. "The laughter ceased abruptly,
something caught you at the throat."

It's natural to wonder what he could have done if he'd escaped
the limitations of blackface, if only he'd been given the chance. But
Williams was given the chance. While the cast was preparing for the
show's move to London, friends and theater professionals strongly

urged him to drop the burnt cork. Blackface was not in the English tradition, and there was fear that the audience would be confused. The company was dropping the use of dialect in the script (but apparently not in the songs) out of the same concern. Williams considered the proposition and seemed excited, for about ten minutes. Then he said no.

It's a terrible irony that the mask of oppression was also, for Williams, the means to freedom. "A great protection," he called it. "I shuffle onto the stage, not as myself, but as a lazy, slow-going negro." Nothing exposed, nothing revealed. For him, it was an actor's mask, a means of escaping self-consciousness. Some have said, with resentment, that as a mixed-race, light-skinned West Indian—and a British citizen, born in Nassau, Bahamas, in 1874—Williams did not think of American racism as aimed at him, even though he'd moved to California with his family at age ten. The blackface made the distinction between who he was and who he played onstage absolutely clear. He was certainly not a man who found it easy to speak out about politics. Yet, in a modern light, his blackface can be regarded as a sign of the invisible mask that no black man of the time could do without. In 1896, Paul Laurence Dunbar, the lyricist for *In Dahomey* and the most well-known black poet of the day, published the poem "We Wear the Mask": "We wear the mask that grins and lies, / It hides our cheeks and shades our eyes,— / This debt we pay to human guile; / With torn and bleeding hearts we smile." An indictment of everyday black American life, Dunbar's poem was also a fair description of the blacks-in-blackface acts so common in the age of *Plessy*.

London audiences turned out to have no problem with blackface. Among Williams's admirers was George Bernard Shaw, who wrote to an actor friend, "The best acting now in London is that of Williams and Walker," adding that he wanted Williams to play Cleopatra's servant in a new production of *Caesar and Cleopatra*. (Alas, this scheme was never realized, and it is not known if Shaw ever approached Williams.) *In Dahomey* was such a hit that it earned a special performance at Buckingham Palace, where Williams sang "Evah Darkey Is a King," mocking black American claims to royal African lineage—"Ef yo' social life's a bungle, / Jes' you go back to the jungle, / An' remember dat yo' daddy was a king!"—to the warmly professed pleasure of the king of England. Williams later said that he was never treated so well as on that day.

The company's next show was *Abyssinia*, its title a historical name for Ethiopia, which, as one of the only African states (along with Liberia) never colonized, was a source of immense pride. There were a few African references in the script, but the show was really just another round-trip fantasy for a cast of African Americans who sang and danced extremely well. And with the biggest budget yet (secured through the business savvy of George Walker), it was an extravaganza, complete with live donkeys and a camel. Williams was again the star, and he soon added a number that became a kind of theme song for him. "Nobody" (music by Williams, lyrics by Alex Rogers) is about a man so hyperbolically luckless and alone that the only possible response is to laugh: "When winter comes with snow and sleet, / And me with hunger and cold feet, / Who says 'Here's twenty-five cents; go ahead get something to eat'? / Nobody!" In Williams's immensely popular recording— it's available on YouTube—he mimics an accompanying slide trombone and seems to vie with it for loopy mournfulness. This tragicomic effect comes straight out of vaudeville and minstrelsy (Kander and Ebb used "Nobody" as a model for the vaudeville pastiche "Mr. Cellophane," in *Chicago*), although Williams gives the entire song an irony worthy of the blues.

Williams was also the star of the duo's third and final show, *Bandanna Land*, a return to the Old South, which they brought to Broadway in 1908. (With a script that includes white characters, this show raises the interesting possibility that white Southerners were played by blacks in whiteface.) Williams seems to have had his biggest success here, performing a legendary one-man poker game; the *Chicago Tribune* was moved to declare him not merely a comedian but an artist. In touring their three big shows and also in their vaudeville turns, Williams and Walker broke the so-called race line in theaters across the country—St. Louis, Philadelphia, Washington, D.C.— where no black performers had played before. As on Broadway, however, the better seats were invariably reserved for whites. One outspoken critic in the black press felt that the team was certainly in a position now to challenge these policies, but the team did not share this view. When Booker T. Washington went to see *Bandanna Land*, he sat in the balcony.

Yet black audiences remained fiercely loyal to Williams and Walker, and the performers were loyal, too, when they felt they had a choice. They made their highly successful recordings with the only black-owned company in the business. Responding to criticism, Walker—their increasingly defensive public voice—pointed out that the payroll for their shows ran to twenty-three hundred dollars a week, that they employed and encouraged a tremendous number of black theater artists, and that they worked out of a "love for the race" and saw their achievements as a public credit to it. In sum, Williams and Walker amounted to nothing less than "a race institution," no matter who sat in the orchestra seats.

One night during the run of *Bandanna Land*, Walker began to slur his speech in a way that was initially taken for a joke but that turned out to be a symptom of syphilis. Both his mind and his muscle control quickly deteriorated: he made his last appearance onstage in February 1909, and died two years later. The Marshall Hotel group was already a thing of the past. Paul Laurence Dunbar had left New York well before he died, in 1906, and, with the relocation of the black community to Harlem, other members of the circle had dispersed. Williams, like Walker, had married a performer in the company, Lottie Thompson, but unlike Walker he preferred a quiet life at home with his wife and his extensive book collection. It had long been rumored that Williams and Walker had their differences and were about to split. But Williams now missed his business partner desperately. The show that he mounted alone, in 1909, *Mr. Load of Koal*, was in the duo's old tradition—three acts and a large black cast—but failed financially. Williams didn't have Walker's ability to push a show into first-class theaters, where expensive tickets drove up profits. In fact, he lacked all of Walker's management skills, and that included the ability to house and feed a company of more than sixty black performers as they toured through, say, Iowa. Although he promised the company of *Mr. Load of Koal* that he would mount another show for them soon, it couldn't have been a surprise when Williams returned to vaudeville, playing solo, in April 1910. It was a very big surprise, however, when just a month later he signed with Florenz Ziegfeld to be the first black headliner in the *Follies* and opened that summer in a show that not only had no other African Americans onstage but permitted no African Americans in its audience, not even in the balcony.

Twenty years later, James Weldon Johnson, in his classic book *Black Manhattan*, still regarded Williams's move as a "defection," echoing what many people felt at the time. Williams responded to attacks in the black press by saying that "colored musical shows" were "at a low ebb right now," and that he could "best represent my race by doing pioneer work." If he was right about the condition of black theater, his own exit capped an irreparable series of losses; it would be a full decade before "colored musical shows" returned to Broadway.

Williams was also abandoning a long if quietly harbored dream of becoming a serious actor. We don't know if he ever learned of Shaw's admiration; what we do know is that the great theatrical producer David Belasco offered Williams a contract just a short time after Ziegfeld did. Perhaps Belasco had read an interview that Williams gave just the year before, in which he spoke of the need for a talented new playwright to tell the story of the Negro's rise in America, and prophesied that the Negro actor would one day rank with the Negro teacher as an elevating force in the community. Belasco did not yet have a play for Williams but promised to find one. Williams appeared very excited and agreed to sign with him, a move that would change his life. Then he abruptly withdrew, rather in the way he'd withdrawn from the chance to be liberated from blackface, during the London run of *In Dahomey*. One may ascribe his decision to salary considerations, lack of confidence, or fear, but it is finally impossible to know why this highly cultivated man preferred to wear a giant rooster suit in the *Follies* of 1910.

Ziegfeld had been putting on the *Follies* for only three years (and was still a year away from attaching his name to the title), but the shows were already known for their beautiful showgirls. A highly publicized clause of Williams's contract—said to be instigated by Williams himself—stipulated that he would not appear onstage with any female member of the company. Presumably, this was meant to mollify those outraged by his presence; another clause stipulated that Williams would never have to tour the South. But even within the *Follies*, there was outrage: a protest by cast members, after the first rehearsal, ended only when Ziegfeld told them he could replace every one of them *except* Williams. He shared the limelight this first season with another newcomer, Fannie Brice, who scored a success singing "Lovie Joe," a brand-new "coon song," so called not because it contained racially deprecating humor but because its sexy bluesiness and Southern inflections gave it a dramatically black "voice." (When one of the producers demanded that Brice sing "more" and "sure" instead of "mo'" and "sho'," she refused: "No Negro would pronounce those words the way you did.") Brice also had a Yiddish-inflected number in the show, but she hadn't yet mastered the accent to pull it off.

Williams was soon the highest-paid member of the *Follies*, and stayed with the show for much of the decade. Some things got easier as he went along; in 1912, the clause prohibiting his appearance with female performers was dropped. Modern historians have discerned a low and steady thrum of racial subversiveness in his performances, particularly in sketches where he played a poor workingman (a redcap, a hansom cab driver) who is clearly smarter than the white fool who has hired him. But Williams increasingly chafed at the shows' limitations: "Singing a half dozen coon songs and telling a few Negro dialect jokes does not satisfy my ambition," he told an interviewer for an African American newspaper in 1915. "I want to be the interpreter of the Negro on the stage." Unfortunately, the path he'd chosen shut him off from real developments taking place in black theater. In 1916, the Lafayette Theater in Harlem (opened in 1912, desegregated in 1913) put on an all-black *Othello* for the tricentennial of Shakespeare's death. That same season, Williams played Othello in a *Follies* sketch in which, as the *Times* described it, he "chokes his Desdemona till he is tired, and then beats her with a sledge hammer, but it only irritates her."

It was a lonely life. The *Follies* usually played New York for a season, then toured the country, and in his time off Williams liked to play vaudeville, where he kept up with his black audience. In either case, he was almost invariably the only black act in the show, and couldn't stay in the same hotel as his fellow players or eat his meals with them. Lottie Williams had retired from the stage in 1908 and preferred to stay home. From 1913, when Lottie's sister died, she and Bert raised her sister's three daughters in a large brownstone in Harlem, where his favorite retreats were the house's library, which he had built for himself, and the neighborhood bar across the street. Williams was a big drinker, and one reason (beyond all the usual reasons) is that bars were the only place that he could easily socialize with his white colleagues. He explained that, when he was on the road, he figured out the other performers' schedules so that he could bump into them in local saloons: "I always said I was waiting for somebody . . . even when I was only waiting for anybody . . . funny what a man'll do for human companionship!" He did not have many close friends, although an exception late in life was his fellow *Follies* star Eddie Cantor, an energetic young white comedian who specialized in blackface and to whom Williams served as a mentor. The pair appeared together, both in blackface, in a famous sketch about a railroad porter and his prissy, college-educated son. Offstage, they continued to call each other "Sonny" and "Pappy."

There's a hint of Williams's wider ambitions in some of the longer monologues that he did in vaudeville or for recordings: a black boy trying to sell a fish to a cruelly indifferent white man, a Southern preacher letting loose. These routines bypass *Follies*-style jokes and display a mordant racial humor on the order of Eudora Welty's. His most famous mime routines, including his one-man poker game, are preserved in a couple of short films he made for Biograph Studios, in the Bronx. For the better part of a century there have been rumors that he appeared in a film without blackface, now lost, although there is no evidence that his dramatic aspirations ever carried him that far. Williams was nothing if not a gentleman, determinedly discreet and publicly unflappable— rather like Duke Ellington, who composed a musical "portrait" of Williams in 1940. He was uncomfortable being where he was not wanted, although this attitude was rooted not in humility but in pride. One of the few stories of Williams responding to racism was told by Eddie Cantor, and it takes place in a St. Louis bar: When the bartender informed him that a glass of gin would cost him fifty dollars, Williams peeled five hundred dollars from a roll of bills. "Give me ten of them," he said.

He left the *Follies* in 1918 and, still under contract to Ziegfeld, joined a smaller, looser, late-night cabaret-style show, the *Midnight Frolic*, which performed on the rooftop stage of the New Amsterdam

Theatre. (George Gershwin was working as the show's rehearsal pianist, one of the last times he held such a lowly job.) He had applied for American citizenship at the start of World War I; in 1917, when the United States entered the fight, he publicly announced his hope that the valor of the "colored troopers" fighting abroad would help to change the racial situation at home. In his new show he introduced "You'll Find Old Dixieland in France" (music by George W. Meyer, lyrics by Grant Clarke), which offered the sophisticated good-time crowd such lines as "With Abe Lincoln in their memory, / They've gone to fight for liberty." But black soldiers won little liberty for themselves, either in the segregated armed forces or after they returned home. During the summer of 1919, white-instigated racial riots tore through more than three dozen American cities. In October, the *Times* reported that forty-eight Negroes had been lynched so far that year. Williams became a citizen in time to see that none of the changes that would give meaning to his status had come to pass.

He rejoined the *Follies* in 1919 and quickly left again, this time for good. He didn't go far; he never had. With Eddie Cantor, he launched a revue-style show, *Broadway Brevities of 1920*, but it didn't outlast the season. That fall, he was shocked to learn just how far another black man had gone in the American theater, when Charles Gilpin, a former chorus boy in one of the Williams and Walker shows, played the leading role in the off-Broadway premiere of Eugene O'Neill's *The Emperor Jones*. The hugely acclaimed show soon moved to Broadway, and Gilpin became the first African American to win a New York Drama League Award. It had all happened very fast: just weeks before the opening, the first choice for Gilpin's role had been a white actor in blackface.

If history was lurching forward, the American stage seemed to be leading the way, however unsteadily. (The Drama League, pandering to the racists among its members, actually disinvited Gilpin from the gala at which he was to be honored, and only reinvited him after O'Neill and the critic Kenneth McGowan ensured that no one else would attend, either. Gilpin got a standing ovation that night.) In the spring of 1921, a new black musical, *Shuffle Along*, exploded on the scene, the biggest hit of its kind since the days of Williams and Walker, with a sixteen-girl *Follies*-style chorus line (including a very young Josephine

Baker) and a score, by Noble Sissle and Eubie Blake, that reviewers found irrepressibly "jazzy." *Shuffle Along* renewed the tradition of black shows on Broadway; some people even credit it with kicking off the Harlem Renaissance, despite the very unrenaissance-like fact that it had a blackface comedy team among its stars.

Williams seemed determined to catch up with these developments. His wife later recalled that he had acquired the script of a serious drama, never identified, which he carried around and called his "bible," hoping it "might do for him what *The Emperor Jones* did for Mr. Gilpin." He was planning to appear in it the following year, in London, where everything he'd become famous for wouldn't stand in his way. Instead, that summer, just a couple of months after *Shuffle Along* opened, he took on a big new musical, his first Broadway-bound venture in thirteen years. Unlike the old Williams and Walker shows, though, and unlike *Shuffle Along*, this show—eventually titled *Under the Bamboo Tree*—had an entirely white cast, except for Williams, who played a porter in a resort hotel, and sang his most memorable number not to another person but to a dog he'd been instructed to drown. It wasn't the kind of racial statement that his black audience had wanted, but it was what he knew how to do. And it was, at least, emotionally honest; Williams spoke of his very real empathy with that dog.

Despite good out-of-town reviews for Williams, the show was soon in trouble. The book had to be rewritten, the musical director was fired, and Williams seems to have worked and worried himself literally sick. The show truly could not go on without him, and so, while ill, he performed through weeks of Chicago winter, ignoring orders to rest and becoming so weak that he couldn't dress himself. In February 1922, the show opened in Detroit, where Williams had started out in blackface more than twenty-five years earlier; if there were any regrets, he had the compensation of leading a first-class company in the first-class Garrick Theater. Nothing was going to keep him from that stage. The comedian Sammy White, who played a tourist in a scene with Williams, described how a terrible croak entered his voice one night and how, sweating heavily, he began to mop his brow, so that the oily cork started coming off on his handkerchief, leaving his face a streaked and mottled mess. The audience, taking it all for part of the act, screamed with laughter. Williams got through the rest of the scene, and the curtain rang down.

He died a week or so later, of pneumonia, at the age of forty-seven. The assessments of his life and career began at once, with Ziegfeld pronouncing Williams one of the greatest comedians in the world. (As the producer of *Show Boat* on Broadway five years later, Ziegfeld may have been responsible for incorporating some of Williams's own history into the landmark show, which contained a scene of savvy African Americans being employed to play Dahomeyan savages at the 1893 Chicago fair, in a number called "In Dahomey.") Some big-name white journalists—Heywood Broun, Ring Lardner—emphatically concurred with Ziegfeld, even while admitting that Williams had been stifled by the *Follies* and the blackface. The black press offered dizzying contradictions, even (and often) within the same critique: he had struggled to humanize the old stereotypes but, by playing in theaters that barred or segregated Negroes, he had become a "facile instrument" of the forces of oppression; his whole career was an example of "lynching one's soul in blackface twaddle," yet wasn't that the only way he could have started a career at all? And hadn't he opened doors for others? What might he have done if he'd had more time? As the years went by, however, and active resistance became the only respected course of racial action, Williams was increasingly regarded as part of a shameful past, better swept away. In 1963, a TV special on the civil rights movement used a film clip of Williams to exemplify the most offensive old-time racial caricatures.

Williams isn't the easiest of heroes. Eventually, though, it became apparent that to turn one's back on him was to turn one's back on a part of our national history: difficult, ugly, embarrassing, a time when the mask of accommodation was the only way for a black man to get by and to preserve, as far as possible, his peace and dignity. An anthology of tributes to Williams appeared in 1923; after that, there was virtually nothing until 1970, when Ann Charters, a white woman, published a slim but thoughtful biography—in which she cites the encouragement of Langston Hughes—that was all too appropriately titled *Nobody*. And Williams remained nobody for decades. In 1981, the Tony Award–winning actor Ben Vereen set out to educate the country about the entertainer he felt had paved his way. At Ronald Reagan's inaugural festivities, Vereen did an introductory routine about Williams, placing him in a sympathetic context and even stating, not quite accurately, that blackface had been a necessity for him and not a choice. He then performed one of Williams's own routines, in full costume and makeup. Unfortunately for Vereen, his introduction was cut from the TV broadcast. Black viewers were so horrified and furious at what they saw—a black man doing what Williams had done all his professional life—that Vereen didn't work again for years.

The first scholarly biography of Williams, by Eric Ledell Smith, was published in 1992 with a subtitle that clearly showed a new approach, referring to Williams as "the Pioneer Black Comedian." Four years later, Thomas L. Riis published a painstaking edition of the scripts and songs of *In Dahomey*. And then, not quite as suddenly as it seemed, minstrelsy and blackface were legitimate and even trendy topics, thanks to causes ranging from the growth of African American studies as a university discipline and the deliberately shocking use of minstrel imagery by artists like Michael Ray Charles and Kara Walker, to the equally shocking use of newer stereotypes by various gangsta rappers and the accusations of a "new minstrelsy" leveled at them—by Spike Lee, most formidably. *Bamboozled*, Lee's scathing film on the subject of minstrelsy, released in 2000, includes a lecture on Williams as a "brilliant" entertainer forced into a degraded tradition, and shows us both an appalling photograph of him in his *Follies* rooster suit and a film snippet of his one-man poker routine. Most notable among the flood of books that have appeared since then are Caryl Phillips's novel *Dancing in the Dark* (2005), an attempt to get inside Williams's mind; Louis Chude-Sokei's smart if at times inscrutably academic study *The Last "Darky"* (2006); Karen Sotiropoulos's bracingly clear history *Staging Race* (2006); and Camille F. Forbes's *Introducing Bert Williams: Burnt Cork, Broadway, and the Story of America's First Black Star* (2008), a closely detailed biography that had its beginnings as a Harvard dissertation. Williams had made it to the Ivy League.

Despite the accumulation of interesting detail, none of these books changed Williams's image. He was seen as an important but passive and somewhat tragic figure who backed away from any substantive efforts to break through the conventions that bound him. Then, in November 2014, the Museum of Modern Art screened *Lime Kiln Club Field Day*, the unfinished and never-before-seen film that the curators themselves had titled, based on its general subject of a fictitious black social club. The footage, dating from 1913, was acquired in a cache of nine hundred film negatives that the museum's founding film curator, Iris Barry, had taken from the vaults of long-shuttered Biograph Studios, in 1938, since they would otherwise have been destroyed. The seven cans containing this film—seven reels in all—were marked "unidentified," hardly making them a priority. When at last their turn came to be transferred to film stock, in the late 1970s, a curator, Eileen Bowser, recognized Williams. Restoration began in 2003, accompanied by an extraordinarily diligent campaign, led by the associate curator Ronald S. Magliozzi, to figure out exactly what it was they had.

What those seven reels turned out to be is the earliest surviving footage for a feature film with an entirely black cast, except for a few minor background roles played by whites. Production shots captured in the footage reveal that it was an interracial production, with white crew members and black actors congenially working together. Three directors—two white, one black—put together some seventy minutes of 35-millimeter film, the unedited material for a romantic comedy that would probably have run some thirty-five to forty-five minutes once duplicate scenes were removed and intertitles added. Although it was never properly assembled, the film appears to have been completed: the pieced-together story line is fully legible. And though it contains its share of racial clichés, involving fried chicken and watermelon, the larger story and the range of characters render this film a radical work for Williams (or anyone) to have made in 1913, or for a long time after.

The setting is a thriving small-town black community, a place of picket fences, picnics, and parades, of comfortably middle-class black families who share a warm and busy social life, and show no special deference toward the friendly old white gentlemen who occasionally cross their path. The story centers on three rival suitors for the affections of a local beauty, played with elegance—and a gorgeous wardrobe—by Odessa Warren Grey, who had been in the cast of *In Dahomey* and who also worked as a fashion designer and milliner. (The character's beplumed hats and sparkling headbands are particularly chic.) Two of the rivals are handsome, sharply dressed young men; the third is Williams, in blackface.

This clearly isn't the lost film of a liberated Williams that people had been longing to find. In fact, given its many outdoor, sunlit scenes, its cast of good-looking actors—none, of course, in blackface—and its many close-ups, the star's stagy makeup appears more bizarre than ever. Even so, the other actors seem not to notice that he looks different or strange; the makeup is invisible to everyone but the audience. What Williams *had* broken with, however, was the psychology that had long accompanied his clownish getup: his character is not a nobody, a loser, or a dupe. He is not only funnier than his rivals but also smarter. And, astonishingly, he gets the girl. The depiction of romance had always been a taboo for blacks in theater, as perilously humanizing as displays of intelligence. Williams, who had never allowed himself an on-stage romance, is seen here in a lengthy and rapturously happy scene, riding a carousel in the open air with his beloved, sharing a lollipop as they go round and round. And there he is, at the climax of the film, walking her to her garden gate and kissing her goodbye. A screen kiss! Williams and Grey did several takes of the kiss, and Williams reacts differently in each of them: he gives a quick little air-punch of self-congratulation; he excitedly shakes his own hands; he holds off shyly at the start, then works his mouth in careful preparation. One hundred and one years after the filming, each of these takes left the MoMA audience giddy with laughter.

Why wasn't the film finished? Why wasn't it considered releasable? The problem may have had to do with its length and ambition, both far exceeding that of other surviving Williams films, but also with its timing. Magliozzi points out that, aside from the fact that all of Williams's films had trouble finding distributors, and were slow to be shown, February 1915 marked a terrible turning point for blacks in cinema: the release of D. W. Griffith's racist masterpiece, *The Birth of a Nation*. In the wake of Griffith's vicious and wildly successful reimagining of Reconstruction, with its black population of fools and brutes exploiting a freedom they did not deserve, it may have been impossible for a film so racially optimistic to see the light of day. The fallout from Griffith's film was crushing. NAACP protests against it had some effect in Northern cities, where theaters were picketed and a few of the more egregious scenes were cut, but were powerless against the larger retrogressive forces that the film either prompted or exacerbated. The revival of the Ku Klux Klan in 1915 was a direct result of Griffith's heroizing of the historical Klan, which had disbanded years before.

An unintended consequence of the protests, however, was the attrition of all black roles in film for a time. White producers had been sensitized to the risk of demonstrations against offensive racial images, but they couldn't come up with any other sort of images of blacks to put on-screen.

Did Williams succeed in changing anything? Years later, the comedian Sammy White, who'd played with Williams in *Under the Bamboo Tree*, reported that Williams, on his terrible last night in Detroit, accounted himself pleased that at least he'd made his final exit on a laugh. Williams was proud of clearing the way both for other comics and for Charles Gilpin's escape from minstrelsy. Yet Gilpin's fate was not what Williams had imagined: overcome by alcoholism during the run of *The Emperor Jones*—he drank too much for even Eugene O'Neill to abide—he was replaced in the London production by Paul Robeson and never fully recovered his career; he died in poverty in 1930. As for the succession of comics who followed Williams, as stars of the *Follies*, in vaudeville, or on Broadway—Eddie Cantor, Al Jolson, Ed Wynn, W. C. Fields—all were white. Only the movies saw the rise of an important black star.

During the early 1920s, some two decades after Williams and Walker first aspired to improve the lot of Negro entertainers, black song-and-dance teams were appearing under names like Dis 'n' Dat, Sleep 'n' Eat, and Brains and Feet. One talented performer who had been working the minstrel circuit since the age of fourteen adopted the name of a horse he had won some money on (or so he claimed) and called his duo Step and Fetch It. Whenever his partner failed to show up or management refused to pay them both, he took the full burden of the name on himself, eventually arriving at the solo billing "Stepin Fetchit, the World's Laziest Man." His story in many ways echoes that of Bert Williams: a West Indian background, a long and groundbreaking career, continuous accusations of making "a mockery of upstanding Negro citizens." However, Stepin Fetchit (Step to his friends) was a boldly assertive man. And, despite the fact that he never wore blackface, he has proved much harder to redeem: his name still stands as a racial epithet and virtual synonym for Uncle Tom.

The first biographies of this long-reviled figure—Mel Watkins's

Stepin Fetchit, 1934

Stepin Fetchit and Champ Clark's horrendously titled *Shuffling to Ignominy*—appeared only in 2005. The two books cannot be confused. Watkins, an expert on African American comedy, writes a wide-ranging, somewhat academic cultural chronicle; Clark, a correspondent for *People*, provides a bluntly anecdotal history. But both authors—one African American, one white—take an unprecedentedly positive attitude toward their unlikely hero and set out to prove that the actor's virtuoso indolence (Fetchit could convincingly fall asleep while standing up) was as much a political as a vaudeville act.

The anthropological notion of wily "trickster" figures—Prometheus, Odysseus, Huckleberry Finn—has long been a staple of African American studies, vital in reclaiming the characters of the old slave tales (Brer Rabbit, for example) as symbols of furtive rebellion, for whom the evasion of work was a significant victory, and the only one they were likely to achieve. The term has become somewhat overused, but Watkins's book presents a stirring heir to the tradition in the man born Lincoln Theodore Monroe Andrew Perry—named for four American presidents—in 1902, shortly after his Jamaican father and Bahamian mother disembarked in the wilds of Florida. Even in childhood, even in church, when the collection plate was passed around, he "would put ten cents in the plate," an acquaintance recalled, "and take out twenty cents change." Although a school dropout, Perry was so far from being illiterate that he supplemented his early income with a regular column for a leading black weekly, the *Chicago Defender*; he also published poetry, most notably on the death of a tuba player in Kansas City. Once he'd won fame as a semi-incoherent mumbler, however, he insisted that his published statements be rendered in dialect, to maintain the illusion. His reasoning clearly belied the linguistic pose: "Sometimes those script writin' men come to me and say Ah ain't readin' their lines clear enough. Most of the time they ought to be glad Ah ain't."

He made his first movie in 1927, shortly before the release of *The Jazz Singer*, in which Al Jolson gave the waning blackface tradition an unsettling new hold on the national psyche. Nevertheless, by 1928, a shuffling, dim, but cork-free Fetchit had signed a contract with Fox and became "the highest salaried colored actor since Bert Williams." The furious racism of *The Birth of a Nation* ultimately had far more influence on the real world—local politics, burning crosses, lynchings—than on the movies. There had been no successful sequel, and Hollywood, after trying and failing to produce one, settled into a racism that was far more gently and comically abusive. Yet now, in the prosperous late twenties, the possibility of real racial advancement in the movie business suddenly loomed. The advent of sound promised a new artistic emancipation, eagerly assured by an industry convinced that mellifluous Negro voices were suited to the new technology and therefore willing, for a remarkable moment, to challenge the prejudices of the society it entertained. "The rich gift of music and of dance makes this race a boon to the singies and the talkies," *Motion Picture Classic* gushed. "A new race has come to the screen."

The revolutionary salvos were two all-black major-studio musicals, both of them set in the post–Civil War South and released in 1929: King Vidor's majestic, nearly operatic *Hallelujah!*, filmed in Tennessee and Arkansas with a cast of local amateurs, and Paul Sloane's critically lauded *Hearts in Dixie*, in which Fetchit, as a shiftless ne'er-do-well named Gummy, danced with a light-footed grace that gave the knowing, twinkle-eyed lie to the physical "miseries" that kept Gummy from working in the fields like everybody else. Gummy's ruse, as Watkins notes, reflects the way that clever slaves at times feigned illness to avoid backbreaking labor. In this light, cool logic and historic defiance underlie Fetchit's characteristic sloth, even if Fetchit himself never made the connection. The actor's professional breakthrough came in a scene where, following the death of Gummy's wife, he briefly extended his narrow comic range to a stunned and tearful sorrow. Despite such moments, *Hearts in Dixie* was racially embarrassing, even in its time. The era's black leaders made their objections known, and the film is virtually unavailable today. Most readers will have to take on faith Robert Benchley's contemporary view that Fetchit, making full use of rare opportunities, was "the finest actor that the talking movies have produced," and, in the age of Chaplin and Keaton, "one of the great comedians of the screen."

All hope for a black Hollywood Renaissance failed with the stock market, later that year; these two films were both its beginning and its end. Fetchit's career soon appeared to have ended, too, either because he courageously fought the studios' more debasing demands or because his personal behavior had become intolerable. The press took opposing sides on whether Fetchit was a heroic crusader or simply out of control, and his biographers offer ample evidence that both were right. In 1930, it was reported that Fetchit planned to produce his own screenplay, *The Dancing Fool*, which would "expel the cotton scenes" and "bring out the modern Negro." In the distinctly unmodern movies he was actually filming, though, he was continually late to the set or outright missing, in a wreck or in a brawl. He drove around town in a pink Rolls-Royce with his name spelled out in neon on the back; he married a seventeen-year-old chorus girl and was promptly sued by another seventeen-year-old for breach of promise; reportedly, a valet delivered his requisite raggedy costume on a gold hanger. He was the world's first black movie star, and he played the role with all the self-entitlement that he was not allowed to show on-screen. (Needless to say, *The Dancing Fool* was never made.) Tales of Fetchit's fantastic wealth and flamboyance could not have been wholly bad for black audiences to read when they got home from the movies. His behavior might even be considered a fair reaction to watching a revolution die.

He went into exile in vaudeville for a few years and returned to Hollywood a humbled man. His new roles included a servant subjected to the screaming racial abuse of Lionel Barrymore, a sniveling sidekick in a John Ford movie, and the butt of Will Rogers's amiably insulting jokes. All the while he was becoming ever more absurdly stylized, his high, whimpering speech nearly vaporizing into the musical spheres. In 1939, the *Times* film critic compared him to James Joyce: "It is now almost impossible to form any idea of what he is trying to say." Fetchit's biographers defend his acceptance of such demeaning roles: he had no choice, really, if he wanted to work. In very much the same way that writers on Bert Williams have interpreted his stage persona, Watkins and Clark each manage to detect a note of insurgency in Fetchit's acting style. Watkins writes of "a surreal obtuseness which so insistently ignored the slights that they were not only deflected but trivialized," while Clark sees the actor's soul concealed in his half-closed eyes, manifesting a "secret and separate self." Both may be correct in claiming that Fetchit's loyal black audience saw such things clearly and recognized a parody of their own methods of survival. There is hardly any other way of explaining why they bought their tickets—

except, perhaps, to enjoy the way the Negro clown inevitably stole the show.

The NAACP failed to notice any radical qualities in Fetchit's performances. By the early forties, its executive secretary, Walter White, had launched a campaign to rid the screen of "subservient, dimwitted, craven, eye-rolling" Negro caricatures, which, in being taken for truth by a white audience, were "doing infinite harm." Stepin Fetchit was far from the only offender. Mantan Moreland, Hattie McDaniel, and many other actors trapped in domestic roles felt that their livelihoods were being threatened, particularly when studio moguls—eager, during the war, to appear to honor the claims of equality—agreed, in March 1942, to enforce the NAACP's demands. But it wasn't only Hollywood that was changing. In 1943, Fetchit volunteered to entertain a black army unit (five more years would pass before the army was desegregated) and was booed as soon as he stepped onstage. In spite of such developments, McDaniel and most of the others continued to play their standard roles throughout the forties. Only Stepin Fetchit, who had been singled out by name, was blackballed.

And yet, typifying the confusion about what Fetchit's character really meant, some of his broadest (and best) performances were in the independent films with all-black casts that he made in the years when Hollywood would not touch him for fear of offending black audiences. His brief turns in *Miracle in Harlem* (1948) and *Richard's Reply* (1949) document all that he might have achieved. Fetchit is as delicately calibrated in his physical clowning as Chaplin or Keaton (if as unvarying in his persona as Mae West), and in the context of an all-black society, with other actors portraying shopkeepers and police detectives and well-bred daughters, he implicates no one by his antics except his unique self: a long and sinuous, dreamily unfocused, narcoleptic moon-calf ("Right now, I'm 'a finish a little nap I started week befo' last"), a marvel of the human condition rather than of a merely racial one, who today seems a creature of the minstrel shows by way of Samuel Beckett.

The burgeoning civil rights movement effectively killed Fetchit's career, just as it had abolished memories of Bert Williams, yet the strength that the movement generated eventually allowed for reconsideration. In 1965, the twenty-three-year-old Muhammad Ali announced that none other than Stepin Fetchit was serving as his "secret strategist." Cynics referred to Fetchit as Ali's court jester, but the young champion offered him the respect of one great showman for another. Around the same time, a newly intense breed of black comedian, unafraid of the old stereotypes, came to view Fetchit as an invaluable ancestor. Dick Gregory—one of the first black entertainers to march in the South, in 1962, and one of the few to wholeheartedly risk his career for the cause—claimed Fetchit as a childhood hero, citing the plain thrill of seeing a black man on the screen. That was enough: no need for hidden meanings or winking tricksters. "To me," Gregory said, being mad at Stepin Fetchit "was like being mad at Rosa Parks." Flip Wilson, in the summer of 1968, asked Fetchit to take a major role in a sketch for a TV pilot, in which a respectable old Harlem junk-shop owner convinces his son, an aspiring lawyer, not to leave the neighborhood. Fetchit's character is serious, even political. "Right here is where we need a criminal lawyer," he advises his son, played by Wilson, "because the worst crime around here is being black." But just when it seemed that he was entering the new era, the door leading out of the past was slammed shut.

That same summer, CBS aired a nationwide television special, written by Andy Rooney, titled *Black History: Lost, Stolen or Strayed*, in which another up-and-coming young comic, Bill Cosby, reminded a new generation that Stepin Fetchit had popularized "the tradition of the lazy, stupid, crap-shooting, chicken-stealing idiot" and that his character remained in the minds of those who had seen his films "as clear as an auto accident." Fetchit's deal with Wilson was swiftly canceled. As Wilson later explained the decision, "The tide had turned against him, and nobody wanted to take a chance." Given that Fetchit was not about to reprise the old "chicken-stealing idiot" but to play an articulate modern black man—apparently the first such role he'd been offered—the cancellation had something of the sense of a life sentence for a rehabilitated man whose crimes had also been his only options. Redemption denied.

"Just because Charlie Chaplin played a tramp doesn't make tramps out of all Englishmen," Fetchit argued, "and because Dean Martin drinks that doesn't make drunks out of all Italians." But the burden for members of a vulnerable race is to be representative: to feel a sickening unease as members of the race are judged by power-ful eyes, to fear that your jokes about each other will be used to twist the knife. Fetchit's late years, mostly spent playing tawdry clubs, were a continual fight against this way of thinking, and his few victories were hardly less bitter than his losses. In 1976, he suffered a stroke while reading a newspaper article that, according to a friend, "blamed him for every black problem this side of slavery." That same year, the Hollywood chapter of the NAACP voted to give him a Special Image Award, but he was too sick to attend the ceremony. He spent much of the last decade of his life—he died at eighty-three, in 1985—in the Motion Picture Country Home and Hospital, largely forgotten except for the insult carried by his name.

"You all have heard about dat straw what broke de camel's back," Bert Williams sang in his 1909 hit, "Believe Me." "Well, a bubble added to my load would sholy make mine crack." More than half a century later, Stepin Fetchit's nightclub routine showed what he had been learning from the brash civil-rights-era comics who had dis-placed him: "My wife and I were just voted the good-neighbor award— we even went out and burned our own cross." The language had changed fundamentally; the experience had not. In an impossible time, these two funny men succeeded in turning tragedy into something painfully hilarious and widely beloved. It was a remarkable achievement. Look-ing back at American racial history, it seems incredible that anyone could laugh.

JAZZBO
GEORGE GERSHWIN

George Gershwin, circa 1930

The audience had grown restless and some people were heading for the exits—the twenty-first piece on the program had just ended—when the clarinet let out an uncorked whoop that riveted everyone in place before the wildly rising cry began to tumble, unmistakably laughing, back down the scale. Nothing like it had been heard before. The tipsy clarinet had hardly been steadied by a burst of brass when a rushing piano part swept the music off to a realm somewhere between Rachmaninoff and ragtime. There was a swoony fox-trot, and a finale that seemed to leave the stage spinning as the audience roared for more. The conductor took several curtain calls that snowy afternoon, February 12, 1924, along with the slender young pianist. Paul Whiteman and George Gershwin, elegant in spats and starched shirts, were bringing jazz to New York's respectable Aeolian Hall. The concert was repeated twice in the next few months (once in the even more rarefied precincts of Carnegie Hall), and the showstopper, Gershwin's *Rhapsody in Blue*, was recorded in June. It's been played many thousands of times since, of course. But that first performance was unique. "Symphonic jazz" was a movement whose time had come and, to beat out the competition, Whiteman had put the concert together quickly. Gershwin composed his contribution in about three weeks. There hadn't been time to finish: the band's arranger, Ferde Grofé, had orchestrated the score, but on the scheduled day a page for a piano solo was still entirely blank, and the composer, at the keyboard, simply improvised. The written direction for the orchestra's entrance in the big bluesy theme that followed read "Wait for nod."

Gershwin, aged twenty-five and the author of various hit songs, from "Swanee" to "Tee-Oodle-Um-Bum-Bo," was suddenly a serious composer and the most famous "jazzbo" in the country. This combination made him a figure of intensely focused expectation. Since the end of the war, Americans had been searching for a homegrown music to reflect the jittery new national rhythms, but the alternatives seemed bleak. The operettas of Sigmund Romberg and Rudolf Friml still flourishing on Broadway were old European hat, the shrieks and toots of "modern" composers like Edgard Varèse were unfathomable, and jazz was widely understood to bear some relation to blacks and bordellos that would make the nation's fair-haired children run riot. The announced purpose of the Aeolian Hall concert was to resolve the pressing question "What is American music?" A gold-plated group of patrons had been assembled: Jascha Heifetz, John Philip Sousa, and Rachmaninoff himself were all seated in the audience, in support of a verdict that Whiteman, as white as his name suggested and the self-proclaimed "King of Jazz," had carefully programmed in advance. To show how far jazz had come from its scandalous roots to his polished dance band's smooth effects, Whiteman opened with the raucous New Orleans–style "Livery Stable Blues"—involving barnyard calls and a tin can—and proceeded through "Yes! We Have No Bananas" to a Victor Herbert suite, and, finally, to the rhapsodic pièce de résistance. A defining moment of the Jazz Age, Whiteman's concert made it clear that few people at the time had any idea what "jazz" was.

The word itself was of mysterious origin. According to F. Scott Fitzgerald, who claimed to have named the age himself, "jazz" originally meant "sex," but broader questions fueled the notorious "jazz debates" of the decade. Blues or ragtime? Black or white? Serious expression or musically illiterate pandering to the masses? The contemporary press was the battleground, and Gershwin himself went into print with a series of articles bearing such eagerly pedagogic titles as "Does Jazz Belong to Art?" and "Jazz Is the Voice of the American Soul," all reprinted in The George Gershwin Reader, edited by Robert Wyatt and John Andrew Johnson. The volume also includes a selection of contemporary reviews, letters, interviews, and studies that trace the course of the composer's fairy-tale career from the Lower East Side to the heights of Gatsbyesque glory, where the suave but ever marveling fellow wrote to his brother Ira, "Flash! Mrs. Dodge Sloan is naming a horse after me. By Sir Galahad out of Melodia."

Given the easy beauty of Gershwin's production and the unpretentious and even naive charm of the man—friends invariably attested to the music as a mirror of his personality—it comes as something of a shock to encounter the anger and bitterness of a large part of the Gershwin debates. Long outliving the quarrels over jazz, these debates adopted many of the same racial and social implications, and continue to offer a view of what Gershwin called the American soul, along with the apparently inseparable issue of our musical style. The voice of that soul, according to Gershwin, is "jazz developed out of ragtime, jazz that is the plantation song improved and transferred into finer, bigger harmonies." Writing in 1926 in the magazine *Theatre*, he reassured a nervous public that he was claiming not that the American soul was "Negroid" but that "it is black and white . . . all colors and all souls unified." This was the ideal behind the work he had planned to call *American Rhapsody*.

Yet, with the possible exception of the original melody of the derided "Livery Stable Blues," no composition by a black composer was played at Aeolian Hall that illustrious day. In accord with the standards of the times, no black musician performed. Nor—as has often been pointed out—did any black composer earn the fame or fortune that Gershwin did by "improving" the hard-won art of the plantation songs. During the decades after the *Rhapsody*, the questions only intensified in the light of developments in both music and society. How had a popular tunesmith composed some of our best-known achievements in classical forms? How had a child of Russian Jewish immigrants come to represent the African American voice? (Implicit in both: How had he dared?) The answers can be found in the unlikely ambitions of an artist who, by writing some of the most fearless and beloved music of the American century, stood like a lightning rod in the storms of an emerging democratic culture.

"Didn't you play anything when you were a boy?" the reporter asked. To which the composer replied, not without pride, "Only hooky." Gershwin credited his great achievement to "the combination of New

York, where I was born, and the rising, exhilarating rhythm of it, with centuries of hereditary feeling back of me." His father, Morris Gershovitz, was a dubious patriarch. He had arrived from St. Petersburg in the 1890s and, dazzled by the possibilities, had gone into a new business nearly every year: ladies' shoes, Turkish baths, a pool hall, even a bookmaking venture at the Brighton Beach racetrack. He had simplified his name and married his Russian sweetheart, Rose Bruskin, whose restless determination more than matched his own. The four Gershwin children—Ira, born in 1896, who everyone quickly forgot was actually named Israel; George, born (but never called) Jacob, in 1898; Arthur, in 1900; and the only girl, Frances, in 1906—grew up in nearly thirty different apartments, from Harlem to Coney Island, but mostly in the thriving ghetto around Grand Street on the Lower East Side. This was not a family tied to tradition. Morris's grandfather had been a rabbi, but Ira was the only one of the three sons to be given a bar mitzvah, and this event appears to have been motivated more by Rose's desire to impress her friends with a party at Zeitlan's restaurant, the local kosher Versailles, than by any residual religious feeling. By the time George came of age, it was clear that his only religion was music.

He had been saved by the piano. On a fateful day in 1910, a secondhand upright was hoisted through the family's Second Avenue window and, to general shock, scapegrace street-fighting George, age twelve, sat down and tore through a popular tune like an old vaudeville pro. He had never studied a note. Many years later, Gershwin recalled the musical epiphanies of his early childhood: sitting transfixed outside a penny arcade as an automatic piano emitted noises that turned out to be Anton Rubinstein's "Melody in F"; feeling a "flashing revelation of beauty" when the strains of Dvořák's "Humoresque" reached him from the school auditorium while he was, in fact, outside playing hooky. But now a piano had flown in through his window like an angel on a mission—which is as good a way as any of explaining how he could play. "Studying the piano made a good boy out of a bad one," he informed an interviewer in 1924. "I was a changed person after I took it up."

His songs poured out of his playing. He said that the tunes came "dripping off" his fingers, although after the piano arrived he studied seriously—Debussy, Liszt, Chopin—for about four years. The word "genius" occurs for the first time in a letter from a teacher who wrote of trying to keep the boy away from jazz. But Gershwin was never much of a formal student. He quit high school at fifteen to become the youngest "piano pounder" in Tin Pan Alley, and the rest of his youthful education was left to what he called "intensive listening": in the concert halls (he favored Russian composers, like himself), at Broadway revues, in the Yiddish theaters, and, increasingly, in the clubs of Harlem. By 1916, the great black stride pianists James P. Johnson and Luckey Roberts were telling Eubie Blake about "this very talented ofay piano player" who could perform their most difficult tricks. The point is not that Gershwin was crossing boundaries but that he didn't recognize that there were any boundaries to cross.

He began imagining "big compositions" while he was still in his teens and his first published songs were being interpolated into the revue-style formats of current Broadway shows. In 1922, just two years after Al Jolson made a sensation of Gershwin's "Swanee"—performed in his customary blackface—Gershwin composed an ambitious one-act "jazz opera" titled *Blue Monday*, which was billed as "a colored tragedy enacted in operatic style." Produced among the skits and high-kicking numbers of the *Scandals* that year, it earned *The New York World*'s verdict as "the most dismal, stupid, and incredible blackface sketch that has probably ever been perpetrated" and was yanked after a single performance. Undaunted, Gershwin maintained his optimistic faith in what he called a "transitory stage" of history, when everyone was awaiting a work that would fuse the nation's disparate musical styles and transcend them all: an American work in the image of America. There was a tension about the age, he wrote, that could not last.

Rhapsody in Blue gave people everything they had been waiting for. Novelty with depth, virtuosity with passion, originality with a tradition strong behind it—their own too-nervous, much-too-fast, thrillingly sad, and ineffably romantic lives, circa 1924, expressed in sound. The indelible clarinet opening was in part the work of the band's clarinetist, Ross Gorman, who jokingly "smeared" Gershwin's seventeen-note rising scale during a rehearsal, to Gershwin's delight, and who provided the descending "laugh"—one can hear it on the original recording—that few clarinetists since have mustered. (Gorman, a master of improbable sounds, could also make his clarinet bark, yelp, and whimper, as can be heard in the recorded number "Barkin' Dog," made with his own band, Gorman's Novelty Syncopators.) Although there is hardly anything in the score that would be identified today as jazz, Gershwin employed every one of the musical elements that defined jazz at the time, starting with Gorman's opening glissando and including horns with wah-wah mutes, copious blue notes, and fox-trot rhythms—rhythms that had their source in W. C. Handy's "Memphis Blues" of 1912. (Gershwin gave Handy a copy of the score, inscribed, "To Mr. Handy, whose early blues songs are the forefathers of this work.") Gershwin had used most of these devices before, but the *Rhapsody*, fifteen minutes long, proved that jazz could provide material for more than a three-minute song or dance, that it could have bigger themes and a more exalted purpose. According to Gershwin, it proved that jazz could have "the quality of an epic."

Gershwin claimed to have conceived the whole composition on a train from New York to Boston, inspired by the "steely rhythms" of the locomotion. From the very start, he heard it as "a sort of musical kaleidoscope of America." It was Ira, the great wordsmith, who talked him out of calling it *American Rhapsody*. Apparently inspired by the mix of color and music in the titles that Whistler gave his paintings (*Nocturne in Blue and Silver, Symphony in White*), Ira suggested, instead, a rhapsody in the key of blue, simultaneously evoking the importance of blue notes in the score, the contemporary chic of everything "blue," and the pervasive melancholy beneath the music's explosive charm.

The initial reviews had plenty of reservations: the piece was structurally incoherent and technically undeveloped. But there was no getting around the fact that something new had taken place. In the *Times*, Olin Downes issued a challenge to both the jazz and the classical sides of Gershwin's radically middle path, correcting Whiteman's racial omissions ("The American Negro," he wrote, "has surely contributed fundamentally to this art") and blasting "the pitiful sterility of the average production of the 'serious' American composer," as exposed by the vitality of Gershwin's work. Until black jazz was given recognition, or dry classical branches again bore fruit, the undivided realm of contemporary music had a single heir.

The phenomenon of Gershwin extended far beyond musical life. The notion that a person may so exemplify an age that, had he not been born, he would have had to be invented is startlingly true of Gershwin, who identified one of the vital sources of his all-American *Rhapsody* as "our vast melting pot." He had been invented: Gershwin's inspiration was first espoused by the poor Russian Jewish musical genius whose "American symphony" is the central (if unheard) theme of Israel Zangwill's play *The Melting Pot*, which was a big success in 1908 and affixed its title forever to New York, where its drama of assimilation takes place. Gershwin gave substance to Zangwill's visionary theme, and he gave it sound. From *The Nation's* welcoming tribute to the *Rhapsody* as "the first distinctive musical phase of the melting-pot" to the *Times's* bright hope that Gershwin would soon produce something "racially important," the work announced a brave new musical world, and specifically a Jewish affinity with African American music, both in its wailing sorrow-songs and in its ebullient long-awaited freedoms. Henry Ford's anti-Semitic Dearborn newspaper had already taken to attacking "Jewish jazz" and its "abandoned sensuousness of sliding notes." (One can practically hear the opening of the *Rhapsody*.) The composer was fully conscious of his cultural role, and he appears to have relished it. By 1925, he was working on a series of piano preludes titled *The Melting Pot* and a successor to the *Rhapsody* that he was calling his *New York Concerto*.

But if Gershwin was a product of the age, he was also one of its heroes: the cultural patron Otto Kahn compared him, as a leader of youth, to Lindbergh. Others were put in mind of Fitzgerald, and there is more than a little of Gatsby in Gershwin's endearingly awkward attempts to master his new social position, as when he announces a "very dignified and sedate" concert, in the magazine *Singing*, and assures readers that none of his numbers "will be cheap or trashy." In appearance, he was immaculately turned out and preternaturally confident and cheerful. But people who came close often remarked on the sadness visible around his eyes or mouth. His many nervous physical ailments (he suffered miserably from "composer's stomach") were a standing joke among his friends. And his letters contain enough references to loneliness to form a leitmotif, like a blues line moaning low under a jaunty melody.

Never married, uncertainly attached to a series of women (preferably married), Gershwin lived surrounded by people and was renowned for his love of parties but also for spending all night at these parties alone at the piano. ("It will be different in every way," a hostess in Cole Porter's *Jubilee* brags of her next soirée. "Gershwin's promised not to play.") If music had an essential role in easing his loneliness, it was also the means of its preservation: an enclosing wall of sound that dazzled yet held off everyone in the room. Kay Swift, by all accounts the most important woman in Gershwin's life, recalled that "nobody would move" while he was playing, "except toward the piano." You had to listen, you might watch, but you could not break the spell to talk or touch; and neither, of course, could he.

The biographers Edward Jablonski and Joan Peyser, among the foremost authorities on Gershwin's life, have laid blame for the vacancy in the composer's personal history on his mother's chilly disposition, and his sister corroborated stories of a woman with a yen for furs "who did not give herself to anyone." Still, George's siblings all managed to escape into the traditional warmth of marriage. In fact, Ira and his wife, Leonore, provided one of several domestic sanctuaries that Gershwin maintained as informal second homes. His own apartment, however, while large enough for three grand pianos, did not contain a single guest room. The melodies that poured out of Gershwin's hands at the keyboard seem to have been an echo of all that he poured in: the close fascination, troubled brooding, sexuality, fantasy, and love that more ordinary people spend upon each other.

Yet if the *Rhapsody*, in particular, contains a portrait of a man or of an era, it is one that has been continually retouched. The most famous recording, Leonard Bernstein's 1959 Columbia Orchestra version—at the Gershwin centennial, it was still the top recommendation of the *Times*—sounds less like twenties "symphonic jazz" than like fifties symphonized Freud. Gershwin's giddy clarinet has become a cat in heat, his lilting central melody a swollen hymn to eros. The following year, Duke Ellington's swinging rearrangement altered almost all the signature elements of the score: even the opening clarinet glissando was no longer a glissando or played by a clarinet. In making the *Rhapsody* his own, Ellington turned it into a work of unadulterated jazz.

The larky gaiety of Gershwin's original is a wholly different experience from either of these classic versions: one can hear it best in Gershwin and Whiteman's 1924 acoustic recording, however rushed and abbreviated (it runs only nine minutes) to fit on two sides of a twelve-inch 78 rpm disk.

And one can best understand its contemporary impact from a scene in *The Great Gatsby*, when a hired orchestra at one of Gatsby's grand parties plays a piece that has just been a sensation at Carnegie Hall—Fitzgerald was writing in 1924—and is titled *Jazz History of the World*. In an earlier version of the novel (discussed in the Fitzgerald essay in this book), Fitzgerald gave the composer of this ambitious composition the rather pointedly Russian Jewish name Vladimir Epstien. And Nick Carraway, unable to distinguish between the music and the champagne he's been drinking, attempted a general account of what he called the music's "themes" and "discords." But all that Fitzgerald retained for the published book was a description of the feeling aroused among the partygoers on that distant summer night, when "girls were swooning backward playfully into men's arms, even into groups knowing that someone would arrest their falls." All grace, no gravity, buoyed on music that reflected a world of expectation and yet marked its end.

In the fall of 1924, the return of Aaron Copland from his studies in Paris and the arrival of Louis Armstrong from the clubs of Chicago began to tear the ideal of an American synthesis apart. Classical music and jazz went their distinct ways—a composer's art and a performer's art; eternal verity and restless improvisation—leaving Gershwin in a no-man's-land that came to be known, with a curl of the lip, as "pops." (In an outstanding book about the *Rhapsody*, David Schiff indicts "a century characterized by the unpopularity of its most prestigious music.") Gershwin's *New York Concerto*, soberly retitled *Concerto in F*, premiered in Carnegie Hall in December 1925: "There would not have been as much excitement," the *Times* reported, "if Brahms had come to town." But a lot had changed since the reception of the *Rhapsody*. The new work was judged a major disappointment, lacking the substance of a real concerto or, equally damning, of real jazz.

Yet revolutionary energy defused in one place was already lighting up another. In the first full-evening music-and-lyrics collaboration of the brothers Gershwin, *Lady, Be Good!*, which opened on Broadway in late 1924, Fred and Adele Astaire performed a song called "Fascinating Rhythm," and the old-world operetta hastened toward a syncopated death. From then until the 1930 hit *Girl Crazy*, in which a young ex-secretary named Ethel Merman sang "I Got Rhythm," the Jazz Age musical coincided with developments in technology to reinvent people's idea of a good time. Recordings began to outsell sheet music, and proliferating radio stations bred a new sort of mass popularity, overwhelming but extremely short-lived. On Broadway, too, the runs were brief and the demand for new shows to fill the theaters was high. Even the Gershwin shows, with their silly librettos, were musical butterflies: light, colorful, and not expected to last. The composer feared that his songs would not long survive them.

Instead, of course, the Gershwin scores led to a renaissance of vocal interpretation. While Gershwin's music was cast out from the redefined borders of jazz, the greatest jazz performers were recording every Gershwin song they could; Ethel Waters covered "I Got Rhythm" almost before the opening-night rafters had stopped shaking at Merman's voice. (An essay by Richard Crawford in *The George Gershwin Reader* lists seventy-nine recorded versions in the song's first dozen years. Max Roach later estimated the number of tunes written on the changes in "I Got Rhythm" as "about ten million.") But Gershwin's ambition to write larger and more enduring forms persisted. In 1928, *An American in Paris*, a "tone poem for orchestra," was performed at Carnegie Hall with a symphony orchestra augmented by saxophones and automobile horns. There were also the experimental shows *Strike Up the Band* and *Of Thee I Sing*, political satires with songs so cleverly embedded in the stories ("Wintergreen for President") that, ironically, most expired with their shows, just as Gershwin had feared. And then, in 1929, Gershwin signed a contract with the Metropolitan Opera to write a full-length work based on the Russian playwright S. Ansky's 1914 drama *The Dybbuk*, about diabolical possession in a village of poor Hasidic Jews.

It was not the first subject that had awakened his interest. In 1926, Gershwin had been excited by DuBose Heyward's popular novel *Porgy*, the story of a crippled Negro beggar, set in Heyward's native Charleston, but discussions bogged down because Heyward's wife,

Dorothy, was turning the book into a play. Later that year, the Habima Players of Moscow, a Jewish company performing in Hebrew, brought Ansky's mystical drama to Broadway, with a score by Joel Engel based on authentic Hasidic melodies. Inspired, Gershwin sketched in some scenes and was soon planning to go abroad to study Jewish folk and liturgical music. The plan suggests that he was inspired, too, by some of the older Jewish members of his musical circle: the Russian-born violinist and composer Joseph Achron, for example, who composed for the Yiddish theater in New York and had been a member of the St. Petersburg Society for Jewish Folk Music, founded by Engel with the aim of collecting the music of the Pale (much as Alan Lomax later collected the folk music of the American South) and of using this material in classical compositions. *The Dybbuk* was an ambitious plan, and Gershwin abandoned it only when an Italian composer obtained exclusive rights to Ansky's play and the Met pulled out.

But the idea of an opera remained, and Gershwin prepared for it seriously. At the height of his fame, he was more of a student than he'd ever been, toiling away at lessons in harmony and counterpoint given by another little-known Russian composer, Joseph Schillinger, who had been recommended to him by Achron. In March 1932, Gershwin wrote again to Heyward and, with the theatrical run of *Porgy* complete, the pair settled on the project that Gershwin called his "labor of love."

From Catfish Row to the Pale of Settlement and back again: worlds that had in common not a shred of language, tradition, or belief but— far more important, for Gershwin—were saturated in and sanctified by music. Heyward's book, like Ansky's play, flows on a stream of song and chant, the open-voiced thanks and lament of a devout people who have long been isolated from modern ways. There is a hint of a musical Eden in Gershwin's description of the South Carolina Gullah Negroes, among whom *Porgy* is set, as a people who express themselves "quite naturally by song and dance." If the comment seems today to carry a racial sting, it is important to remember that this was precisely how Gershwin saw himself. As for Heyward, he had grown up poor, was orphaned young, and, like Gershwin, had dropped out of high school; stricken with polio at sixteen, he had nearly lost the use of his arms. Personal history had drawn him to the story of a crippled beggar aflame with pride, a real individual whom he had read about in the local papers, not as a condescending outsider but as one who recognized his own. (James Baldwin later wrote that Heyward "knew more about Bess than he understood and more about Porgy than he could face.") Years later, recalling the weeks that Gershwin spent in the South, going to church services and listening to spirituals, Heyward wrote that the visit had felt more like "a homecoming."

Gershwin began composing with "Summertime," in December 1933. He was determined to write not just his own orchestration but his own spirituals; only the cries of the Charleston street vendors, some of the eeriest vocalizing in the opera, were drawn directly from life. Ira, always close at hand, provided the urbane lyrics for the drug-dealing villain, Sportin' Life ("It Ain't Necessarily So"), while Heyward sent the libretto (honed from his wife's play) and the more pastoral lyrics from his home. The letters between Gershwin and Heyward form a wonderful record of their collaboration, in warm sympathy on the fundamental points: the necessity of an all-black cast (a decade after *Blue Monday*, Gershwin wants no part of Jolson's attempt at a blackface version) and as much emotional truth as possible. ("I have cut out the conventional Negro vaudeville stuff," Heyward assures the composer about a scene from the play.) But Gershwin is adamant (against Heyward's advice) on using operatic recitative for the speech of the blacks and spoken dialogue—flat, gruff, a break in the flood of music—for the intruding whites. The distinction is like that between Shakespearean characters who speak poetry and those limited to prose.

Porgy and Bess was not produced at the Metropolitan Opera; it was only in 1955 that an African American soloist, Marian Anderson, finally broke the color line and sang on that stage. Instead, it was taken on by the adventurous Theatre Guild, which had already produced Dorothy Heyward's play but had never before attempted an opera, or anything on this scale. Some of the cast were seasoned performers from vaudeville or Broadway—John W. Bubbles as Sportin' Life, J. Rosamond Johnson as Lawyer Frazier—but much of the rest consisted of conservatory-trained singers who would have had operatic careers if the country's major theaters had not been closed to them. Abbie Mitchell, in the role of Clara, who opens the opera with "Summertime," had started off as a star of African American musical theater at the turn of the century, performing alongside Bert Williams in *In Dahomey*; at age fifty-two, she had recently sung the lead in *Cavalleria rusticana* at the Mecca Temple in New York. Ruby Elzy, who sang Serena, had attended Juilliard but was best known as Paul Robeson's co-star in the 1933 film *The Emperor Jones*. And the youngest of them all, Ann Brown, a doctor's daughter from Baltimore and another polished Juilliard graduate, had so bewitched Gershwin that he recast the role of Bess in her image: a delicate, light-skinned woman, rather than the darker, earthier Bess of the book. In response to Brown's prodding, he also found a way to let her sing "Summertime," writing an unplanned third act reprise. ("I have decided to drop the trio and let you sing your favorite melody," Brown remembered him telling her: "Are you happy now?")

The original choice for Porgy had been Paul Robeson, but he was performing abroad at the time. The man who ultimately took the role, Todd Duncan, had a master's degree from Columbia and was on the faculty at Howard; he had appeared in the recent production of *Cavalleria rusticana* with Abbie Mitchell. Duncan later spoke of auditioning for Gershwin with an eighteenth-century Italian aria because he refused to conform to the idea that blacks ought to sing spirituals, and he had nothing but disdain for popular songs. When Gershwin immediately offered him the leading role, Duncan coolly replied that he'd have to hear the music first. In a luminous account of this reverse audition, Duncan describes his conversion from skepticism to tears as Gershwin played and caterwauled at the piano ("My voice is what is known as small," Gershwin liked to say, "but disagreeable") and summed up his wonder at the results with the inevitable question: "Where did this man get this from?" Or, as Duncan later told Ned Rorem, "I literally wept for what this Jew was able to express for the Negro."

After eleven months of composition and nine months of orchestration—this from a man who could turn out a song in an hour or two—*Porgy and Bess* went into rehearsal in August 1935. Of all his accomplishments, Gershwin was proudest of the thickly contrapuntal orchestral writing. ("Get this, Gershwin writing fugues!" he crowed. "What will the boys say now?") Although a hit in Boston, the four-hour show was severely cut before it reached New York, where many of "the boys" had been sharpening their knives since 1924. Cultural hopes occasioned by the *Rhapsody* had long since been deflated. On opening night, in October, the Alvin Theatre was packed with showbiz celebrities, but few classical musicians were in sight. (Aaron Copland, listing the country's most notable composers the following year, found room for Piston, Strang, Salzedo, and Citkowitz but refused to scrape as low as Gershwin.) The *Times* sent representatives of both drama and music; the drama critic objected to the use of operatic recitative (a device he seemed never to have heard before), while the music critic complained of the number of Broadway-style songs.

There were some ecstatic accounts. Marcia Davenport, in the magazine *Stage*, called *Porgy and Bess* the first true opera since Strauss, and wrote with something like the old melting-pot ardor of the scene of mourners at a wake, "its rhythms Negroid, its soaring, minor cadences yearningly Hebraic." Performing in the climax of that scene, the soprano Ruby Elzy was widely praised for the savagely beautiful aria "My Man's Gone Now," which concludes with a rising cry that Davenport characterized as "a wail, a minor arpeggio for which the composer's direction is *glissando*": a tragic pendant to the tipsy clarinet of *Rhapsody in Blue*.

Of the reviews that were out for blood, the composer was reportedly most wounded by Virgil Thomson's assertion that "Gershwin has not and never did have the power of sustained musical development." Thomson's review (which can be found in *A Virgil Thomson Reader*) is a dizzying mixture of perspicacity and poison. Asserting that Gershwin was a charming but not, of course, "serious" composer and had adhered far too uncritically to his "melting-pot sources," Thomson conceded that *Porgy and Bess* was fully alive despite being afflicted by "fake folklore" and—as the phrase appeared in the journal *Modern Music*—"plum-pudding orchestration." In Thomson's collection, appearing under his own aegis, the phrase is "gefiltefish orchestration." One suspects that the editor of *Modern Music* found this choice of delicacy too distasteful to publish.

Thomson's charge that *Porgy and Bess* was racially invalid—"Folklore subjects recounted by an outsider are only valid as long as the folk in question is unable to speak for itself, which is certainly not true of the American Negro in 1935"—had some uneasy support from black musicians. Duke Ellington was quoted as objecting to Gershwin's dramatic characterizations, and to the opera's lack of a Negro musical idiom, but he claimed to have been misinterpreted. Still, it's understandable that many African Americans found aspects of the opera objectionable. Despite Heyward and Gershwin's lofty aims, the characters in *Porgy and Bess* are, after all, poor and superstitious; they speak in an uneducated dialect; the hero is a cripple and the heroine an addict. Porgy's upbeat anthem "I Got Plenty o' Nuttin'" might be intended as a noble Rousseauian cry of freedom, but it could also be taken as a bitter historical truth, and one that the simple hero all too easily accepts.

Porgy and Bess closed in just over three months, losing its entire investment. The sudden demise of his most beloved work prompted Gershwin to leave for Hollywood in the summer of 1936. He'd had a big success there five years earlier, but he was not particularly welcome now. The boy genius had fallen down hard. *Porgy* bore the dangerous mark of highbrow miscalculation, and—unlike Berlin, Porter, or Rodgers—Gershwin hadn't had a Broadway hit in a long time. ("I had to live for this," he grumbled, "that Sam Goldwyn should say to me, 'Why don't you write hits like Irving Berlin?'") Given Gershwin's record of maladies, increasingly violent headaches were dismissed as just another of his nervous symptoms; his unprecedented swerves into foul humor were chalked up to the experience of failure. Doctors, finding nothing wrong, suggested psychiatric help, while members of his circle suspected him of being self-indulgent, even when his motor coordination began to falter.

He was living then with Ira and Leonore in a large house in Beverly Hills. Long afterward, Ira recalled a night when George spilled food at dinner and Leonore ordered him to leave the table. Ira was still trying to exorcise his memory of the look in George's eyes when he helped him get upstairs. He was spending most of his time lying down by then, the headaches were so bad; but he was moved to a smaller house nearby. There was no more piano playing, the house was dark—sunlight hurt his eyes—and he complained that all his friends were leaving. On Friday evening, July 9, 1937, George Gershwin went into a coma, and there was no one with him but a nurse and the valet whose job had once been to keep people away.

In the hospital the following day, a brain tumor was detected. One of the country's leading neurosurgeons, vacationing on a yacht in Chesapeake Bay, was brought to shore by a military craft sent out by President Roosevelt's personal physician. But it had been too late for a long time. Emergency surgery was performed early Sunday, and that morning Gershwin died, at the age of thirty-eight. The body was sent back to New York, and, despite terrible rain on the afternoon of the funeral, at Temple Emanu-El, there was, *Variety* reported, "a turn-away attendance." That fall, a memorial concert was broadcast from the Hollywood Bowl, where Fred Astaire sang "They Can't Take That Away from Me," and Ruby Elzy performed a lacerating "My Man's Gone Now." In published accounts of Gershwin's estate, which was estimated at more than $400,000, his most profitable musical property was listed as *Rhapsody in Blue*, assessed at $20,125. His least valuable work, *Porgy and Bess*, was worth $250.

Barely five years later, in 1942, a New York revival of *Porgy and Bess* scored a commercial triumph, largely because Gershwin's operatic recitatives were replaced with spoken dialogue, and the running time was cut to two and a half hours. The orchestra size was also reduced, although the original leads—Duncan, Brown, and Elzy—repeated their roles. This production earned the kind of reviews that Gershwin had craved: even Virgil Thomson discovered that the work's "inspiration is authentic and its expressive quotient high." But, if Gershwin was cheated of his vindication, he was also spared the fury of the next wave of reaction.

In 1953, another major revival of *Porgy and Bess*—starring the young Leontyne Price, fresh out of Juilliard—prompted James Hicks, the reviewer for the Baltimore *Afro-American*, to declare Gershwin's labor of love "the most insulting, the most libelous, the most degrading act that could possibly be perpetrated against the Negro people." In the following decade, Harold Cruse's widely read volume *The Crisis of the Negro Intellectual* sought retribution for the injustices done to Negro artists. "The Gershwin-type musicians achieved status and recognition in the 1920s for music that they literally stole outright from Harlem nightclubs," Cruse wrote. *Porgy and Bess* was nothing more than "a symbol of that deeply-ingrained American cultural paternalism practiced on Negroes ever since the first Southern white man blacked his face." Cruse called for a boycott of the opera by all black musicians and insisted that it ought to be performed only by whites in blackface.

Fortunately, few musicians agreed. Whatever Duke Ellington felt in the thirties, in 1953 he cabled Robert Breen, the director of the new production, "Your Porgy and Bess the superbest, singing the gonest, acting the craziest, Gershwin the greatest." For generations, black musicians have kept this score in a state of grace. Sidney Bechet's incandescent recording of "Summertime" is as close as one may come in this world to hearing Gabriel welcome you home; Billie Holiday sang the song as though the world contained no home at all. (Holiday once claimed that she had turned down the part Ruby Elzy played in *Porgy* because she couldn't bear to sing "My Man's Gone Now" night after night: "It's too sad. It's the saddest song ever sung.") In 1959, a bloated movie by Otto Preminger made Gershwin's entire premise seem a stale mistake, but the bad air was blown away by Louis Armstrong and Ella Fitzgerald's two-voiced brass-and-silk *Porgy* album, and by Miles Davis's equally blithe reconfiguration of the score. Looking in *The New Grove Gospel, Blues and Jazz* these days, one will find Gershwin mentioned only as an adjunct to Davis's *Porgy* recording. But close the book and listen—to Herbie Hancock's Grammy-winning *Gershwin's World*, to Marcus Roberts's distinctly personal "Rhapsody" on *Portraits in Blue* (with a band that mixes jazz musicians and the Orchestra of St. Luke's), or, for that matter, to the Minnesota Klezmer Band's *Gershwin the Klezmer*—and he is everywhere.

In our daily lives, in our elevators or our memories, we know the tunes even when we don't know exactly what it is we know. When the New York City Ballet orchestra launches into George Balanchine's Gershwin ballet, *Who Cares?*, some people in the audience inevitably start to sway and bits of piping lyric escape into the air, uncontainable, from those who don't realize they have begun to sing. Gershwin was planning to compose a ballet when he died—but what wasn't he planning to do? In the last months of his life, he told his sister that he had not yet "scratched the surface" of his aspirations. He was thinking of a big work about Abraham Lincoln, he was asking Heyward for new ideas, and there was always his original idea of "an opera of the melting pot, of New York City itself," which would "allow for many kinds of music, black and white, Eastern and Western, and would call for a style that should achieve, out of this diversity, an artistic and an aesthetic unity." We'll never know what we lost when the sounds and colors—Eastern and Western, jazz and classical, black and white—divided behind him. A brilliant 1986 Glyndebourne Festival Opera production of *Porgy and Bess*, directed by Trevor Nunn and conducted by Simon Rattle, successfully reestablished the work's recitatives, its dignity, and its composer's goals. Gershwin was lauded as an operatic genius. Not long after, the English musicologist Wilfrid Mellers, impressed with the composer's empathy for his characters, described Gershwin's only opera as the understandable work of "an archetypical White Negro and a poor-boy Jew."

Many of the old controversies resurfaced, however, in the 2012 Broadway revival, which expanded the show's title to *The Gershwins' Porgy and Bess* but, in the spirit of the 1942 version, cut the show itself to two and a half hours, including intermission, and cut Gershwin's orchestral forces to the size of a traditional pit-band. More controversial still, the director Diane Paulus and her writing partner, Suzan-Lori Parks, reshaped Heyward's scenes and dialogue to modern standards of racial sensitivity. Some of these changes were theatrically valid and evaded old embarrassments; others added new ones. "I Got Plenty o' Nuttin'," moved to the morning after Porgy's first night with Bess, was no longer an introductory statement of character—or what Paulus called a "happy-darky song"—but a celebration of renewed virility, as Norm Lewis, performing the song with a winking slyness, made "nuttin'" a code word for sexual pleasure. On the other hand, "Summertime," a lullaby meant to be sung by a pensive young mother to the infant in her arms, lost its tonal shimmer and its inwardness when presented as a duet for a more sociologically uplifting mother and father. And the same carefully responsible father, urged by his wife not to go to work in a terrible storm, replied with thudding rectitude, "How is our boy gonna get his college education if I don't go out?"

All these changes and cuts, plus rumors of an imposed happy ending (ultimately abandoned) raised a furor in the New York press even before the curtain rose on the first performance. And yet, as many public doubters came to admit, the production worked, if not as the ideal *Porgy* for all time, then as a reasonably adapted *Porgy* for this particular time. Thanks in large part to Audra McDonald's gritty, emotionally scathing Bess, and in even larger part to the sturdy power of Gershwin's music, *The Gershwins' Porgy and Bess* was dramatically potent and served to introduce many people to the wonders of the score. It ran for nine months, and the audience night after night was a mixture of people black and white—not as common a sight on Broadway as one might hope in the second decade of the twenty-first century. In one of the articles that Gershwin wrote in defense of jazz, he stated that "true music" must always "repeat the thoughts and aspirations of the people and the time." And he added, "My people are Americans. My time is today." Ninety years later, his music still holds us together.

THE SILVER SPIRE
THE CHRYSLER BUILDING

The Chrysler Building, June 17, 1930

On a mild October day in 1929, the architect William Van Alen stood at the corner of Fifth Avenue and Forty-second Street, terrified, as he stared at a spot a few blocks east and very high up. Nearly eighty stories in the air, from out of a dense web of steel, the tip of a needle gleamed and began to climb; Van Alen later wrote that the spire of the Chrysler Building had emerged that day "like a butterfly from its cocoon." But this butterfly stood one hundred and eighty-five feet tall and weighed twenty-seven tons, and nothing like the operation of securing such an object at such an altitude had ever been attempted before. Van Alen reported that he physically shook whenever he thought about the possible danger to people on the street, who had received no warning of the architectural coup taking place above their heads. The previous week, the *Times* had announced that the Chrysler Building's framework was complete, after less than a year of construction, and that the building had reached its full height of eight hundred and eight feet, or sixty-eight stories. These figures allowed Walter Chrysler's competitors to sit back on their foundations and gloat: he had, with remarkable docility, ceded his goal to build the tallest building in the world. Although the newspapers had been following the skyward contest almost foot by foot, no reporters or photographers were on hand to share Van Alen's anxious vigil. The spire, a triumph of nerve as much as of ingenuity and steel, was meant to take the city by surprise. The highest thing on the Manhattan skyline rose into view in ninety minutes flat.

As it happened, the exquisite execution of this insane plan was kept so secret that the newspapers failed to report it at all, and historians have never known exactly what day or even what month the renowned event took place. The eminently practical architectural historian Christopher Gray, in a brief introduction to a volume of rediscovered photographs, *The Chrysler Building: Creating a New York Icon, Day by Day*, published in 2002, scoffs at the notion that the spire's emergence actually came as a surprise: How many workmen had to be in on the plan? But, regarding a date, he offers only that it must have been erected sometime in October or November; that is, after Chrysler's long-standing rival, the Bank of the Manhattan Company, down at 40 Wall Street, had gone as high as it could go. One of the many gripping photographs that follow, however, catches the drama nearly in the act.

The photograph shows a small celebratory flag—a sure sign that a building has just "topped out"—flying like an exclamation point above the tapering spire, which thrusts straight up from the still-skeletal ovoid ridges of the building's not-yet-famous crown. Both structures are in their raw-steel state. In fact, the building's ineffably metaphorical crown had only recently assumed its distinctive form. The quintessential jazz baby of buildings turns out to have been, in several vital aspects, an improvisation: a riff on height and speed that kept altering shape as dares and provocations forced it higher, the perfect symbol of an age of endless possibilities. According to the book's catalogue, the eureka-moment photograph was taken on October 23. How eerily apt that the last risky upward rush seems to have happened on the eve of Black Thursday, October 24, when the stock market brought the boundless world that the Chrysler Building represented crashing down.

These photographs are themselves a remarkable souvenir. Large in format, nearly tactile in detail, they have been printed from a cache of negatives, many on flammable silver-nitrate film, found in the crumbling office of an elderly photographer who was going out of business. In another week, their rescuer, David Stravitz, writes, they would have been sold off and converted into silver. This magic, mercurial aura suits the subject well. Still, these are utilitarian pictures, most of them taken by a commercial firm for the purpose of getting the contractor paid. The majority are dated in bold white print at the corner of the plate, and some bear inscriptions on the order of "Boiler Room Vault Wall." No one intended these as works of art. Yet, from the moment that the site is blasted down to bedrock, in November 1928, to the slow strip-tease of scaffolding in 1930, from workers straddling the majestic eagle gargoyles to taxicabs the size of pumpkin coaches lined up in front of Schrafft's below, these coolly objective records can inspire intense emotion.

Although the photos were discovered in the late seventies, it seems particularly fortuitous that they were first published in 2002, less than a year after the attack on the World Trade Center, when it was so heartening to see images of a great building going *up*. And if, as seems inevitable with historical photographs, the surrounding cityscape evokes nostalgia for a New York unreservedly optimistic and in bud—a freshly painted ad for five-dollar shoes appears on a wall suddenly exposed by construction; a movie theater offers Laurel without Hardy—these pictures are most valuable not in evoking what we have lost but in meticulously detailing what we still have right before our eyes: the Art Deco wonder of the world, its eagles still fiercely guarding Lexington Avenue against all incursions of reality.

For nothing in the old carnival city appears quite as fantastic as William Van Alen's pulsing automobile-age vision, materializing with all the cathedral-age craftsmanship that Walter Chrysler's money could buy. "The fulfillment in metal and masonry of a one-man dream," a critic called the newly completed building, yet historians have had reason to disagree about which man's dream it represents, and whether its mythic symbols derive from German Expressionism or from Coney Island. By the time the elaborately inlaid elevators made their first run up to the splendiferous Cloud Club, in the summer of 1930, a new "tallest building in the world" was under construction down on Thirty-fourth Street, and Chrysler and Van Alen were at each other's throats. But in their own brief flight toward the clouds, they managed to perfect, as much as F. Scott Fitzgerald or George Gershwin, the uniquely American style of the honky-tonk sublime.

The Chrysler Building would not look the way it does if Dreamland had not burned down in 1911. Coney Island's white-towered fairway had been the brainchild of a real estate entrepreneur named

William H. Reynolds, whose reputation for public mayhem was such that when a short circuit in the Hell Gate exhibit set the entire blockslong place ablaze, some newspapers assumed that it was just another stunt. Financially drained and cured of his taste for artificial fantasy, Reynolds turned his attention to the real-life fantasy of Manhattan, where he proposed to erect the tallest building in the world. Although the Woolworth Building beat him to the punch, in 1913, and the war slowed him down, by the time the late-twenties boom began, he had got hold of a choice piece of land at the new city hub around Grand Central Terminal and had hired William Van Alen to execute the design.

As the association suggests, Van Alen had a reputation of his own as a showman, albeit one in thrall to the most coolly modern materials and means. Scant record of his early life exists, but his beginnings were apparently modest: a Brooklyn boy, born in 1882, he enrolled in night classes at the Pratt Institute after the sudden death of his father, in 1897—Jacob Van Alen was struck by a locomotive while crossing the Long Island Rail Road tracks—and found work as an office boy in an architectural firm by day. A few drafting and design jobs later, he won the Paris Prize in 1908 for his drawing of a grand opera house; in the three years that he spent getting wisdom at the École des Beaux-Arts and the café Les Deux Magots, he was transformed. One architecture critic wrote that Van Alen was the only student to return from Paris without a boxful of books. He went on to quote the young architect's credo, and whether the indicated oddities of speech were meant to reflect traces of France or Brooklyn or sheer revolutionary intoxication, we will never know: "No old stuff for me! No bestial copyings of arches and colyums [sic] and cornishes! [sic] Me, I'm new! *Avanti!*"

There was no cornice on the first building that Van Alen designed when he got back to New York; in 1915, this was something of a guerrilla tactic. And he did not mellow with age. During the twenties, in partnership with H. Craig Severance, he designed a Madison Avenue shoe shop that dispensed with the usual dully inanimate display of shoes; instead, in an enormous oval window, two cobblers plied their trade. The combination of glass and theater was even more striking in a Childs restaurant on Fifth Avenue, where six stories of windows rounded a corner, and the multitiered display of ladies at lunch was rumored to have inspired Ziegfeld. Van Alen's most radical design, however, was his original plan for the Reynolds skyscraper, which featured a jewel-like glass dome and a base in which triple-height showroom windows were topped by a full dozen stories with glass-wrapped corners, creating an impression that the massive tower above rested on air. Nothing as artistically or technologically ambitious had been attempted before, nor was it attempted then. Had it been built, both Van Alen's career and the poker game of New York architecture would have played out very differently.

Reynolds evidently disapproved of this advanced and costly scheme. The official "Reynolds Building" design, published in August 1928, was a far more conservative venture, with an Italianate dome that one critic said looked like Governor Al Smith's derby hat, and with a brickwork pattern on the upper stories that cleverly (and cheaply) mimicked corner windows and is a recognizable feature of the Chrysler Building today. In fact, this design displays the central forms of the existing building exactly: tower, flanks, setbacks, window runs. Yet it differs in everything that makes us think of the Chrysler as unique: the glittering fantasy that defied the austere new modernist ethos (Lewis Mumford awarded the building a "Booby Prize" for 1930) by turning decorative detail into architectural essence. The transformation began that October, when Reynolds defaulted on his lease and Walter Chrysler was ready with the money, reportedly two million dollars, which got him the property, the design, and the architect, too.

The money came from a personal account. Chrysler had been searching for a site for his business headquarters since he'd set up his corporation just three years earlier, during which time it had risen from thirty-second place among car manufacturers to third. But this was not a corporate acquisition. Chrysler wanted the building as a project for his sons, who had suffered the misfortune of growing up rich, and whom he wished to feel "the wild incentive that burned in me from the time I first watched my father put his hand to the throttle of his engine." Like his father, who had been a locomotive engineer on the Union Pacific, Walter Chrysler was a hands-on mechanic for most of his life. He had little formal education and used to lie about graduating from high school, but as his biographer Vincent Curcio shows, his feeling for machines was akin to genius.

Born in Kansas in 1875, Chrysler started out at sixteen sweeping
train sheds for ten cents an hour. At thirty-two, he was master mechanic
for the entire Chicago Great Western line. When he moved to the ail-
ing Buick car company, in 1911, he saved General Motors a fortune by
replacing old wood-carriage techniques with methods suited to steel.
He was earning a million dollars a year when he moved to New York
in 1920 to take over the Willys-Overland Motor Company, and by the
time his engineers were test-driving the first Chrysler car, in 1923—
"We had dreamed about it as if we had been its lovers," he wrote—he
and his family were ensconced on a vast French Renaissance estate in
Great Neck (not far from Scott and Zelda Fitzgerald's), complete with
a boathouse and pier on Long Island Sound. In good weather, he liked
to sail his yacht to work.

One of the many real-life Gatsbys of the era, Chrysler had got rich
enough fast enough to marry his beautiful Daisy—actually named
Della—only to realize that the true love of his life was his car. As a
young husband and father, he blew the family savings and went deep
into debt to buy a brand-new Locomobile, whose ivory body he recalled
for decades as his "siren's song." He didn't long so much to drive it,
though; he waited three months for that. He wanted to dissect it, and
he worked in his garage over every valve and knob until he could have
built the vehicle from scratch. "Had I been Aladdin," he wrote, "I'd have
taken that old lamp apart to see if I could make another, better lamp."

His own better dream machine made its debut in January 1924,
at a show in the lobby of the Commodore Hotel. The first line of
Chryslers came in a range of "King Tut" colors (the sensational discovery of the tomb had taken place just two years earlier) aimed at the
average middle-range pharaoh: pyramid gray over desert sand was a
popular combination. The distinctive winged cap of Mercury atop the
hood served as a silvery pun—it was the radiator cap—but it was also
a fair promise of speed: these cars were beating uphill-racing records
that summer. *Fortune* later noted that Chrysler had produced the perfect car for the twenties, "a period when desires had supplanted needs."
What better definition of being rich? And it was not long before he
determined to produce the perfect building. It might be taken as a
sign that the 1928-model Chrysler was called the Silver Dome.

•

A skyscraper is a psychological phenomenon. Economics have always supplied a justification, but in truth the added costs of building very high—deeper foundations, elevators taking up floor space—were often unrecoupable. In 1929, the American Institute of Steel Construction released a study that reported diminishing returns above the sixty-third floor in Midtown Manhattan. Nevertheless, it was only the stock market crash that killed a host of plans for edging up toward where profit was near to nil. The Chrysler crown begins at the building's sixty-sixth floor and officially rises to the seventy-seventh, but all the spaces above seventy-one are so cramped and contorted that these "floors" have not been rentable for anything but radio equipment. From the seventy-fifth level up, the jack-o'-lantern "windows" are open to the winds. Skyscrapers are about power and longing for transcendence and, as everyone will tell you, about sex: the Empire State Building was known for a time as Al Smith's Last Erection. But the great creators themselves were concerned with an even more profoundly American drive: advertising. And with seeing that the other guy didn't get there first, particularly if the other guy was somebody you knew.

Walter Chrysler took over the building process quickly, and it seems that nothing was too fantastic to be considered. In March 1929, the press offered details of an "artistic dome" in the form of a giant star "with thirty points set up on end"; it was to be surmounted by "a sculptured figure sixteen feet high," whether of Walter Chrysler or some other deity was not specified. And then, in July, the Bank of the Manhattan Company, designed by Van Alen's former partner H. Craig Severance and under construction at 40 Wall Street, announced that it was building straight up to eight hundred and forty feet, or more than thirty feet beyond the Chrysler Building (which went unmentioned), making it the tallest building in the world. Soon after that, on August 30, Al Smith announced his first plans since losing the race for president: he was supervising the construction of a new office tower, to be known as the Empire State Building—eighty stories tall, or exactly a thousand feet, and eat our dust. And the man who had hired Smith and put the plan together? John J. Raskob, a former finance chief at General Motors, who had helped Walter Chrysler get his corporation started, and who, some believe, had expected more than he got in return.

The Chrysler Building: Creating a New York Icon, Day by Day is a strictly figurative title. Sadly, the book contains not a single photograph

from September 1929, when all hell broke loose as plans for the top of
the building were stretched upward, in response to the summer's
bulletins, while construction forged steadily on. Van Alen noted mildly
that "it was necessary to resort to the unusual" because of the
"after-consideration nature" of what he'd had to do. A drawing published at the time shows that he had been planning a more reasonably
compact form of the crown we know—six rounded tiers instead of
seven, a lesser spire—but the change from stable semicircularity to
elongated gothic tension, in one of the most complex geometric structures built before Frank Gehry's museum at Bilbao, supplied a shock
that still registers on the eye.

Tension was part of the process. A photograph from August 30
shows open sky beyond the sixty-first floor. Through September, curved
beams akin to immense steel barrel staves were manufactured in a
New Jersey shipyard and assembled into vaults on-site. By October 7,
when the shutter clicked again, a dozen new floors sprout a crazy maze
of steelwork, at the top of which, on October 14, an enormous plat-
form is mysteriously perched. It is indeed hard to imagine that anyone
who could count believed the news that the building had topped off
at sixty-eight stories; or failed to realize that something was, literally,
up. Still, it would have been difficult to predict the scale of the cloud-
piercing "needle"—delivered in five unassuming segments and assembled in the central shaft—which brought the Chrysler Building to a
title-clinching one thousand and forty-six feet four and three-quarter
inches. And not a possible quarter inch more, as Raskob and Smith
were well aware when, a few weeks later, they announced that plans for
the Empire State Building had been ratcheted up to a nose-thumbing
thousand and fifty feet.

But as Louis Sullivan showed in his pioneering skyscrapers, there
is more than one way for a building to appear transcendently tall.
And, as Walter Chrysler knew, unlimited amounts of cash and glamour
always help. Although he had lost the race for supremacy in height, as
an architectural patron Chrysler now managed to do what not even
Louis XIV had done before him: he enlisted the sun as a worker in his
atelier. As construction on the Empire State Building began nearby—
plans soon added another two hundred feet, and an airship-mooring
mast for dramatic effect—the Chrysler crown and spire, hidden under

scaffolding, were clad in a revolutionary metal that looked like an alloy of steel and light. The use of diamond-honed Enduro KA-2 steel, developed by Krupp in Germany after World War I and exhibited for the first time in 1926, was Chrysler's most significant decision. He had it tested for months, to be sure that no amount of exposure would tarnish its almost metaphysical silver glow. When the top of the building was revealed, in 1930, critics marveled at the incandescence that made it a beacon even to ships far out at sea. Not a single metal sheet has ever been replaced, and on clear days the Chrysler tower is still outshone only by the sun itself.

But the first extensive architectural use of stainless chromium-nickel steel provided more than a gleaming surface for Van Alen's design; it appears to have provided an inspiration. Conjecture about the source and meaning of the Chrysler's majestically heaped-up arches and triangles has ranged from car wheels (with spokes) to a chorus girl's headdress (with feathers) to Angkor Wat. In Van Alen's mind, the origins seem related to the imaginative leap from glass and brick to the possibilities of steel, as signified by the peculiar March announcement of an "artistic dome" that would have been, in essence, a work of sculpture: a human figure standing on "a star with thirty points set up on end." Luckily, the figure never made it off the drawing board. But the giant star may still be seen, visibly transformed into architecture, in the crown's radiating burst of jagged, sharp-cornered windows. People will always make their own associations; that is part of the building's power. But anyone who looks up and counts will find that there are exactly thirty triangular windows—thirty star points set on end—per side.

Also clad in the new metal's glow were the nine-foot-high pineapples, colossal radiator caps, and fierce eagle heads that animate the building's corners like grotesques looming out from a medieval cathedral. It seems odd today that such extravagant fantasy was denounced at the time as being too commercial: "advertising architecture," Lewis Mumford sneered. True, the Chrysler decorative scheme offered a newly overt kind of self-display: a brick frieze depicting hubcaps zipped around the thirtieth floor, punctuated by those imperial radiator caps with wingspans of fifteen feet. It was noted, by contrast, that the Woolworth Building had not been covered in big nickels and dimes. Yet so fixed has this notion of advertising become that the building's most magnificent ornaments, the glowering thrust-necked eagles, are often presumed to derive from automobiles, although no eagle ever decorated a Chrysler. In fact, the perfect model eagle glowers just a block away, thrusting its head straight out from behind the wing-capped god Mercury—who looks, under the circumstances, oddly like the radiator-capped god Mercury—on the monumental pediment over the main entrance of Grand Central Terminal.

Like many railroad stations, the original Grand Central, built in the nineteenth century, was studded with sculpted eagles; the pediment of the building that replaced it, in 1913, evokes this aquiline tradition. But the towering Chrysler eagles evoke the power that trains and steam and shrieking speed once had over the national imagination—not surprisingly, considering that they were designed by a man whose father was killed by a locomotive for a man whose father was an engineer. There is a boy's sense of scale and wonder in all the building's details and public spaces, whether they look backward to Kansas or forward to a sort of Emerald City, which a population of office workers entered every day through granite portals shaped like Egyptian tombs and flecked with mother-of-pearl. Yet, after passing through the lobby, with its *rouge flamme* marble walls, and riding up in elevators styled like tiny Parisian drawing rooms, most people found themselves set down amid plain white walls and ordinary windows, in the usual banality of modern office space. Van Alen did what he could to keep this sad phenomenon at bay, with elaborate radiator grilles and patterned doorknobs, but the economic reality of so many floors had to be conceded. The ultimate distinction of Manhattan's Dreamland was the size of the bill.

Only at the level of the Cloud Club did fantasy resume. Occupying three linked stories at the base of the crown, this executives' lunch club (which doubled as a speakeasy in its early years) was a stylistic riot of Georgian lobby, Tudor lounge, and Bavarian bar. The main dining room, however, was pure cosmopolitan Fred-and-Ginger "Cheek to Cheek": faceted blue marble columns with white-ice sconces that melted into a vaulted ceiling painted with clouds. Not many people got to see these clouds; membership was reserved for the likes of E. F. Hutton and Condé Nast. But for fifty cents anyone could go up to the observatory, on the seventy-first floor, where the steeply tilted walls reflected structural necessity but appeared to be inspired by Expressionist film sets, principally the angular madhouse of *The Cabinet of Dr. Caligari.* (German movies made a deep impression on architectural thought during this period, if not very often on architectural practice.) The observatory was open for only a few years. But photographs reveal that a decor of painted sun rays and ringed-Saturn lighting globes gave the ominously shattered space an unlikely, naive sweetness—an optimism that seemed to emanate from the prominent reliquary-like case in which, there at the summit, Walter Chrysler enshrined his first set of machinist's tools. The room embodied an essential characteristic of the Chrysler and Van Alen enterprise: the determined American innocence that turned Krupp steel into a crown of stars and revamped the geometry of angst into an Art Deco heaven for the workingman.

A different characteristic of the enterprise was revealed in June 1930, one month before the Cloud Club opened, when Van Alen placed a lien on the building in order to receive the balance of his fee. Although he eventually won his case, word that Walter Chrysler had accused him of taking bribes from subcontractors seems to have lost him his reputation. Little else explains the sudden end of his career. The Depression, limited construction, the war: all may account for even an eminent architect's failure to get much work. But, aside from a few experiments with prefabricated housing—there is something heartbreaking about the shape of the great Chrysler portals being refitted for a shower stall—Van Alen, "the Ziegfeld of his profession," seems to have had no further jobs at all, even during the postwar building boom. Walter Chrysler, writing his autobiography in 1937, failed to mention Van Alen's name, referring only to "architects" and to his own hand in the work.

In 1941, a year after Chrysler's death, a notice in the *Times* mentioned that Van Alen was working on plans for an underground-garage project. And then, silence—extending to his death, in 1954. The *Times* ran no obituary. He left his money to establish an architectural scholarship fund and to care for his wife, Elizabeth Bloodgood, who, by the time of her death, in 1970, seems to have thrown away whatever papers or letters or drawings still existed. There were no children. And there are no biographies, no archives. One of the few photographs we have shows Van Alen dressed up as the Chrysler Building at the Beaux Arts Ball in 1931: encased in silver metal cloth trimmed with eagle epaulets, he peers out from under an immense tiered headdress that is fastened down below his ears, so that he appears to be caught partway through the painful metamorphosis by which he vanished, whole, into his work.

The building has gone through its own vicissitudes. By the time the Chrysler family sold it, in 1953, the sleek glass style of Van Alen's initial design was more in keeping with prevailing architectural standards. According to the rules of the reigning International Style, ornament was a crime, and the Chrysler Building was a major culprit. Little loved and subject to a succession of sometimes ruthless owners, it went through years of degradation. The tower sprang leaks; garbage piled up in the service areas. An exodus of tenants during New York's darkest period brought occupancy down to a deathly seventeen percent; foreclosure proceedings began in 1975. But tastes were already changing. Postmodernism and suburban burnout and maybe even Saul Steinberg's drawings played a part in making urban eccentricity beautiful again. Landmark status came in 1978, and the current fizzy night lighting— said to be Van Alen's original scheme—was switched on in 1981. The giant real estate company Tishman Speyer, which took over in 1997, did a spectacular lobby restoration and some vital repairs before truly bringing the building into the modern age and selling ninety percent of it to the government of Abu Dhabi, in 2008. Presumably, the whole building is staying where it is. The land beneath it is still owned by Tishman Speyer, which continues to manage the property. And despite its compromised New York credentials, today the building stands proud. Current tenants display a sense of loyalty so strong that even those who never knew the place in its prime are aggrieved by the destruction of the Cloud Club.

Astonishingly, the club kept its doors open until 1979, and after that remained more or less intact through an odd alliance of neglect and hope. Tenant Christmas parties were held there through the late nineties. Then, in March of 2000, the Art Deco Society of New York issued a bulletin accusing Tishman Speyer of tearing the place apart.

The company refused access to the press—invoking tenant privacy—but Christopher Gray, in his introduction to the book of construction photographs, reassured us that the decor "partly survives." Whom to believe? A sneaking desperado visit, via the fire stairs, by a reporter with a pounding heart, revealed, alas, that everything is gone; the place had been stripped down to the fireproofing on the columns where the white-ice sconces used to be, down to the brick on the inner side of the building's arches. One tenant reported that dumpsters were piled with bits and pieces free for the taking. It appears that DaimlerChrysler's plan to locate an exclusive headquarters here was abandoned, midway through renovations, when the German-American merger proved so financially dismal that it quashed the upbeat symbolism of the move. This destruction was not illegal—only the facade and lobby have been landmarked. But it was shameful. And the greatest shame lies in the fact that, for so many years, no one had the wit to find a use for this unique setting. The chance for any public space is gone; deprived of the mirrors and clouds, the fabled rooms appear merely inconvenient and startlingly small. But oh, the starrily triangulated views!

On May 1, 1931, at the opening ceremony for the Empire State Building, Mayor Jimmy Walker, cheerfully facing impeachment, congratulated the builders for providing "a place higher, further removed than any in the world, where some public official might like to come and hide." Al Smith, in his derby hat, read a telegram from President Hoover, and Edmund Wilson recorded his impression that, from these heights, the Chrysler crown and spire appeared "now dwindled, a tinny-scaled armadillo-tail ending in a stiff sting-like drill." The following year, F. Scott Fitzgerald, in the midst of a breakdown that seemed to mirror the country's own condition, went up to the Empire State observatory, on the hundred-and-second floor, to get his bearings. And with a shock, he felt that he understood it all: the delusions of the past, the present unbearable loss. The realization came to him, he wrote, as it came to everyone who had looked out from this godlike height for the first awful time: New York had limits, the green-and-blue expanse into which it faded on all sides went on forever, but—how could we have known?—New York "was a city after all and not a universe."

The Chrysler observatory, monumentally overshadowed, had lost most of its business by then. Decades later, when the World Trade Center was nearing completion, architects for the Empire State Building considered replacing its famous upper profile with a tower that would rise to a hundred and thirteen stories; two designs were published but sheepishly withdrawn. The new building at One World Trade Center, completed in 2015, has seen changes in every aspect of its design since its inception after 9/11, except for its symbolic height, a patriotic 1,776 feet (including its 408-foot spire). It is now the tallest building in the Western hemisphere, a claim not likely to last long. A recent surge in skyscraper construction in Midtown Manhattan has proved bitterly controversial, in part because apartments for the super-rich are stealing sunlight from the streets below and, worse, from Central Park, but also because the new buildings make no claims on the imaginations of the people who live among them.

The issue of how tall our tall buildings ought to be has always vexed us. Louis Sullivan thought that illusion was as important as actual size—"the glory and pride of exaltation must be in it"—while his student Frank Lloyd Wright, sworn enemy of the urban landscape, liked a strong cornice, to show that a building was, "emphatically, *finished!*" Le Corbusier argued that New York's skyscrapers were "much too small." But William Van Alen, sworn enemy of the cornice, created a skyscraper that never visibly finishes at all. Anyone who looks up from the street will see. The Chrysler spire rises to an impossible slenderness that disappears gradually, like a bird flying out of sight: it becomes increasingly difficult to follow, but that doesn't mean it isn't there; our senses merely fall behind. This street-level vision may provide some consolation against Fitzgerald's sense of loss: somewhere in the empyrean, infinitely tall, the Chrysler Building is still rising.

TOUGH GUY
DASHIELL HAMMETT

Dashiell Hammett, circa 1933

At a party in Hollywood in the spring of 1935, Dashiell Hammett was asked by Gertrude Stein to solve a literary mystery. Why is it, she began, that in the nineteenth century men succeeded in writing about so many different varieties of men, and women were limited to creating heroines who were merely versions of themselves—she mentioned Charlotte Brontë and George Eliot—yet in the twentieth century this situation was reversed? Nowadays, Stein pointed out, it was the men who portrayed only themselves, and why should this be so? Stein reasonably assumed that Hammett, a hard-drinking ex-detective whose photograph had appeared on the cover of his latest novel, *The Thin Man*, about a hard-drinking ex-detective, might be in a position to know.

The party that evening was given in Stein's honor, and Hammett was the one person in Hollywood she'd asked to meet. Although he had at first taken the invitation for an April Fools' joke, such tributes were no longer much of a surprise. Hammett had been "duh toast of duh intellectuals" (in Edmund Wilson's disgusted phrase) ever since *The Maltese Falcon*, published in 1930, had introduced a new type of tough-guy hero in matching tough-guy prose: a tight-lipped, street-smart style, determinedly flat despite flickers of amusement, and startlingly devoid of the familiar processes of consciousness. Readers were riveted, and critics were quick to announce the newest development in the creation of an American language. It was the kind of achievement that Stein and other literary radicals had been struggling for in their brave obscurities and unread treatises, and it had emerged from the least likely source: cheap detective stories that large numbers of people actually liked to read, based on the real experience of a man on a job that just happened to involve unlimited amounts of violence, sexual intrigue, and moral devastation.

For years, Hammett had plied his trade in magazines like *Mystery Stories*, one of about seventy "pulps" then on the market—"pulp" as a category denoted the low quality of the paper, and presumably also of the contents and the readership. He produced about ninety stories (and five novels) in the dozen active years of his career, many of them for badly needed money, and many clearly executed beneath the level of his engaged attention; he was capable of knocking out five thousand words a day. Of course, he also produced whiz-bang tales that exhibit the best of what the pulps could offer, and a few that transcend formula in the strict music of Hammett's deadpan dialogue, or in the verbal loop-the-loop of lines like "Give me my rhino instead of lip and I'll pull my freight" (which in context makes perfect sense). Also beyond formula are occasional set pieces that suspend the action in an almost hallucinatory spell; these read like intrusions from a different genre or a darker mind, as when the detective in "The Tenth Clew" nearly drowns and spends several pages succumbing to the not-unpleasant drag of going under. At the top of his game, as in the surprisingly buoyant story "The Scorched Face," published in 1925, he demonstrates how imaginative wit can transform even the crudest material into an exquisite whirring toy, with cops chasing crooks in perfect circles, round and round.

But the most extraordinary aspect of Hammett's stories is their long and echoing influence: in the pulps, Hammett not only developed a literary style but helped to set the style of an era. The indelible characters that he went on to produce in his novels—Sam Spade, Nick and Nora Charles, even Asta the schnauzer (or, on-screen, the wire fox terrier)—were resilient enough to launch careers in radio, comic strips, and, of course, movies, where Hammett's low-down glamour and stark masculine charm have been a distinctive force from the early thirties to the Coen brothers. In the long and fractured hall of cultural mirrors, it is easy to lose track of the original: the Kurosawa film *Yojimbo*, based on a Hollywood film noir adaptation of Hammett's novel *The Glass Key*, was itself the basis for the Coen brothers' Hammett-inspired film, *Miller's Crossing*. When Bob Dylan allows that his favorite film is Truffaut's *Shoot the Piano Player*, in which Charles Aznavour replays Humphrey Bogart playing Hammett's idea of a modern urban hero, we must acknowledge that there is still a lot, for better and worse, that we owe him.

This quintessential masculine style was the work of a writer who grew up believing that just being a man was a fair guarantee of moral corruption. Samuel Dashiell Hammett was born in 1894 in southern Maryland, on land that could have passed for a farm if his father had not been preoccupied with drinking and women and looking for easier ways to make a living. His beloved mother, who suffered from tuberculosis, is reported to have held to the loudly voiced conviction that men were a no-good lot. Sam, her bright and curious middle child—one biographer has him reading Kant at thirteen—was given reasonable proof of her view when he was forced to leave school at fourteen to help with his father's latest failing business. There followed several years of predictable menial jobs, and predictable drinking and resentment, until he joined Pinkerton's National Detective Agency, becoming a detective at twenty-one. The job caught his imagination; for the rest of his life, he told different versions of a story about being asked to find a stolen Ferris wheel.

In June 1918, longing to get away from home, Hammett enlisted in the army, but he'd got no farther than a camp in Maryland when he contracted influenza; by the following spring, he had full-blown TB. Most of his remaining time on base was spent in the hospital, and he was discharged with a small disability pension after less than a year of service. He was twenty-five, six feet one and a half inches tall, a hundred and forty pounds, and a physical ruin. And there was nowhere to go but home again, coughing like his mother now and drinking like his father.

The early twenties was a period of continual, debilitating illness. Once he had gained a little weight, he left his family for good; he skipped his mother's funeral a few years later, and it was twenty years before he saw his father again. Rejoining Pinkerton's, he headed west, where agents were in demand for brutal union-busting work. He was back in the hospital in a matter of months. In 1921, barely convalescent, he married a pretty and pregnant nurse; they moved to San Francisco, where, through medical rather than moral failings, he was unable to support his small family. He worked for Pinkerton's again until his next collapse. Resigned at last to being incapable of physical work, he haunted the library, read enough to make up for his interrupted schooling, and began to write. He aspired, above all, to be a poet.

Although Hammett's poetry meant the most to him, the detective stories that he was also turning out paid the bills. His best market was a crime-story pulp magazine called *Black Mask*, which specialized in a new kind of all-American violence—no more mischief in the vicarage—and where he was publishing regularly by 1923. This was the year his TB flared up dangerously and his weight went down to a hundred and thirty-one. At times, he wasn't able to cross his bedroom without relying on a line of chairs to hold him up. Poor, sick, unemployed, drinking to forget his condition until his condition forced him to stop drinking, Hammett sat down and, out of the black-and-white depths of the detective world, fashioned a new myth of the indomitable American male.

"I want a man to clean this pig-sty of a Poisonville for me, to smoke out the rats, little and big. It's a man's job. Are you a man?" The speaker is the leading tycoon of a western mining town, who has brought in union-busting thugs and can't get rid of them. The detective he is hiring is not impressed with the terms of the offer. "What's the use of getting poetic about it?" asks the Continental Op, which is short for an operative of the Continental Detective Agency. Middle-aged, short, and woefully overweight, Hammett's Op, who made his debut in 1923, is nevertheless the first fully hard-boiled hero in American letters. He believes that emotions are a nuisance during business hours, and all his hours are business hours. He shoots a beautiful woman in the leg rather than let her walk out on a rap. Hammett wrote thirty-seven stories and two novels about him without giving him a name, and without providing a single character who gets close enough to want to call him by one.

"I don't like eloquence," the Op says in "Zigzags of Treachery" (1924). "If it isn't effective enough to pierce your hide, it's tiresome; and if it is effective enough, then it muddles your thoughts." This is a rare confession of a sentiment that became the basis of Hammett's style, which manages to leave out almost everything that can't be expressed in a crayon drawing or summed up in a shrug, and which relies, in its warmest descriptive passages, on words like "nice." ("Her eyes were blue, her mouth red, her teeth white," he writes of one beauty, "and she had a nose. Without getting steamed up over the details, she was nice.") For all his cheery comic-strip bravado, Hammett's reticence ties him to the generation of war poets who rejected the muddling eloquence that had lured men to the front; given his poetic ambitions, the connection may be more real than seems likely for a mystery writer. It also ties him to Hemingway, to whom Hammett was relentlessly compared by critics, and whose war-bred indictment of all "abstract words such as glory, honor, courage" was the first commandment of the era's literary faith.

The term "hard-boiled" had come into favor as soldiers' lingo during World War I, when it was used to describe the tougher species of drill sergeant; it was given literary currency in the twenties by *Black Mask*. Hammett, having missed the war, tested his hero's physical courage against armies of crooks and crooked cops, and his moral resistance against beautiful women, that newly revamped danger to soldier and noncombatant alike. The beginnings of film noir are evident three years before the talkies, in Hammett's 1924 story "The Girl with the Silver Eyes," in which the Op confronts head-on the destruction a female can wreak. In a scene that still holds tremendous tension, the lowest hophead stool pigeon on the West Coast, one Porky Grout, plants himself squarely in front of the Op's speeding car to protect the all-too-seductive girl from being nabbed: the Op sees a crazily determined white face looming up against the glass, then the windshield flies off and the road is clear again. "She had done that to Porky Grout," he reminds himself after he has nabbed her anyway, and she is inching ever nearer to him across the seat of his Porky-spattered car, "and he hadn't even been human! A slimy reptile whose highest thought had been a skinful of dope had gone grimly to death that she might get away." When the girl makes her inevitable play for the Op—and freedom—he has his answer ready. "You're beautiful as all hell!" he shouts, flinging her back against the door. Then he hauls her in for arrest.

There is something of inverted chivalry in the attitude: the power attributed to women to delude and destroy, the fear, the need for self-protection. Many blame the era's sexual jitters on the experiment of female emancipation, and it is tempting to compare it with the waves of sexual fear inspired by black men after the country's earlier emancipation—fear based on the assumption that retribution was on its way. The Op is, after all, protecting his honor from ravishment. If one adds the new social threat posed by women to the questions about manliness and courage that the war set loose, one hardly knows how to weigh the contribution of a writer's individual psyche. Hemingway's biographers have based equally credible cases for his machismo on his experience in the war, which ended with an explosion in a trench and shrapnel in both legs, and on the sexual confusion of his early childhood, when his domineering mother dressed him in his sister's clothes. Hammett's life offers neither shrapnel nor infantile cross-dressing to elucidate a controlling masculine myth that was more strictly defined and tightly defended than even Hemingway's, an ideal so stoically closemouthed that it eventually stranded him in silence.

"Spade had no original. He is a dream man," Hammett said. "He is what most of the private detectives I worked with would like to have been." Hammett worked on *The Maltese Falcon* for nearly a year. The novel made its debut in 1929, as a serial in *Black Mask*, but it was, as Hammett knew, a different order of achievement from anything he'd ever done. Of its type—just the kind of qualification that enraged Hammett—it is a flawless work, nearly classical in its austerity, its smooth meshing of parts, and the unnamed presence of so many big, old-fashioned themes: trust and guilt and the great Jamesian theme of renunciation, which Hammett claimed to have adapted from *The Wings of the Dove*. Whatever its source, *The Maltese Falcon* takes on the same daunting task as the most resounding lyric novels of the twenties—*The Sun Also Rises*, *The Great Gatsby*—by seeking a personal language to express a unique point of view.

It is the point of view of a man to whom Hammett gave his own first name, Samuel, and the physical appearance of the devil—a heavily muscled "blond satan" (Hammett was reading Spengler as well as James, and probably had Nietzsche's "blond beast" in mind), with long yellow eyes and a wolfish smile. Evidence of the bruised idealism and anger that suggest the moral heights from which he has fallen is confined to the slightest shifts in his physiognomy: a deepened line, a flush of red. Most of the time, however, Spade is inscrutable, and the reader is put in something of the position of a timorous heroine in a pulp romance. *The Maltese Falcon* very quickly became what we would today call a crossover hit, bringing not only highbrows but women more usually inclined toward those pulp romances to a genre not known for attracting either group. Over "the magnificent Spade," Dorothy Parker confided, she'd gone "mooning about in a daze of love such as I had not known for any character in literature since I encountered Sir Launcelot at the age of nine."

A devil ought to be able to handle even women who are beautiful as hell, and Spade gets his chance with Brigid O'Shaughnessy, the paradigmatic femme fatale. To Brigid's predictable coloring-book attributes Hammett added a body "erect and high-breasted," "without angularity anywhere." Hammett's editor worried about the steaminess of her rapport with Spade—and also about the obvious homosexuality of the novel's crooks—but Hammett refused to make any substantial changes. Spade forces Brigid to strip to be sure she hasn't palmed a thousand-dollar bill, and he goes to bed with her. But Brigid is just another cold-blooded killer in heels, and so in the end, of course, he turns her in.

Three movies were made of *The Maltese Falcon*, the first in 1931, a year after the publication of the book. It is not surprising that the novel had such appeal for Hollywood, although Hammett had originally voiced very different aspirations. In March 1928, he had written to his publisher, Blanche Knopf, about his plans to adapt the "stream-of-consciousness method" to a new detective novel. He was going to enter the detective's mind, he told her, reveal his impressions and follow his thoughts: this was to be Sam Spade as Leopold Bloom, not Launcelot. But a few days after sending the letter, Hammett received one himself, from the head of the Fox Film Corporation, asking to look at some of his stories. He promptly fired off a second letter to Knopf, informing her of an important change in his artistic plans: he would now be writing only in "objective and filmable forms." *The Maltese Falcon* may have been the first book to be conceived as a movie before it was written.

John Huston's version of *The Maltese Falcon* (1941)—the third to be made, and arguably the first classic of film noir—is mostly faithful to the book. There were just a few necessary changes: Bogart's Spade doesn't get to sleep with Mary Astor's Brigid, and he doesn't make her strip. But there is a larger concession to Hollywood sensibilities. In one of the most wrenchingly beloved of all movie endings, Spade forces himself to resist Brigid's pleas and hands her over to the cops. Astor stares straight ahead, unblinking, as the bars of the elevator gate close her in, like the bars of the prison she's headed for. Hammett, however, closed the book with a chilling coda: Spade returns to his office on Monday morning, to the ranks of small, corrupted souls and ways, and, with a shiver, realizes that this is where he belongs. It is the only time we get a glimpse inside his mind.

One section of *The Maltese Falcon* could not be filmed, and for many readers it is the most important story Hammett ever wrote. A dreamlike interruption in events, it is a parable that Spade relates to Brigid about a man called Flitcraft, dutiful husband and father of two, who was nearly hit by a falling beam while walking to lunch one day. Instead of going back to work, Flitcraft disappeared. "He went like that," Spade says, in what may be Hammett's most unexpected and beautiful phrase, "like a fist when you open your hand." His narrow escape had taught this sane and orderly man that life is neither orderly nor sane, that all our human patterns are merely imposed, and he went away in order to fall in step with life. He was not unkind; the love he bore his family "was not of the sort that would make absence painful," and he left plenty of money behind. He traveled for a while, Spade relates, but he ended up living in a city near the one he'd fled, selling cars and playing golf, with a second wife hardly different from the first. The moral: one can attempt to adjust one's life to falling beams but will return to the same old patterns as soon as the shock wears off. What else is there to do? And yet, as Spade reports, Flitcraft continued to finger the small scar that he got from the beam that day—"well, affectionately."

"How perfectly fascinating," Brigid replies when Spade is finished, and changes the subject back to herself. Others, however, have assumed that Spade here reveals the existential dilemma at the bottom of his soul; this three-page parable has lent Hammett's entire body of work a philosophical aura, as though he were a kind of Albert Camus *avant la lettre*. The parable can also be used to justify the fact that Spade forms no lasting connections with other people. Why bother in a world where all is so easily undone? By extension, it justifies Hammett's own unsteady record in the same regard. At the time that he was writing *The Maltese Falcon*, Hammett was no longer living with his wife and children—they now had two small daughters—ostensibly because of the danger of infection presented by his TB. But he had already launched a series of affairs, and in the fall of 1929 he moved to New York with a writer named Nell Martin, to oversee his new novel's publication. He was no Flitcraft, however; his absence was painful to his family, and he left almost no money behind.

That fall, in the few months that he lived with Martin, Hammett wrote the only one of his books in which the hero betrays the basic principle of the masculine code: he runs off, to New York, with his best friend's girl. *The Glass Key*, the darkest and most dire of Hammett's works, was his farewell to the hard-boiled genre. Like a bad Hollywood dream, the book is filled with ominous Freudian signposts— the breakable key, an attack of writhing snakes, a killer who murders his own son—and with an out-of-control violence that brings its worst to bear on the hero himself. In the book's longest sustained episode, Hammett's tall, thin, tubercular stand-in is beaten repeatedly by sadistic thugs. It isn't a fight scene but a torture scene, bordering on the surreal, and it goes on for several sickeningly drawn-out pages. "He's a . . . a God-damned massacrist, that's what he is," one of the thugs observes, demonstrating that Freudian notions had sifted down even to the bottom of the social snake pit. Then he turns to the hero just to check: "You know what a massacrist is?"

By one definition, it's someone who gets what he thinks he deserves. But whatever Hammett felt he deserved at the end of 1929— and whatever his variously afflicted protagonists suggest that he felt he deserved at any time—what he got was great reviews, fame, and fortune. *The Maltese Falcon*, published in early 1930, was found to exhibit both the "absolute distinction of real art" and the "genuine presence of the myth." Sam Spade was a "real man"—at last!—coming after so many high-minded, effeminate detectives; one reviewer judged Hammett's writing to be better than Hemingway's, "since it conceals not softness but hardness." Hammett quickly became a star, a dazzling man-about-town, with his chiseled features, his taste for fancy suits, and his titillating detective past. He was soon on his way to Hollywood, to write scripts for actors who would merely play the hard-boiled hero that Hammett really seemed to be.

L illian Hellman knew what she wanted the moment she laid eyes on him. It was November 1930. He was just coming off a bender, and was perhaps a bit rumpled, as she recalled, but he was without doubt "the hottest thing" in Hollywood. She was twenty-five, married to a well-connected writer named Arthur Kober, and had a job reading scripts at MGM. They were at Bing Crosby's opening at the Roosevelt Hotel when the lights began to dim, and Hellman, at a table with her husband and Darryl Zanuck and the Gershwins, caught a glimpse of the tall, angular figure passing by; she found out his name and was off so fast she was able to walk him the rest of the way to the men's room. By March, she was his darling Lily, in 1932 she got a divorce, and the rest is the stuff of expertly manipulated legend: nearly thirty years of love and loathing and consuming faithlessness and ultimately unbreakable regard. Hellman was gutsy and smart and ambitious—everything that a small Jewish woman without beauty had to be even to enter, much less conquer, the worlds she did. At the start, she might have been mistaken for a muse. There is no other way to explain the extraordinary change that marks *The Thin Man*, which Hammett called a detective novel but which is really an amiable social comedy, its hero a married ex-detective who is supported by his wonderfully smart-mouthed wife while he enjoys a new career as a nearly full-time drunk.

He started the novel in New York, in late 1932, when he had blown every cent of his Hollywood money on lavish hotel suites and weeklong parties and a lot of other things he couldn't remember. (For the better part of a year, he couldn't remember to send any money to his wife and children.) That fall, he sneaked out of the Pierre Hotel, leaving a thousand-dollar tab, and checked into a fleabag joint managed by Nathanael West, who rented out rooms to writers on the cheap. By May 1933, he had finished the manuscript. Hammett told Hellman that she was his inspiration for Nora Charles, a tribute indeed—even if he told her that she was also the book's silly young girl and the villainess—since Nora, aside from being beautiful and rich and twenty-six, was one of the most clever and engagingly open heroines of the day. It is easy to see why Nick can't sustain any serious violence with Nora there to interfere whenever he's about to do something that will get him hurt. ("I know bullets bounce off you. You don't have to prove it to me.")

It was Nora's sexual openness that got the manuscript rejected by the major magazines, until *Redbook* finally ran an expurgated version, in December 1933. Her teasing question to Nick after he'd wrestled with a female suspect—"Didn't you have an erection?"—had to be changed, although, just a month later, Knopf not only published the book with the line intact but based an ad campaign around it. ("Twenty thousand people don't buy a book within three weeks to read a five word question," the ad proclaimed, while dropping a discreet mention of "page 192.") A great many people did buy the book, the cover of which displayed a full-length photo of Hammett, dapper in tweeds and a hat, leaning on a cane. The movie version, released the following year, starts rolling with the same photo of the author, looming high and handsome on the screen. Nevertheless, devoted Hammett readers dismissed *The Thin Man* as a travesty, bitterly complaining that Nick Charles—lazy, rich, soft, even (the final insult) married—was not the man that Hammett used to be.

If anyone appeared to be that man anymore, it was Lillian Hellman. In 1933, Hammett suggested to Hellman that she try writing a play based on a story in a recent true-crimes collection, about two schoolteachers ruined by the lies of a vicious pupil. *The Children's Hour* had a great success on Broadway the following year, and Hellman went on to become the leading female playwright in American theatrical history. By her own account, she owed much of her success to Hammett, a close and demanding reader of her work who pushed her to rewrite until she'd reached her highest standard. Their professional relationship appears to have continued this way for nearly two decades, up to and including Hellman's 1951 play, *The Autumn Garden*, a family drama involving a cruelly womanizing alcoholic artist named Nick, who causes enormous pain to his smart and loving wife, Nina, and who carefully hides the terrible secret that he hasn't finished a painting in twelve years.

The private travails of the Hammett-Hellman relationship seem to have been accurately exposed here, except for the fact that Hellman had learned to practice a matching promiscuity, which her lover referred to, with apparent pride, as behaving like a "she-Hammett." Yet even after their relationship ceased to be sexual, in 1941, when, as Hellman relates, he took his revenge for a single rejection on her part by refusing to sleep with her ever again, her jealousy remained formidable. Hammett's biographer, Diane Johnson, who happened to be an attractive young woman, reported feeling under attack by Hellman even after Hammett's death. During his lifetime, Hellman took the only revenge that she could, by means of the art that Hammett had taught her to perfect. Still, it might be argued that Hellman's account of Nick's artistic impotence was almost charitable: by the time *The Autumn Garden* premiered on Broadway, in March 1951, Hammett hadn't published a creative word in seventeen years.

It was not difficult, during much of this time, for the world to overlook his silence in the continuing swirl of glamour and second-hand success. In the thirties, Hammett wrote story lines for two *Thin Man* movie sequels and several other films, moved back and forth between New York and the Beverly Wilshire Hotel (where he preferred either the penthouse or the King of Siam's suite), dreamed up plots for a Hearst comic strip printed under his name, and steadily drank himself out of his mind and into Lenox Hill Hospital, where he experienced a complete breakdown in 1936. In 1938, he announced a new novel, but he soon returned the advance, with a note saying that he was afraid he was "petering out." That same year, MGM paid him eighty thousand dollars but turned down his draft for yet another *Thin Man* sequel. It was the last year that Hammett commanded such easy and enormous sums, which was just as well, as a matter of principle if not of economics, for by this time he was almost certainly a member of the Communist Party.

Hellman, a famously indefatigable supporter of the Soviet state, has often taken the blame (or, occasionally, the credit) for Hammett's political conversion, and clearly the man whose original line of work included union busting hardly seems to have been a natural fellow-traveler. But it was more likely the Spanish Civil War—and the intrepid involvement of Hemingway, among others—that offered him a chance to assert a moral course in the midst of his spectacular dissolution. It is no disparagement of the authenticity of Hammett's principles to note that speaking at rallies and petitioning F.D.R. on behalf of the Loyalists also provided a creditable alternative to facing the battles of the blank page. Moreover, his new political sympathies took nothing away from his national allegiance, and when the next opportunity for heroism arose, in the fall of 1942, this forty-eight-year-old alcoholic with scars on his lungs and an FBI record managed to enlist as a private in the U.S. Army. His determination to serve was so immense that, when he was told he couldn't be sent overseas because his teeth were rotted and infected, he had them all extracted by an army dentist. Hellman, who was far from being in control of Hammett's politics or anything else, remembered meeting him for a soft-boiled dinner at the '21' Club before he shipped out, and before his dentures arrived; this time when she laid eyes on him, she started screaming. But what galled her more than anything was that he'd called the day he enlisted the "happiest day of my life."

These were his happiest years, too, as he recalled them, although he saw no combat and faced no tests of courage. Nor was he the kind of man who thrived on male camaraderie. On the contrary, he doesn't appear to have had any close male friends, and he acquired none now; women were always more willing to bridge his emotional gaps. But in the army, Hammett seems to have finally found peace. He was stationed in the Aleutian Islands, the farthest he was ever to travel, and his days consisted of tasks that were easy to fulfill, and of writing letters that fulfilled his personal obligations with a similar, mechanical ease. "It may be that most of the time I don't want to think about the outer world," he admitted to Hellman, in 1944, in response to her accusations about his reasons for enlisting. In 1945, he told her that if he could stay on there, he would be able to write a new novel. But after his transfer to the base near Anchorage, with its distracting bars and brothels, he gave it up.

In all the years he was busy not writing, Hammett's literary legend only grew. Raymond Chandler, who published his first story in *Black Mask* just as Hammett was bowing out, complained, "If a character in a detective story says 'Yeah,' the author is automatically a Hammett imitator." Chandler, like James M. Cain and Ross Macdonald after him, paid tribute to Hammett but vigorously distinguished himself from the master's example. Mystery aficionados may rattle off the easy distinctions between Hammett and Chandler—San Francisco versus Los Angeles, Sam Spade versus Philip Marlowe, the stylistically bare versus the near baroque—but the essential difference is that Chandler displayed the recognizable goals of a gifted novelist with a lively interest in psychology and detail, while Hammett, at his best, was not any recognizable sort of writer at all. Here, in a giddy bit from "The Scorched Face," the Op and a helpful cop combine forces to break down a door:

> It shook, but held. We hit it again. Wood we couldn't see tore.
> Again.
>
> The door popped away from us. We went through—down a flight of steps—rolling, snowballing down—until a cement floor stopped us.
>
> Pat came back to life first.
>
> "You're a hell of an acrobat," he said. "Get off my neck!"
>
> I stood up. He stood up. We seemed to be dividing the evening between falling on the floor and getting up from the floor.

What sort of style is this, poised between blank verse and slapstick? Chandler, in a particularly Oedipal mood, wrote that he doubted Hammett "had any deliberate artistic aims whatever." He wasn't the only one to believe that Hammett's so-called style was merely an outgrowth of the required just-the-facts language of his Pinkerton reports. Yet Chandler undermined his claim by further attacking Hammett for writing nothing that was not "implicit in the early novels and short stories of Hemingway," who was himself nothing if not an artist aiming high. Hammett left no doubt that he'd read Hemingway: in the 1927 story "The Main Death," a bored young wife sits smoking and reading *The Sun Also Rises*, which had been published the year before. But Hemingway was also surely aware of Hammett; in the same novel, he distinguishes between the easy bravado of the new hard-boiled style and his own far more complex understanding of a man's attempt at unrelenting strength. "It is awfully easy to be hard-boiled about everything in the daytime," Hemingway's war-wounded hero, Jake Barnes, confesses, "but at night it is another thing."

For all his literary repercussions, it was in the movies that Hammett made his deepest mark. No author has been better served by Hollywood: in the thirties, the breezily underhanded charm of William Powell and Myrna Loy as Nick and Nora turned a single novel into the longest-running major film series of the era; the last of the five *Thin Man* sequels was made in 1947. Sad-eyed, lisping Humphrey Bogart, whom *The Maltese Falcon* made into a star, brought Hammett's influence to a peak when his Sam Spade became the original for another long, if unofficial, series. During the next few years, Bogart drew the masculine ideals of Hemingway (*To Have and Have Not*) and Chandler (*The Big Sleep*) into the persona of a single seen-it-all tough guy with some well-guarded soft spots, whose willingness to lose everything but his honor was just what the country needed while getting through the war. The noble renunciation of love for wartime principle at the end of *Casablanca*, made a year after *The Maltese Falcon*, is unthinkable without Spade's renunciation of Brigid for far less noble motives. The plane that takes Ingrid Bergman up, the elevator that takes Mary Astor down—both leave Bogie conveniently alone with a buddy and his personal peace restored. There is a strange sort of justice in the fact that the truculent antihero brought into existence by the traumas of the First World War should have provided the materials for the most romantic (if no less truculent) hero of the Second. Hammett, in originating the type, performed a national service more significant than anything he did in the army.

Reluctantly returning to the "outer world" in 1945, Hammett continued to earn fame and reasonable fortune through frequent radio adaptations of his books, which were based on scripts that he refused to write or read or even to discuss. Living quietly, he divided his time between Marxist-style politics and Bowery-style drinking, in New York and on Hellman's Westchester farm. Beginning in 1946, he lectured on crime fiction and "the possibility of the detective story as a progressive medium in literature" at a Marxist school in lower Manhattan. But the revolutionary possibilities of the genre became apparent sooner than expected. That same year, Albert Camus arrived in New York for the American publication of *The Stranger*, a novel of murder and existential sangfroid that had been inspired, as the author later revealed, by American detective stories and their fast-talking American prose. Camus, dark and handsome in his trench coat, told people how pleased he was whenever his resemblance to Humphrey Bogart was pointed out.

At Christmas 1948, just a year after William Powell took his final turn as the adorably drunken Nick Charles, doctors at Lenox Hill told Hammett that he could either give up drinking or die. He surprised everyone who'd ever known him by promising to stop, and then wholly shocked them by putting the bottle down for good. When Hellman later told him how he had defied expectations, his reaction was wide-eyed amazement. Of course he had stopped. He had given his word.

For those who reasonably mourn the tragic toll of alcohol on American writing, it might be pointed out that sobriety did nothing at all for Hammett's work. Whatever he had used the liquor to drown had long ago gone under, and there was nothing left but time. In 1950, while briefly planning a new novel, he assured a friend that there was no need to worry over lapses in artistic productivity: "Nobody dies young anymore."

Hammett's word of honor became an issue of national import in 1951, when he was called before a federal judge in New York to name contributors to the Civil Rights Congress bail fund, of which he was a trustee. This was privileged information. The CRC was a Communist-sponsored group, and the fund was used to gain the release of defendants accused, under the notorious Smith Act, of advocating the overthrow of the government; four had recently jumped bail and couldn't be found. There is significant doubt that Hammett even knew the names that he refused to reveal. He himself never said one way or the other, and he pleaded the Fifth to every question asked. The outcome was, as he had to know—given the example of others who had testified—almost inevitable: a verdict of contempt of court and a sentence of six months in jail.

Hellman said she found it irritating when Hammett told people, as he always did, that his time in jail had not been bad at all. The conversation was no sillier than that at a New York cocktail party; the food was awful but one could drink milk; and it was possible to be proud of work well done even when that work was cleaning toilets. In fact, the months that Hammett spent in jail, mostly at the Federal Correctional Institution near Ashland, Kentucky, entirely broke his health. He was still in his late fifties but, returning to New York, he couldn't get down the steps of the plane without stumbling and stopping to rest. (Hellman, who went to meet him at the airport, says she stayed out of sight for a while so he wouldn't see her see him.) And his punishment was far from over.

He had become, according to *Hollywood Life* and other publications, "one of the red masterminds of the nation." Walter Winchell took to calling him "Dashiell Hammett and sickle" and "Samovar Spade." All radio shows based on his work were canceled. The IRS attached his income, now nearly nonexistent, for unpaid taxes going back to his time in the army; his federal debt was ultimately calculated at more than a hundred and forty thousand dollars. In 1953, he was called before a Senate committee, chaired by Joe McCarthy, that investigated the purchase of books for State Department libraries overseas. His own works were removed from the shelves until President Eisenhower, a Hammett fan, volunteered that he didn't see anything the matter with them.

Dead broke and weak and chronically short of breath, Hammett struggled with his last attempt at a novel, called *Tulip*, and managed to write a couple of chapters. He was living alone in a cabin on a friend's estate north of New York City, and an interviewer who sought him out in the mid-fifties described a pathetic has-been, still wearing his pajamas at noon and explaining that he kept three typewriters around "chiefly to remind myself I was once a writer." When getting on by himself proved impossible, he moved into Hellman's East Side apartment, where he spent the last two and a half years of his life. Lung cancer was diagnosed in late 1960, and he died just a few months later, in January 1961. Hellman has written movingly of rubbing his shoulder when the pain came on, pretending it was only arthritis and hoping that he thought so, too. She tells of entering his room one night, near the end, and finding he had tears in his eyes for the first time in all the years she had known him. "Do you want to talk about it?" she asked. She recalls that he replied, almost with anger, "No. My only chance is not to talk about it." And he never did.

So she did it for him. Hellman's first publication about Dashiell Hammett was a captivating introduction to a volume of his stories, *The Big Knockover*, which she published in 1966. Cynics (and few hardened Hellman observers are anything else) point out that she had bought the copyrights to all his works for a well-calculated pittance, snatching them away from his legal heirs. With her next books—*An Unfinished Woman* in 1969, *Pentimento* in 1973, and *Scoundrel Time* in 1976—she launched the Hammett-and-Hellman industry and made a bundle. Just as her plays dropped into the oblivion of the old-fashioned, well-made melodrama, the instinctive dramatist rewrote a life in which the plays hardly figured at all. At the center of Hellman's memoirs is an adventurous political heroine who is loved by a man of almost unearthly moral and physical beauty. In prose that echoed his own spare style, Hellman updated the early Hammett myth and turned him into one of the most romantic heroes in modern fiction: an unforgettable "Dostoyevsky sinner-saint," a stern idealist who preferred silence to the risks that words inevitably posed to the clear and simple truth.

The fact that Hellman's volumes were filled with outright lies— "every word," as Mary McCarthy famously charged, "including 'and' and 'but'"—was well recognized by the time she died, in 1984, bluffing and suing all the way to the grave. She had not, in fact, traveled to Nazi Berlin to deliver money hidden in a smashing fur hat to an anti-Hitler group; she had not tried to raise money for Hammett's bail in 1951; he had not sent her a note after he'd been sentenced, pleading that she get away to safety. She had simply fled, in fear, to Europe. The list of self-aggrandizing lies is nearly as long as McCarthy implied, and biographies of Hammett are valuable to the degree that the authors steered clear of her "cooperation." (Richard Layman's *Shadow Man* remains the most coolly reliable; Joan Mellen's scathing *Hellman and Hammett* exposes the deceptions one by one.) Looking over Hellman's so-called memoirs now, one regrets the compulsive mendacity, principally for demeaning her own courageous testimony before the House Un-American Activities Committee, in 1952, and for making us suspicious even of what we wish to believe about her and about the man she seems to have truly loved. But, given the evidence of a woman who couldn't speak without disastrously improving on reality, and a man who couldn't speak at all, how are we to judge? The mystery of Dashiell Hammett may remain forever unsolved.

Hammett himself tried to find a solution in *Tulip*. Begun after his release from jail and abandoned in 1953, the would-be novel centers on a rambling and very un-Hammett-like dialogue between two men, called Pop and Tulip, who have come together to hash out Pop's single overwhelming problem: he can no longer write. Hellman included *Tulip* in the collection of stories she published after Hammett's death as a sign of what he was moving toward in his quest for a new literary life. But the idea for the book can be traced all the way back to Hammett's conversation with Gertrude Stein, in 1935, when she asked him why modern men could write only about themselves. Hammett had replied that the answer to her question was simple. In the nineteenth century, he said, men were confident and women were not. In the twentieth century, however, men had lost their confidence; they could imagine themselves as a bit more intriguing, perhaps, or better-looking, but they could venture no further because they were too afraid to let go of whatever they happened to be. He had thought of writing about a father and son, he told her, just to see if he could create a hero different from himself.

Judging by Hammett's answer, the many novels that he abandoned over the next two decades were attempts at breaking through the fears and limitations that he'd long disguised as forms of strength. *Tulip*, however, details a weary internal standoff: the pair of leading characters openly signify experience and creativity, and they agree only on the fact that they cannot get along. "Of course things get dull when you reason the bejesus out of 'em," the lively Tulip scolds, in an attempt to get Pop writing again. Tulip is an odd name for a man, and one thinks inevitably of Lily, and of the whole crushing weight of the feminine imperative against which Hammett defined himself: the tireless urging to feel, to connect, to talk talk talk. But perhaps the most dispiriting aspect of the story is the revelation that Pop and Tulip are not old friends, not a man and a woman, not father and son, but simply parts of the same resignedly unhappy man. When Pop explains, "I had always beaten Tulip by not talking," he admits that he has finally beaten himself.

Silence was always at the edge of Hammett's style. The white space on many of his pages nearly equals the quantity of print, the short lines of dialogue snapping off as soon as the necessary thing is said, if not before. He made inarticulateness into a method and a heroic mode of being; few American writers—not even Gertrude Stein—came so close to the radical purity of words stripped down to their far-from-routine nakedness. Noun, verb, primary color; no echoes, few implications. Small wonder that so much of his writing falls flat. The whole enterprise was nearly impossible, like the ideal of living a life of absolute honesty, free of hypocrisy, new every day. It was a treacherous ideal, part nobility and part pathology, and it brought him, as a writer, to the very end of words. Yet in a few short years Hammett turned out a few short books that have yielded a chorus of voices and a phantasmagoria of beloved images—Sydney Greenstreet frantically hacking at a lead bird with a penknife, William Powell lying on his back and tipsily shooting lights out with a popgun, Bogart grabbing Mary Astor for one short, hard kiss—before the gift just went, like a fist when you open your hand.

THE COLLECTOR
PEGGY GUGGENHEIM

Peggy Guggenheim at her home in Venice, 1964,
with an Alexander Calder mobile and a Picasso painting

Entering Picasso's studio in Paris, in 1940, Peggy Guggenheim found the master surrounded by a group of admirers. Her artistic mission for the past several months—to buy a picture a day—was widely known. Most artists and dealers, anticipating a German attack, were desperate to sell anything they could before packing or hiding their works and fleeing the city. Léger, Giacometti, Man Ray: all eagerly delivered their work to the gawky American heiress, and few objected to her haggling over price. There were not many buyers, after all. "People even brought me paintings in the morning to bed," Guggenheim reported, "before I rose." She rarely bought on impulse, though, because she knew exactly what she was after. She had a list, compiled by experts, of artists who should be included in a first-class modern collection, and it had not taken her long to acquire a painting or a sculpture by almost every one. The great exception, who ignored her pointedly as she hovered in his studio, finally glanced up to inform her that she had arrived at the wrong location. "Madame," Picasso said as he dismissed her, "you will find the lingerie department on the second floor."

Madame did not experience the rebuke as an extraordinary setback. This is not surprising, as she had barely registered the war as a setback to her plans to open a splendid new gallery in Paris. On April 10, 1940, the day after Hitler's troops entered Denmark and

Norway, Guggenheim rented an enormous apartment on the Place Vendôme, and she went so far as to have the little plaster cherubs chopped off the walls and the place suitably repainted for the display of her treasures before, at last, she admitted defeat, just weeks before France did the same. Dangerous weeks, it might be said, for a woman with a prominent Jewish name. By her own account, however, Guggenheim seems to have been disturbed mostly by the French refusal to protect her art. Léger had advised her to ask the Louvre for storage space, but the august museum pronounced her entire collection not worth saving. "A Kandinsky, several Klees and Picabias, a Cubist Braque, a Gris, a Léger," Guggenheim fumed, along with Surrealist paintings by Miró, Ernst, de Chirico, Tanguy, Dalí, Magritte: all this had to find refuge in a friend's barn in the Vichy countryside. She herself, though, was happy to stay put. She was enjoying the attentions of a new lover, who was prevented from leaving Paris, she said, because his wife was too ill to be moved. And so, as the bombing reached the factories on the outer boulevards, and trains crowded with refugees in direst need poured into the city, she sat in cafés and drank champagne.

"I can't imagine why I didn't go to the aid of all those unfortunate people," Guggenheim wrote in a memoir published shortly after the war. "But I just didn't." She dutifully recorded her escape from Paris— on June 12, 1940, two days before the Germans entered the city—to join her art in the relative safety of the Vichy-controlled south of France. It was only once all her precious collection had been discreetly packed amid a large supply of blankets, sheets, and pots and pans, in five wholly unprovocative crates of legally exportable "household goods," and had been shipped without disturbance to America, that she continued on her way to Lisbon, leaving behind a trail of rumpled beds and moral quandaries. She managed to board a Pan Am Clipper flight to New York in July 1941. At forty-two, Guggenheim had been living abroad for nearly twenty years, and she was bringing back with her the chaotically extended family that she had acquired: her ex-husband and their two teenage children, her ex-husband's soon-to-be ex-wife and their children, and the painter Max Ernst, who counted as family because he was already, in Guggenheim's mind, her husband-to-be. In her memoir, she recounted the reasons that she had fallen in love with Ernst: "because he is so beautiful, because he is such a good painter and because he is so famous."

Despite the memoir's occasional flush of naive charm, it is hard to think of another book that so determinedly assassinates the character of its author. By the time Guggenheim began writing it, in 1944, her dream of a first-class modern gallery had become a reality, not on the Place Vendôme but above a corset shop on West Fifty-seventh Street, and she was presiding over an art world so tumultuously new that no one could have made a list of who the important figures would turn out to be. And yet almost every major artist of mid-twentieth-century America—Pollock, Rothko, Motherwell, Cornell, Nevelson, de Kooning—showed at Guggenheim's Art of This Century, as the gallery was called: it was the place where American art came into its own. With it, Guggenheim achieved a professional reputation for daring and for an instinctive grasp of talent that not even the publication of her self-mortifying self-appraisal, titled *Out of This Century*—one reviewer called it *Out of My Head*—was fully able to destroy. To complete the job, it seems, we have biographers.

Guggenheim's achievements have long been obscured by accounts of her personal life, and particularly by judgments of her moral status as a woman and as a mother. A stunningly hostile biography, Anton Gill's *Art Lover: A Biography of Peggy Guggenheim*, published in 2003, claims that "the jury remains out" on the question of whether Guggenheim had a good eye, as opposed to merely having good advisers, but betrays no difficulty in passing judgment on her otherwise. According to Gill, she responded to the prevalent sexism of the male art world of her time with "a mixture of low self-esteem and aggression, aided by money"; regarding her private life, he states as categorical "her inability to give anything in return for what she took." As he tells it, Guggenheim was an inadequate friend, an inept wife, and, to cite his most frequent and furious charge, a catastrophic mother. Her "most successful relationships," he writes, "were with animals and works of art," but his book is more informative about Guggenheim's feelings for her Lhasa apsos than for the talents of Jackson Pollock, to whom she gave his first four one-man shows.

Gill's focus is far narrower than that of Guggenheim's previous biographer, Jacqueline Bograd Weld, author of *Peggy: The Wayward*

Guggenheim (1986), a good and still enjoyable book that nevertheless introduced the sort of malicious gossip that supports a number of Gill's charges. But malicious gossip seems almost unavoidable when it comes to Guggenheim. (Another woman subject to such gossip, Yoko Ono, who was friendly with Guggenheim, notes in Guggenheim's defense that "when a woman is powerful others will go to any lengths to criticize her.") Even the best of the biographies, Mary V. Dearborn's richly detailed and largely sympathetic *Mistress of Modernism: The Life of Peggy Guggenheim* (2004), is forced to spend a good deal of time rehashing the reputation that its subject had by then acquired: "The general assessment was not only that she was unimportant but that she was a fright, a predator, and finally a joke." The most recent portrait, a slim volume by Francine Prose, titled *Peggy Guggenheim: The Shock of the Modern* (2015), also aims at countering the long-entrenched assessment, stating straight-out that Guggenheim was (among other things) "loyal, generous, brave," and also, of course, "passionate about art." But the old accusations rankle. Reflecting the continuing quandary of how to deal with charges that remain disturbing—sexual promiscuity no longer seems to count as a problem—Prose offers the almost touchingly hairsplitting distinction, "It's not at all clear that Guggenheim was a 'bad mother,' though she was a self-involved and frequently neglectful one."

All these biographies struggle, with varying degrees of success, to maintain a hold on the reason that Guggenheim is worth reading about at all: in a brief five-year period of her life, she helped change the course of twentieth-century art. And she owed her achievement not only to her money but to the force of her personality—to the same willfulness and lopsided passion that got her into so much trouble everywhere else. It was Guggenheim's inexhaustible brio that made her gallery a unique phenomenon, with Guggenheim herself continually patrolling and touching and talking, or standing at the door and asking people as they left, "What did you think of the paintings?" And then, if they didn't seem to understand what they had seen, adding with a shrug, "Come back again in fifty years."

Nothing less than the war could have brought her back to America. She associated the entire country with her awful childhood;

"one long protracted agony" is how she remembered it. Both of her grandfathers—"my stable-born grandfather, Mr. Seligman," and "Mr. Guggenheim the peddler"—had fled the oppression and restrictions of their lives as Jews in Europe in the mid-nineteenth century, arriving in America with no money and no English and nothing but their explosively unleashed initiative to explain how Mr. Seligman came to found a vast international banking house and Mr. Guggenheim to acquire a large part of the mineral wealth of Colorado. From her birth, in 1898, Peggy Guggenheim (her given name was Marguerite) had a prescribed place in New York's German Jewish aristocracy. The house she grew up in, on East Seventy-second Street, had a Louis XVI parlor, a Louis XV dining table, and a dark servants' stair that gave her nightmares. It was a fairy-tale world, complete with monsters and curses. Her adored father spent most of his time away with his mistresses, her mother was addled and wholly distracted, and she was left to the care of vicious nurses, one of whom threatened to cut out her tongue, and whose forced outdoor exertions induced in her a lifelong terror of Central Park. Yet her upbringing did not strike her as unusual. "I don't think there were any good mothers in those days," she wrote.

In 1911, Peggy's father, Benjamin Guggenheim, abandoned his family entirely and moved to Paris; in April 1912, coming back for a visit, he went down on the *Titanic*. Peggy was nearly fourteen, and she later claimed that she never got over the loss. Seeking emotional ballast, she clung to her beautiful older sister, Benita, who was the first and most constant love of her life, and whose attentions she vied for with her equally beautiful younger sister, Hazel. Yet even this solace was turned to pain by what appeared to be the greatest curse of all, blooming day by day right in the middle of her face: the Guggenheim nose. A potato nose, as her grandfather's was usually called; her version, if on occasion more poetically compared to a sponge or a peony, was viewed as equally outsized and grotesque. As a result, her youth was filled with racking attempts at "being beautified," which culminated, in 1920, with a primitive nose job that for a long time only made the offending object worse, except insofar as its swellings allowed her to predict inclement weather.

Guggenheim cited two other sources for the sense of inferiority that plagued her early life: a lack of money, and the oppression and restrictions of being a Jew in America. Seeking independence, Benjamin Guggenheim had broken not only with his wife and children but with the economic partnership of his brothers, and his death left his daughters in the position of poor relations until their mother came into her own inheritance. The family moved to smaller quarters and had to cut down on servants. It was during this dismal period that mother and daughters were "politely but firmly" turned out of a hotel in Vermont for being Jewish, in a particularly humiliating but hardly novel display of anti-Semitism. In the town on the New Jersey shore where Guggenheim's various uncles had built vacation homes that included replicas of the Petit Trianon and a Pompeian villa, the nearest hotel would not admit Jews; she reports watching happily as the place burned down one summer. But she reserves her greatest disgust for the family villas themselves, for the Victorian pomp and suffocating closeness of the new ghetto that effectively walled her in.

She made a bid for freedom as soon as her father's estate was settled, in 1919, and she inherited four hundred and fifty thousand dollars—a greater sum than anyone expected, although a pittance by Guggenheim standards. (Her accountant later estimated that her inheritance would have been on the order of two hundred million dollars, had her father remained with the family business.) In any case, it was quite enough to allow her to vault the ghetto walls when at last she spied a place to land on the other side. Harold Loeb, Peggy's cousin and the family's artistic rebel, asked her to help keep accounts in a small bookstore that he subsidized, in the area around Grand Central, and the experience was a revelation: the discovery of a world full of people whom she later recalled as "so real, so alive, so human" precisely because "their values were different" from hers. When Loeb moved to Paris the next year to work on a novel, she followed. "I soon knew where every painting in Europe could be found," she wrote, "and I managed to get there, even if I had to spend hours going to a little country town to see only one." She particularly adored Venetian painting, and when an acquaintance assured her that the works of Bernard Berenson would be too difficult for her, she read every volume that she could get her hands on.

This ravenous intellectual and aesthetic hunger seemed to disappear immediately upon her marriage, at twenty-three, to a dazzling bon vivant and painter named Laurence Vail, an American raised in France, whom she gleefully titled "the King of Bohemia." Artistic, popular, ostentatiously at ease in the world, and decidedly not Jewish, the golden-haired Vail was to Guggenheim an enthralling figure, and she guilelessly reports how she pushed him all the way to the altar. (She was so sure he wouldn't show up for the wedding that she didn't buy a dress.) In the same lightly rueful tone, she goes on to detail how, during the years of their marriage, he would knock her down in the street or "walk" on her stomach or, when he was truly furious, rub jam into her hair. The violence has an absurd, cartoon quality that keeps the pain from seeming real, unlike the pain of the King of Bohemia's frequent reminders that his wife possessed neither the beauty of a consort nor the artistic talents of a rightful citizen. As Guggenheim sums up his argument, "All I had to offer was my money," upon which Vail graciously consented to live.

Bohemia is a cruel country. Unprotected by the bourgeois rules of polite behavior that she had so gladly left behind, Guggenheim appears to have borne the insults and humiliations of her new society with a kind of perverse pride, even when they were no different from the insults and humiliations she had always known. She mildly noted that when, at a party in Paris, Man Ray's mistress, Kiki, called him a "dirty Jew," it was her mother, visiting after the birth of Peggy's first child, who was "outraged" and "told Kiki what she thought of her." Guggenheim herself offered no response. Bohemia does not seem to have been tarnished for her even after Harold Loeb was brutally caricatured by his friend Ernest Hemingway in *The Sun Also Rises*, in 1926, as the pitifully overeager Jewish character Robert Cohn, whose most memorable trait is his ability to withstand any amount of verbal abuse without complaint. But then, in the same year, Laurence Vail completed a novel of his own—*Murder! Murder!*—which contains a viciously anti-Semitic portrait of the author's barely disguised wife, who moves her lips in her sleep "as she dreams of sums." Guggenheim reported that she "took offense" at the original manuscript, and that Vail obligingly rewrote it. This only suggests how much worse the book must once have been.

Bohemia is especially cruel for children. Populated largely by adults bent on fleeing the responsibilities of adulthood, the culture readily supplied new justifications for the same old failures of mothering and fathering that Guggenheim had endured herself. The Vails' son and daughter, Sindbad and Pegeen, seem to have suffered from a more or less benign neglect even before their mother ran off with another man.

By the late twenties, the perils of motherhood for all the Guggenheim sisters were chillingly clear. Benita, after several attempts to have a baby, died in childbirth, in 1927, and Guggenheim wrote that it was this death, coupled with Vail's heartless attitude to the loss, that brought her marriage to an end: "I felt virtually as though I had been cut in two." About her children, she suddenly felt that she "had no right to have any," a comment that may shed light on the single incident that even she found too disturbing to recount: the death of her sister Hazel's two small sons, the following year, when they plunged from their mother's grasp and off a rooftop in New York. The fact that Hazel was not charged with murder was widely assumed to be a result of the family's legal interference. Yet Guggenheim wrote of 1928 simply as the year in which she fell madly in love with a brilliant alcoholic writer whose affectionate nickname for her was Dog Nose. As she saw it, the privilege of going off with this man meant that she had to give up one of her children, in order to be fair to her husband. She chose to keep the girl, a pensive three-year-old flaxen-haired waif. Guggenheim later wrote that the intensity of her longing for her son, who was five, nearly destroyed the new relationship, but by then there was no way back.

She spent the next decade of her life administering first to the needs of the alcoholic writer and then to the unfaithful Communist who eventually took his place—and for whose sake she joined the Party, her bank account notwithstanding. She was nearing forty and sick with a sense of personal failure when a friend suggested that she open an art gallery as a diversion from suffering over men. She acted quickly: aided by half a million dollars that she inherited on her mother's death, in 1937, and closely guided by Marcel Duchamp, she opened Guggenheim Jeune in London in early 1938. And at last she found a way to direct her thwarted needs and desires. "The instant I felt it I wanted to own it," she wrote of a small rounded brass sculpture by Jean Arp. "I fell so in love with it."

Arp's *Head and Shell* was the first work to enter her collection. She now had two major expressive outlets, art and sex, and they often seemed to work in tandem: for the next year and a half, she became known for exhibiting the most avant-garde artists, but even better known for her affairs with them. Her sexual career from this point on is legendary, primarily because she proudly made it so, detailing conquests ranging from the Surrealist master Yves Tanguy to the young Samuel Beckett (who, whenever she asked what he planned to do about their relationship, replied, "Nothing"). By the time she closed the gallery, after two seasons, in June 1939, she had lost a good deal of money but gained a Don Giovanni–like list of names. Still, it was a pair of men who would never make it onto her list—the eminent critic Clement Greenberg, and Jackson Pollock, who reportedly said that you'd have to put a towel over Peggy's head to fuck her—who changed the meaning of her life.

In the early forties, New York was filled with refugee artists—Mondrian, Dalí, Léger, Tanguy, Breton, Duchamp—whose work had defied the Nazi ban on non-naturalistic art, and who were invigorating the local art world with their ideals and practices. There was no shortage of galleries and museums to show this revolutionary work, but Guggenheim was not intimidated. The Museum of Modern Art had opened in 1929, but had by 1940 acquired, according to Guggenheim, the look of a millionaires' yacht club. In 1939, her own uncle Solomon had established the Solomon R. Guggenheim Collection of Non-Objective Painting, just around the corner from MoMA on East Fifty-fourth Street, but in his mid-seventies Uncle Solomon was infatuated with his young German curator, Hilla Rebay, who with suitable non-objectivity had filled the place with the works of the little-known Rudolf Bauer, who happened to be her lover. Guggenheim certainly depended on advisers—Alfred Barr, James Johnson Sweeney, Alfred Putzel—but she was the only one to decide what got shown in her gallery, and its atmosphere was unlike any other in town.

Art of This Century opened in October 1942, at 30 West Fifty-seventh Street, as both a gallery with art for sale and a museum for Guggenheim's collection. Designed by the émigré architect Frederick

Kiesler, it was divided into four highly theatrical spaces: Surrealist paintings were shown in a black cave of a room, projecting at angles on what appeared to be sawed-off baseball bats (a "faintly menacing" effect, according to the *Times*), while abstract and Cubist works hovered on weblike cables above a floor painted brilliant turquoise (Guggenheim's favorite color). The simpler Daylight Gallery housed changing exhibitions of lesser known and newer works—the only works for sale—while the Kinetic Gallery featured interactive art like Duchamp's *Boîte-en-valise*, a leather suitcase containing a box containing tiny replicas of much of Duchamp's work: a portable oeuvre suitable for an artist-refugee, its contents were viewable only by staring into an eyepiece and turning a large wheel. At the gallery opening, a benefit for the Red Cross, F. Scott Fitzgerald's grown-up daughter, Scottie—a living link between one age of New York glamour and the next—was photographed peering into the Duchamp. Guggenheim herself wore one earring by Tanguy and one by Calder, to display her professional impartiality between the Surrealist and abstract modes.

In truth, though, she had her favorites. From the time she succeeded in bullying the broke and miserable Max Ernst into marriage, in December 1941—"I don't know if he was miserable because he was going to marry me or some other reason"—Guggenheim did everything that she could to support his brand of delicately mannered Surrealism. Ernst's unhappy former dealer, Julien Levy, implied that she'd thought up the gallery and the marriage as a package deal. Defending the movement, she very neatly (if crudely) cut off all disagreement: "With regard to Surrealism," she replied to a negative critique by no less a figure than Klaus Mann, "he seems to be in perfect accord with Hitler."

Nevertheless, Ernst left her after hardly more than a year for the beautiful young painter Dorothea Tanning, a Surrealist who worked in a notably Ernst-like mode. He had already chosen two of her paintings for Guggenheim's second exhibition, which was entirely devoted to women artists. (Each of the fifty-five exhibitions that Guggenheim mounted is documented in the absorbing volume, *Peggy Guggenheim and Frederick Kiesler: The Story of Art of This Century*, published under the auspices of the Guggenheim Foundation in 2004.) Ernst had visited the studios of all thirty-one women in the show, and he later joked that he had slept with all but one, who was not home, but whose maid obliged him instead. His speedy departure, a terrible blow to Guggenheim's overtaxed heart and ego, happened to coincide with an argument she had over money with his fellow Surrealist André Breton. It was as a result of these highly untheoretical developments that one sophisticated European style fell out of favor in New York's most adventurous art establishment, and American painting—largely ignored by both MoMA and Uncle Solomon—literally had room to come into its own.

Jackson Pollock's name was misspelled the first time he showed one of his works at Guggenheim's gallery, in early 1943; by the time of the "Spring Salon of Younger Artists," she had got it right. The critical response was favorable, and, in an unusual arrangement, Guggenheim offered to pay Pollock a hundred and fifty dollars a month to quit the custodial job he held at her uncle Solomon's museum and do nothing but paint, in order to produce enough work for a one-man show that fall. In exchange, his paintings were hers to sell, if she could. Clement Greenberg, who had recently shifted his intellectual focus from Marx to Mondrian, was away in the army for most of the year, and played no direct part in these early events. Shortly before he was inducted, Greenberg had written approvingly of Guggenheim's collection and of the new energies of abstract painting, but he had made no firm case in its favor. It was Greenberg's experience in the army that ultimately altered his perception of the significance of abstraction and made him adamant about its place in American art.

If Guggenheim had glided through wartime Europe with barely a nod to the dangerous realities of being a Jew, she displayed a new political awareness in New York, at least insofar as politics applied to art. One of the epigraphs in the catalogue of her collection was from Adolf Hitler, describing the "corruption of taste" in modern art and asserting the need to sterilize the offending artists along with the rest of the insane. Another epigraph, wholly contradictory—as contradictory as the contents of the catalogue itself—was from the English art historian Herbert Read, who explained that neither the Fascists nor the Nazis had been able to produce great art because the spiritual aspect of creativity "works only in the plenitude of freedom." On the opening of the gallery, Guggenheim herself issued a statement about displaying art at a time "when people are fighting for their lives," circumstances that made her fully conscious of a responsibility to serve the future.

But Greenberg had a far more intense and personal reaction to the war. The son of Russian Jewish immigrants who had abandoned all religious observance to become "atheistic socialists," as Greenberg put it, he was overwhelmed by the dangerous realities of being a Jew during his eight months of military service, although he never left the country. Stationed at a POW camp for German soldiers in Oklahoma, he was deeply shaken by the ranks of confident young prisoners going about their self-appointed exercises in preparation for Hitler's victory. He later described 1943 as the year that he began, as a Jew, to feel physical fear. Back in New York that autumn, he started writing about both art and literature from an increasingly close and often explicitly Jewish point of view. A long article on Sholem Aleichem as "the Jewish Dickens," in *The Nation*, quickly veered into a discussion of what Greenberg saw as the essential virtues of the Jews, including their "examining and comparing intellect"—a quality that, by early 1944, he was identifying as "a Jewish bias toward the abstract."

Greenberg did not apply his notion of this essentially Jewish bias to the art of painting; but then Hitler had done that already. Instead, over the next few years, he turned the Nazi equation of abstraction with Jewish decadence on its head, arguing that a new sort of art was emerging in New York City that was fully representative of the principles that were required to win the war: an abstract art that was positive in spirit, heroic in scale, free, imaginative, and unquestionably American. Guggenheim, who had not wanted to come back to the country at all, was now very nearly cast as a patriot; her private escape into art began to take on the tone of a campaign for world liberation.

Greenberg expressed some reservations in his review of Jackson Pollock's first one-man show, at Guggenheim's gallery, in November 1943, but he nevertheless compared the Wyoming-born painter to Melville, Hawthorne, and Poe. Greenberg was particularly impressed by an immense mural-sized canvas that Guggenheim had commissioned for the foyer of her East Side town house; nearly twenty feet long, it was the largest work by far that Pollock had yet done. (The public got to see the mural when she opened her house in conjunction with Pollock's second exhibition, in the spring of 1945.) Guggenheim herself described the mural as "a continuous band of abstract figures in a rhythmic dance," and recounted how it had been painted in a single night of poured-out inspiration, just before the show's opening, after Pollock had sat numbly in front of the enormous canvas for weeks. The truth of this dramatic story has been questioned; Pollock told his brother that he had painted the mural the previous summer. Nor is there any evidence for the equally dramatic and continually repeated story that the painting proved too long for the wall and that the ever-helpful Duchamp calmly proposed cutting eight inches off one end (while Pollock went off to locate Guggenheim's liquor supply), remarking that, with this kind of painting, it really made no difference.

Which of these myths of modern art appears the more significant—the frenzy of inspiration or the practical adjustment of the dully repetitive result—depends on one's attitude to Pollock's work or, perhaps, to modern art itself. Although Guggenheim was not initially impressed with Pollock, she appears to have developed her own purely instinctive response to what she called his "wild and frightening" painting. She sponsored no other artist so resolutely, no matter who tried to cajole her into it. Although her financial arrangement with him garnered her a large number of his works, as cynics inevitably point out, she never sold one for more than a thousand dollars. And it was through her manipulations that MoMA bought its first Pollock, in 1944. If nothing else, the behavior that she put up with may be considered evidence of her commitment. (The drama of the mural installation ends, rather famously, with Pollock wandering into a party at Guggenheim's apartment later that night and urinating into the fireplace.) "I dedicated myself to Pollock," she declared, and she came to think of him as her "spiritual offspring."

By the end of the war years, the gallery owner and the critic were virtually the twin engines of the new American painting. Guggenheim exhibited it; Greenberg explained what it meant and why it mattered. During this fraught period, Greenberg made the case that abstract art in New York had become a moral phenomenon, and that it fulfilled on painted canvas many of his early political ideals: the urban concord of Mondrian's *Broadway Boogie Woogie*, the defeat of nihilism in Pollock's passionate intensity, a general ascetic standard that stood opposed to the "restless rich" and their complacent way of life. Off the canvas, however, ascetic ideals were not much in evidence. Guggenheim liked to claim that every night while she lived in New York she went to bed drunk. She gave frequent parties, where she served cheap Scotch and potato chips to guests who ranged from Joseph Cornell to Gypsy Rose Lee; one night Max Ernst angrily overturned an ashtray on Greenberg's head, crowning him King of the Critics, upon which Greenberg socked him in the jaw. Considering the gap between what Greenberg preached and the general uproar that Guggenheim inevitably set in motion, it is difficult to understand how he believed that a memoir by her would aid his cause.

Yet it was Greenberg who encouraged her to get down to work, beginning in the summer of 1944. Although it has been claimed that Greenberg also read each chapter of her book as it emerged, this does not seem likely. Greenberg's review, which appeared under the pseudonym K. Hardesh—Hardesh is Hebrew for Greenberg—in *Commentary*, in 1946, is a furious judgment hurled down from the heights of Sinai. "As a Jew," Greenberg wrote, "I am disturbed in a particular way by this account of the life of another Jew." Although he believed that Guggenheim displayed fine critical alertness with regard to the bourgeois world that she had rejected, she was incapable of criticizing the bohemian world that she had so gratefully claimed in exchange. Greenberg's few words of praise for Guggenheim were made in a comparison with Gertrude Stein, a woman of similar background who had entered bohemia through literature, while Guggenheim "flew in on money and a kind of vitality that amounts almost to genius."

He didn't carry the comparison any further, although it is evident that Stein's 1933 memoir, *The Autobiography of Alice B. Toklas*, was the model for Guggenheim's own surrealistically naive tone. And then there were the paintings, the painters, the parties: all the most celebrated elements of Stein's world were reestablished in Guggenheim's, yet Picasso chose to paint Stein's portrait and he threw Guggenheim out of his studio. It was through sheer strength of character that Stein became a heroine of bohemia—or, as she would have preferred it, a hero—while Guggenheim was, in Greenberg's terms, a victim, a position he found troublingly emblematic. "In the list of the martyrs of bohemia, Jewish names stand out," he observed, citing Modigliani, Pascin, and Soutine. He might well have added Guggenheim's cousin Harold Loeb, whose savaging in *The Sun Also Rises* provides the likeliest answer to the mystery of why Stein broke with Hemingway after the book appeared. It is difficult to imagine Guggenheim taking such a stand; indeed, if she was offended by Greenberg's denunciation, she never let on. But, of course, that was precisely Greenberg's point.

Guggenheim's own view of the possibility of belonging to any sort of world had grown exceedingly bleak. As soon as the war was over, she began looking for a place to live in Venice, having decided that "I would be happy alone there." During her remaining time in New York, she gave a one-woman show to her daughter, Pegeen, now a pensive twenty-year-old waif who painted canvases of sad little families of blank-faced dolls. And the great collector acquired, at last, a major Picasso, *Girls with a Toy Boat*, which she claimed to find "madly amusing." Her main worry in closing up shop was what would become of Pollock—she had raised his monthly payments to two hundred and fifty dollars—and it was with difficulty that she finally secured another gallery's agreement to show his new work if she subsidized him for one more year. The last exhibition at Art of This Century took place in May 1947. Commemorating its scant five years of existence, Greenberg wrote that Guggenheim's position in history was assured and that her departure was a serious loss to living American art.

"I am where I belong, if anyone belongs anywhere nowadays," Guggenheim wrote to Greenberg from Venice later that year. She had bought an unfinished eighteenth-century palazzo, in which she planned to live quietly with her paintings and her dogs. All ideas of retreat vanished, however, when she was offered an entire pavilion for the display of her collection at the Biennale of 1948, the first international art exhibit there since before the war. This was a major event, and Guggenheim's pavilion was the focus of attention: "the explosion of modern art after the Nazis had tried to kill it," as her Italian secretary later said. Guggenheim was thrilled when Bernard Berenson visited, even if he responded to her avid declaration that he had been the first person to teach her about painting with "My dear, what a tragedy that I wasn't the last." Although she was laying plans to turn her palazzo into a museum, it did not seem likely that many visitors to Venice would come to look at what she had to show.

The real explosion happened the following year. In August 1949, *Life* ran a story with a banner headline reading JACKSON POLLOCK: IS HE THE GREATEST LIVING PAINTER IN THE UNITED STATES? Citing the testimony of a single, unnamed but "formidably high-brow New York critic," *Life* ventured to answer with a resounding yes. Moreover, the article featured a large photograph of Pollock dressed in jeans and cowboy boots, a cigarette dangling from his lips, displaying all the allure of the James Dean–style heroes of the approaching fifties. America fell in love with Pollock's image, if not with his art. He was famous, and yet his work remained nearly impossible to sell until 1956, when he died the quintessential fifties-hero death—in a car crash, drunk, at the age of forty-four—and prices started going through the roof. Guggenheim had long since become incensed over the absence of her name in the stories of his astonishing rise; she'd complained that Pollock didn't even answer her letters. When Greenberg called from New York with news of his death, she is said to have replied, "I don't give a damn."

In Venice, she found a home at last. In the city that gave the world the word "ghetto," she now owned one of the last privately owned palazzi along the Grand Canal, equipped with her own gondola and private pier. Instead of the traditional family colors and coat of arms to adorn them (which neither her stable-born grandfather Seligman nor her grandfather Guggenheim the peddler had been able to provide), she displayed a shield of her favorite turquoise striped with white, and heraldic images of her Lhasa apsos, which emerged from Venetian workshops looking like shaggy little lions.

At the age of fifty-one, she took up naked sunbathing on her roof—directly across the water from the windows of police headquarters—and developed an attitude to sampling the local men that her friend Mary McCarthy compared to her attitude toward the local olives and crusty bread. She herself was delighted with this image, and when one of her guests inquired, "Mrs. Guggenheim"—as she was known in later years—"how many husbands have you had?" she shot back, with perfect Mae West timing, "D'you mean my own, or other people's?" It is easy to point to the indisputable loneliness and the inability to maintain a relationship that lie behind the pose. But one may also allow for the cockeyed bravery that McCarthy expressed in terms of Guggenheim's "huge, gay, forgiving heart," and which seems to be summed up in Guggenheim's reply to Max Ernst's inquiry about whether he might visit her with his wife. "Come to Venice," her telegram to him read. "All is oblivion."

Even Guggenheim's most trusted methods of achieving oblivion failed her when, in March 1967, she received the news that her daughter had committed suicide, in her home in Paris, at the age of forty-one. Pegeen, who had four young sons and was in the midst of a stormy second marriage, had consumed a fatal mixture of pills and alcohol. Her husband claimed that he had rescued her from seventeen earlier attempts, but Guggenheim steadfastly refused to believe that the death was not an accident, because, she said, "I know she would have never deserted her children." She was still arguing against the charge of suicide in an updated version of her memoir published in 1979, the year of her death. Although she could rage in her own defense, Guggenheim clearly came to feel that the blame belonged to her alone, as did many people around her, including her son and ex-husband. "Sindbad and Laurence once said to me 'You killed Pegeen,'" she admitted in her final years, "and sometimes I think I did."

Guggenheim's shortcomings as a mother are all too clear, and can perhaps be best understood in terms of her inability to stop being a child herself. But there may be more than one contributory reason for Pegeen's tragedy. It does seem worth noting that two of Laurence Vail's three daughters by his second wife also attempted suicide, and that, according to interviews with them in Weld's 1986 biography, their father maintained some sort of sexual involvement with both. This isn't to say that Vail had an incestuous relationship with Pegeen, but the field of damage in this family was very wide, and the boundaries of childhood were consistently blurred. "We were like two sisters, friends, having lovers," Guggenheim said of her relationship with Pegeen, in her own last years. And she added, "Her death has left me quite bankrupt."

When she was asked in those late years to name her greatest achievement, Guggenheim answered that the first was Pollock and the second was her collection. But the painting that meant the most to her was Picasso's *Girls with a Toy Boat,* in which two rather sweet if monstrously misshapen little girls, playing at the ocean's edge, are depicted with protuberant breasts and pregnant bellies. When Guggenheim opened her museum to the public, in 1951, she placed this painting in the entrance hall, above Giacometti's tabletop bronze *Woman with Her Throat Cut.* It was several years, she pointed out, before she realized that the painting was not funny but disturbing and profound, and that its "poor little girls" were not really enjoying themselves; rather, they were preoccupied with "their destiny as women." She did not specify what she thought this destiny was, but, to judge from her reaction to this image of two childlike sisters or friends, already swollen with their own children, she believed that she had lived something very like it. In the bedroom of the palazzo, Guggenheim always kept a portrait of herself and Benita as little girls. And in the public space of the museum she established an exhibit of the works of Pegeen Vail, a room filled with naive paintings of detached and doll-like figures, which she referred to as Pegeen's tomb.

Guggenheim died of a stroke in 1979, after a long and wretched physical decline, at the age of eighty-one. Her ashes were buried in her garden, near the graves of her many dogs, which were marked with a plaque reading "Here Lie My Beloved Babies." The anxious question of what would happen to her beloved paintings and sculpture had been answered just a few years earlier, when, after being assiduously courted, she agreed to return to the fold and leave everything—the art and the palazzo, too—to the Solomon R. Guggenheim Foundation in New York, which would maintain her collection in Venice as a semi-independent Guggenheim outpost. Although she'd long ago dismissed the New York Guggenheim's grand Frank Lloyd Wright building as "Uncle Solomon's garage," a show of her collection there, in 1969, had left her profoundly moved at the sight of her treasures "descending the ramp like the nude descending the staircase." (She seems to have been more gratified only by a show of her collection at the Louvre, in 1975, which she regarded as "a great revenge for me.") There have been complaints over the years about the institutionalization and commercialization of Guggenheim's palazzo: there is little sense anymore that it was ever a home, and other collections now share its rooms and bring its holdings up to date. Yet it is hard to imagine that she would argue with its status as the most visited modern art museum in Italy and the second-most-visited museum in Venice, after the Palace of the Doge.

Guggenheim was calmer and quieter in her last years. She liked to say that floating in a gondola was the nicest thing in her life since she gave up sex. The impulse was never quite vanquished, though. "If she takes your hand, I suggest you let her," Mrs. Alfred Barr advised Saul Steinberg about proper behavior during a gondola ride; it would cost him so little, she said, and would give her so much pleasure. She became an honorary Venetian citizen, and year by year she learned virtually all the city's churches and its frescoes, its hundred and fifty canals, and the names of most of its four hundred bridges. Every day, she would glide along in the late-afternoon sun, sometimes accompanied by a famous visitor, but more often alone, as she had predicted when she planned to make Venice her final home. "You fall in love with the city itself," she reported with the sense of an important goal finally achieved. "There is nothing left over in your heart for anyone else."

BORN FOR THE PART

KATHARINE HEPBURN

Katharine Hepburn, 1942

Jo March chopped off her hair and wrote thundering dramas and moved alone to New York just after the Civil War but found happiness in a last rainy scene under an umbrella with her kindly older suitor; Lady Cynthia Darrington set altitude and distance records on the earliest solo flights but went down in flames for love of a married man; Tess Harding was *The New York Chronicle*'s ace political columnist and the second-ranked dame in the country, after Mrs. Roosevelt, but swore to give it all up for life in Spencer Tracy's kitchen. Cutting a path across history, in the guise of more than forty varied screen heroines who shared a singular face and accent, Katharine Hepburn embodied the most sought-after strengths of modern women, and then habitually followed a man into confusion and defeat. The strengths—intelligence, independence, gall—were the memorable part, and formed a dramatic premise in themselves. The dire or merely domestic outcomes of so many of her movies can be easily dismissed as the requirements of a less enlightened age, or as a sign of the ongoing bewilderment about how a truly "modern" woman's story might conclude. But since Hepburn's own story has ended—she died at ninety-six, in 2003—we may be able to learn how such a woman actually lived out an uncensored and unedited freedom, since we have always somehow known that, despite four Academy Awards and a dramatic range from Louisa May Alcott to Eugene O'Neill, for half a century Katharine Hepburn was really playing herself.

She was ostentatiously modern—"more modern than tomorrow," the filmland magazines promised; "You've never seen anything like her!"—from her first screen appearance, in 1932, in Hollywood's take on a creaky British melodrama called *A Bill of Divorcement*. Yet there was nothing in her impersonation of a British ingénue named Sydney that violated an ensemble acting style still bound to the Victorian stage. At twenty-five, Hepburn was as stilted as John Barrymore, who played to the galleries as her half-mad father. The novelty was not in what she did but in what she was. With her starved, whippet-like grace and charged intensity, she herself appeared slightly mad. But the same characteristics also made her seem—as George Cukor, the director, had gambled—like a distinctly new type of woman, poised between the nervy and the nervously overwrought.

The quality of a nearly feverish radiance continued to excite audiences even when her character was neither modern nor threatened with hereditary insanity. By the fall of 1933, *Little Women* was breaking box-office records at Radio City, with Hepburn as America's beloved Jo billed alone above the title. *Variety* crowned her the second-most-popular female star in the country, right behind Mae West. Between them, these two unprecedented creatures neatly divided the possibilities: Brooklyn and Bryn Mawr, vaudeville and the classics, flesh and bone—or rather flesh and the ravenous Puritan spirit that consumed it. Still, even if Hepburn looked like Mae West's clothes hanger, and seemed as rigid as her own New England scruples, it was she who outlasted every change in the rules of a country that couldn't quite decide whether such women should exist.

The idea that Hepburn *was* the parts she played quickly became a studio gambit. Publicizing *Little Women*, Cukor announced that she'd been "born to play Jo," since she came from just the same sort of large, sternly wholesome New England family that Alcott's fable was about. And, besides, he added, "she's tender and funny, fiercely loyal . . . Kate and Jo are the same girl." So, too, Kate and Tracy Lord, the imperious "virgin goddess" of *The Philadelphia Story*, of 1940, were the same rare girl—part of the lore of the play was that it was written for Hepburn by her old friend Philip Barry, after months of observation of the same large, although now apparently quite wealthy and eccentric, New England family. When, in 1941, *McCall's* named

Hepburn its Woman of the Year (borrowing the title of yet another film written for her), the magazine specified that it was honoring her not as an actress but "as a woman" and "a raving individual." Given the indisputable evidence of movie after movie, the country looked to Hepburn as a figure who merged all our contradictory fantasies of aristocratic lineage and republican conviction, of high spirits and high morals: she was a big-screen Eleanor Roosevelt, but with the beauty that only Hollywood can grant as a reward.

"I'm just something from New England, that was very American and brought up by two extremely intelligent people who gave us the greatest gift that man can give anyone—freedom from fear," she recalled of her childhood. These words only hint at the lifelong gratitude Hepburn displayed for her parents and the domestic paradise they'd built; as an adult, she returned home often and in all her troubled times. ("That's very unusual, isn't it?") Some twenty Hepburn biographies have given increasing attention to this very unusual family romance. The most prodigiously researched, Barbara Leaming's *Katharine Hepburn*, devotes a quarter of its pages to events that occurred before its subject was born.

Dr. Thomas Hepburn was a urologist who worked toward the public recognition and treatment of venereal disease. Katharine Houghton, his loving wife, campaigned for legal birth control and led the battle for woman suffrage in Connecticut, but was always home in time for tea. In a sprawling house in Hartford, these high-minded individuals raised six exceptionally bright children who swung on the birch trees in the backyard and won blue ribbons for diving and tennis and anything else that was up for the winning. The family was so immoderately strong and fearless and happy that there was never any need to mention the suicide of Mrs. Hepburn's father or of her father's brother or even of Dr. Hepburn's own oldest brother—Uncle Charlie—since there was nothing to be done about these matters and, as their famous daughter later remarked of her parents, "They simply did not believe in moaning about anything."

The oldest children, Thomas and Katharine, were born one and a half years apart—Tom in 1905, Katharine in 1907—and they formed a little club unto themselves. Early photographs show a pair of nearly identical freckled cherubs, hand in hand. By the age of ten, Kathy is sporting cropped hair and a boy's wardrobe, ready and able to follow her big brother into anything. In March 1921, the pair, aged thirteen and fifteen, took the train to New York City with their mother and stayed several days in the Greenwich Village house of one of her suffragist friends, their "Aunty Towle." They saw Pavlova dance on a Wednesday, and on Thursday their mother went back to Hartford. On Friday, they went to a movie with Aunty—it was *A Connecticut Yankee in King Arthur's Court*, and Tom complained that a scene of a hanging gave him "the horrors." On Saturday night, after supper, Tom played his banjo to entertain them, and on Sunday morning, when the children were to get the train home, Kathy went upstairs to Tom's attic room and found that he had hanged himself from one of the rafters.

It would seem to require an Electra or an Antigone, not a wholesome American heroine like Jo March, to produce the sentence with which Katharine Hepburn, in her autobiography, described what happened next: "In a state of numb shock I cut him down and laid him on the bed." This is not quite accurate. The police report contradicts her memory of horrified competence with its account of a young girl clinging hysterically to her brother's body as she attempts to hold it upright. The noose that Tom had fashioned out of a torn bedsheet had proved too long, and when he jumped from a packing case his feet had hit the floor; he'd had to pull hard against the line in order to strangle himself. Tom needed not to be cut down but to be raised up, and his sister was still supporting his body in her arms when the doctor arrived. In *Me*, published in 1991, Hepburn was still worrying over the truth of one particularly tormenting part of her story—that is, whether her brother really came to her the night before to say "You're my girl, aren't you? You're my favorite girl in the whole world." She knew that she had repeated these words to others but wondered, seventy years later, if Tom had ever really said them.

Dr. Hepburn insisted that his son's death was the result of a boyish stunt gone awry, and tried to get the newspapers to retract their accounts of suicide. But however he managed to alter the truth for the public, or for himself, he could not alter it for his daughter: the sole family witness to the will it took for Tom to go on dying once his feet were on the ground. This was a memory she knew to keep to herself. She saw her mother cry for what she swears was the first and only time ("She was stalwart") on the trip to the crematorium, and reported that she herself now acquired the skill of shedding tears when tears were called for: "This was what I thought I should do. People die—you cry—but inside I was frozen."

Are there families in which suicide runs like intelligence or cancer? Two days after Tom's death, news arrived of the death of another of Dr. Hepburn's brothers: he had run his car's engine with the garage door closed. For the family, it was not difficult to annul the existence of an uncle who had lived as far away as Annapolis. It must have exacted more of an effort in the case of Tom, and yet, once the facts of his death were satisfactorily revised, he was not spoken of at home again. When Kathy became too moody to continue at school, the family brought in tutors; she later recalled how she enjoyed playing golf during her free time in the afternoons. She went on to Bryn Mawr, where she received poor grades but a great deal of attention—for the way she dressed, for her snooty manner, and, when all else failed, for jumping into the campus fountain. It was now that she decided to make a career out of expressing emotion in front of as many people as she could get to watch.

From her first weeks in New York, in the summer of 1928, Hepburn walked straight into leading roles. But she was frequently thrown straight out as soon as she got near the stage. What was so attractive at an audition was precisely what went wrong in performance: electrifying tension and insufficient control. Under pressure, her voice rose to incomprehensible heights and speeds. She hired a vocal coach and took movement classes with Pavlova's former partner, Mikhail Mordkin. Still, she was fired at least four times in the next two years. She was even fired from a play that Philip Barry wrote with her in mind, *The Animal Kingdom*, suggesting the remarkable fact that she couldn't yet play herself.

She finally had a hit in a Broadway version of *Lysistrata* called *The Warrior's Husband*. Playing the Queen of the Amazons, she made her entrance running down a flight of steps with a dead stag over her shoulders, but in the end she was happily overcome by a stronger man. It is a success worth noting, for this was a character that she would repeat in some ways for the rest of her life. The surrendering Amazon won her a screen test, reportedly excruciating, but George Cukor saw past the extravagant emoting and the Theda Bara makeup—he said she looked like "a boa constrictor on a fast"—and pushed the reluctant powers at RKO to give her a chance. What he'd loved, he said, was the way she swooped to put down a glass, with her back to the camera, and then turned to do the scene with her eyes suddenly filled with tears.

She got to Hollywood in July 1932, and was as pointedly outrageous there as she'd been at Bryn Mawr, only now Bryn Mawr was part of the act. She was an East Coast aristocrat, the *Mayflower* in skirts—or, rather, in slacks, since the *Mayflower* didn't need to dress, which made the biggest impression of all on the folks from steerage who ran the studios. Her publicity stressed how she hated publicity; she didn't pose for pictures, except when caught unawares with a rented pet monkey on her shoulder. She was probably an heiress. She would soon go back to playing Shakespeare, or O'Neill. Her personal life was mysterious, and there were rumors about those slacks and her women companions. In fact, she'd left behind in New York a fairly new and barely used husband—one Ludlow Ogden (Luddy) Smith, a college beau acquired in a moment of professional discouragement, whom she quickly bequeathed to her family as a kind of permanently hovering extra brother. She was also having an affair with her agent, Leland Hayward, who was then married to his first wife for the second time. There were many reasons to maintain a veil of mystery, even aside from its excellence as a tactic.

In 1933, the magazine *Picturegoer* made a stab at rending the veil with an astrological treatise titled "What Her Birth Date Means to Katharine Hepburn." Born in early November 1909, she was a Scorpio and therefore "strongly individual, very uncompromising, critical and judicial in a clear, decisive fashion." Exactly right, of course, except that she was born on May 12, 1907. That an aspiring movie star should take two years off her age is less than notable; it's rather meek. That she conscientiously changed the month and the day, however—and for decades biographies listed Hepburn's date of birth as November 8—is more problematic, since the birth date she'd taken over, with her parents' knowledge and consent, was her brother Tom's.

•

"I wasn't afraid. Not for a long time. When I lost a part, I thought it was because I was a genius and geniuses always have a hard time," confides the giddy little starving genius of an actress Hepburn played in *Morning Glory* (1933), which won her an Academy Award. Determined but pure-hearted Eva Lovelace has come to New York to be very famous, to play Juliet and Lady Macbeth, and to die at her zenith onstage, preferably as Cleopatra grandly ending it all herself. Audiences loved Hepburn best in roles like this, part swan and part odd duck, where her patrician quiverings were framed in awkwardness and aspiration. The most exquisite of these hybrid creatures appeared two years later, in *Alice Adams*—her best early performance, as Booth Tarkington's desperate dreamer trapped in the banality of Main Street, putting on airs and wasting her ambition on the kind of small-town suitor that Eva Lovelace had fled for her life. Given an excuse to be as flutteringly absurd as she often was anyway, Hepburn is heartbreaking.

But no one concerned with her career seemed to understand the mixture of comedy and pathos that gave these movies their appeal. Her next four films were box-office fiascoes, and none worse than the cross-dressing cult favorite *Sylvia Scarlett* (1935), Cukor's vague Shakespearean reverie on Hepburn as a boyish girl who passes herself off as a girlish boy. On the edge of professional disaster, she took on tragedy queens and Victorian damsels, and toppled right over into the abyss. *Mary of Scotland* (1936), a clanking opera-without-music, survives mainly as fodder for speculation about the star's affair with her director, John Ford. There is something understandably alluring, almost patriotic, in the mating of these two distinctly American birds of prey, and their respective biographers have been at odds over the extent of what went on. (Ford was, and remained, a very married man.) But, for all that her directors fell under her spell, Cukor's Hepburn sent audiences fleeing in confusion and Ford's put them out cold.

When everything fails, you laugh. That was the lesson of Depression movies, and Hepburn learned it very late. While the studio dawdled over whether she should play Empress Josephine or Sarah Bernhardt, she went off in a Theatre Guild touring production of *Jane*

Eyre, which she hoped to lure Ford into filming. When neither her performance nor a headlining affair with Howard Hughes made Ford jump at the project, she returned to Hollywood and, in the spring of 1937, took on one more movie tailored just for her. The role of the ambitious actress Terry Randall, in Edna Ferber and George S. Kaufman's Broadway hit *Stage Door*, was converted into another Hepburn vehicle, reflecting the audience's latest view of the fading star: an heiress, a bit of a pompous ass, a self-conscious tragedienne whose ghastly "calla lilies are in bloom" speech was lifted from one of Hepburn's own stage flops—*The Lake*, which had earned her Dorothy Parker's famous verdict that her acting "ran the gamut of emotion from A to B." The only difference was that this time it was all meant to be funny.

Stage Door may be the warmest ensemble comedy Hollywood ever produced. In the embracing camaraderie of its rooming house filled with aspiring actresses, for most of whom careers and mutual loyalty are crucial and for whom men offer little more than a way to a role or a steak dinner—where getting married is an admission of defeat—it may also be the only truly feminist film Hepburn ever made. Not that anything of the sort was intended. Under Gregory La Cava's improvisatory, seat-of-the-pants direction, the script changed from day to day and the movie just sort of happened as it went along. (It finally had so little in common with the play that Kaufman said it ought to be called *Screen Door*.) Originally, one of the two leads—Hepburn or Ginger Rogers—was to be married off to the big producer, played by Adolphe Menjou, but somehow that plotline disappeared: what happened between the women was so much more interesting.

The cast was delectable—Lucille Ball and Eve Arden threw in the salt and pepper—but it was Rogers who got things cooking. "She gave him sex and he gave her class" was Hepburn's expert sizing up of Rogers's trade-off with Fred Astaire. But the wisecracking blonde gave Hepburn something equally important: the kind of populist foil that she learned she couldn't do without. Easy banter, teasing jabs, a clear-eyed American common sense that tried Hepburn's mettle and made her unbend: she got all that from Rogers, and not from any actress again. That's a loss, because Rogers challenged Hepburn to be a decent, feeling, regular human being, while her later replacements— above all, Spencer Tracy—challenged Hepburn only to be a more regular dame.

Stage Door was a moderate commercial success, but the two madcap heiress movies that followed—Howard Hawks's now canonized *Bringing Up Baby* (with Cary Grant and the leopard and the dinosaur bones) and Cukor's *Holiday* (Grant and Hepburn fleeing the oppression of wealth)—were box-office flops. However adorable the highly advertised "new Hepburn" was designed to be, and however much the buoyancy and liberal spirit of these films have won them contemporary fans (recent scholarship has found that *Baby* demonstrates the decline of the patriarchy and the collapse of the phallus), audiences at the time were simply irritated. Hepburn seemed more unbearably superior than ever, as—in both films—Grant played up to her (rather than down), her character won every round, and the high speed of screwball comedy turned her voice into a drill. Reviewers blamed her for headaches and exhaustion. In 1938, she made the theater owners' dreaded list of stars whose very names had become box-office poison.

With RKO fed up and offering her no roles that she was willing to play, she took herself off to Fenwick, her parents' Connecticut seashore home, for the summer and fall of 1938. Philip Barry had spent time there, too, not as a suitor but as a playwright fascinated by the suitor situation, particularly as it involved the constant presence of her far-too-cheerful ex-husband. (Luddy took photos of her visiting beaux—Hayward, Ford, Hughes—and liked to assure visitors that he was the sanest member of the family.) It was Luddy who had come from the Main Line Philadelphia society that Barry gave the Hepburns as a background in *The Philadelphia Story*. When Barry showed Kate the play, she thought it good enough to invest in the production and, in one of the smartest moves she ever made, to secure herself the movie rights (with money borrowed from Hughes). She left only one important contractual escape: all bets were off if she landed the role of Scarlett O'Hara.

But Atlanta was burned again without her. David O. Selznick insisted that audiences disliked her too intensely, and, in any case, she lacked the "sex qualities" needed for Scarlett. And so *The Philadelphia Story* went ahead and opened on Broadway in March 1939, to reviews nearly as apologetic for past abuse as they were enthusiastic about the work at hand. The show ran for more than four hundred performances, and Hepburn was suddenly back on top, thanks as much to her business acumen as to her acting. She sold the movie rights for her new hot property to MGM, a much bigger and richer studio than RKO, and got Louis B. Mayer to agree to her terms: herself in the starring role (of course), a large degree of script control, and Cukor to direct. She tried to get Spencer Tracy and Clark Gable for the roles of her ex-husband and an interfering reporter; she'd never met either, but they were the biggest male stars in the country (aside from Mickey Rooney). Mayer managed to persuade her that Cary Grant and James Stewart would be adequate to the tasks. Thus, with some rather more delicately balanced notions of masculinity than she'd intended for her opposition, she made the movie in which the shrew was tamed and finally forgiven by her men and the country alike.

For Hepburn's real populist foil—whether represented by Rogers or Stewart or Tracy—was, of course, the moviegoing population of the United States, which has always exalted its aristocrats right up to the point of revolution. As Tracy Lord, Hepburn has a cold perfection that is denounced as the source of everyone's troubles, particularly the men's. The actress's social and moral affronts were now firmly tied to her deficit in "sex qualities": her character is reprimanded as a "prig," a "perennial spinster," and one of "a special class of the American female, the married maiden." The silent opening battle tells it all. Grant storms out the door, she throws his golf clubs after him, he storms back to give her a shove—and over she goes, stiff as a poker. It's a slapstick routine, a Punch and Judy show, and it was put in right at the start to make sure no one missed the point: this woman has to learn to bend.

Apart from cinema's eternal little girls—like Lillian Gish and Mary Pickford—Hepburn was probably the least sexual beauty ever to become a movie star. The lack of femme fatality may be ascribed to her uncommon self-possession: the stubborn vertical bracing of that pratfall also kept her from assuming the conventionally vulnerable (or predatory) female sexual postures. This is the Hepburn women still want their daughters to watch. But Hepburn can also appear just too tightly wound and scrubbed—she enthused about taking several cold showers a day—for anything as stickily human as sex. In the entire range of her movies, it is difficult to call up an image of her in a clinch or a kiss or an unembarrassed sexual situation: except for *Woman of the Year*, the 1942 film that followed *The Philadelphia Story* and that forms nearly a genre in itself.

Woman of the Year was her first movie with Spencer Tracy, whom she still hadn't met when she offered Mayer the terrific script that Ring Lardner, Jr., and Michael Kanin had written for her, with her collaboration, and told him she wouldn't let MGM make it without giving her Tracy this time. How determined she was to capture the rough-on-smooth sexiness that Ginger gave to Fred was made explicit in her choice of directors: "I had to explain to Cukor"—whose reputation as a "woman's director" was privately attributed to his homosexuality—"that this script had to be directed by a very macho director from the man's point of view and not the woman's. I'm sure that George was very disappointed."

The macho replacement was George Stevens, her director in *Alice Adams*, who had worked with Laurel and Hardy and was known for his touch with comedy. He was also known for his touch with his leading ladies, on-screen and off. The first we see of Hepburn in *Woman of the Year* is a fabulous outstretched leg in a silk stocking and a high-heeled shoe—who knew she had legs?—and the rest of her is hardly less alluring. The role is a radically new female fantasy: a political columnist whose family is intimate with the Roosevelts and who converses brilliantly in half a dozen languages. (We hear her do Bryn Mawr shades of Spanish and German and Russian, but Mayer vetoed Yiddish; the virgin goddess might lay herself down, but the Connecticut shiksa remained inviolate.)

Hepburn's Tess Harding is everything Jo March and the generations of world-seeking girls who modeled themselves on Jo ever dreamed of becoming, a woman immersed in a life of adventure and achievement and importance. In her relationship with Tracy, who plays a sportswriter for the same paper, she's the intellectual force and the big success. Reversing all the clichés, it's he who gets upset when she's preoccupied with her work or fails to notice that he's bought a new hat. And she's the sexual aggressor, too: in one breathtaking scene (considering that it's Hepburn) they neck for a bit, clinging tight, and she shocks him by casually preparing for him to stay the night. Retribution inevitably arrives, of course, with marriage and the familiar accusations: she's heartless, thoughtless, too self-involved to be a mother or a wife—in fact, he points out, she isn't really a woman at all.

And so, in one of the most lyrically funny and politically reviled episodes in American movies, Hepburn cooks Tracy breakfast in order to win him back. She's scheduled to launch a battleship that morning, but it can wait. In a nearly silent sequence that parallels the opening of *The Philadelphia Story*, she sets to work: fielding squares of toast as they sail through the air, gingerly tapping down an obscenely drooling waffle maker, hitching up a shoulder strap with a colander—she's part Pavlova and part Stan Laurel. Weeping, she tells Tracy she wants to quit her job ("What are ya gonna do, run for president?" he snarls) and be a proper wife. The screenwriters were only the first of many to be outraged by this ending—feminist film criticism hardly has a sorer point—which was tacked on after the film's completion, apparently when women in the preview audience found the star's perfections threatening. (The original ending had her outcheering Tracy at a baseball game.) Hepburn, due to her contract, had practical control of the story, of the director, and pretty much of L. B. Mayer, and she took personal credit for the change. Yet the rub is not that she was willing to compromise her principles for the sake of success. If she hadn't, she would have stopped making movies right along with Mae West. More disturbing is the possibility that Tess Harding's crazed capitulation didn't seem to her to be a compromise at all: that it was love.

At thirty-four, Hepburn was a star again through her own formidable efforts, and she had also finally "discovered what 'I love you' really means." Her definition of the phrase veers from the traditional to the alarming. "It means I put you and your interests and your comfort ahead of my own," she wrote. It means "total devotion." In practice, it meant that if "he didn't like this or that," she continued, "I changed this and that. They might be qualities which I personally valued. It did not matter. I changed them." The man she loved, as much of the world is aware, was Spencer Tracy. The life she described after more than two decades of celebrated devotion sounds relatively simple. "Food—we ate what he liked. We did what he liked. We lived a life which he liked. This gave me great pleasure. The thought that this was pleasing him."

The great, secret affair was not much of a secret at the start. While *Woman of the Year* was playing at Radio City, in February 1942, Sheilah Graham informed readers of her Hollywood column that the two stars "got on like a house afire" and that "the love scenes in the picture are extremely convincing!" There seemed little reason to keep things quiet, since Hepburn was divorced and Tracy's affairs with his co-stars were notorious; by the time they met, he was known to be spending more time at the Beverly Hills Hotel than with his wife and children. Later legend often portrays Louise Tracy as a Catholic who would not hear of divorce. In fact, Louise was Episcopalian—it was Spencer who was Catholic, if limited in observance to playing priests and racking up guilt.

Louise was, however, something of a saint. Although the modest wife and the glamorous movie star may seem polar opposites, they were all too alike in their unremitting ideals of love and the sheer blind strength they offered in its service. Louise was someone Hepburn might have played, if Hepburn had ever been able to convince as a mother: when the Tracys' first child, John, was born deaf, in 1924, Louise devoted herself to teaching him to speak and live normally. She succeeded against all odds, and went on to establish the John Tracy Clinic in a small bungalow in Los Angeles, in 1942, just a few months after the Sheilah Graham tidbit appeared. Over the years, the clinic grew into one of the country's largest centers for the education of deaf children, and Louise earned one humanitarian award after another; it was remarked that she even looked a little like Eleanor Roosevelt. She and her husband continued to pose together for pictures, for the clinic, as late as 1962, which was the next time that any significant publicity appeared about Tracy and Hepburn.

For those who know the partnership as a series of sophisticated comedies of sparring, loving equals (in which he got top billing, every time), it may come as a surprise that the next movie to match the description—*Adam's Rib*—did not get made for seven years. In between, the pair stumbled together through a number of misfits in various genres, from a political melodrama to a wholly implausible western. Alone, Tracy had some success in a couple of war movies (he was the only big male star at MGM who didn't enlist). Hepburn pushed hard to get the studio to risk making O'Neill's *Mourning Becomes Electra*—even for her, though, Mayer stopped at incest—and then settled into the likes of Pearl Buck's *Dragon Seed*, a film all too accurately described as a "Not-So-Good Earth." In any case, her criterion for an acceptable part soon came down to whatever wouldn't keep her away from Tracy for long.

The studio found this a reasonable use of her time, since Tracy, one of the most infamous drinkers in Hollywood, needed constant supervision to stay sober. Garson Kanin, scriptwriter and courtier to the royal pair, tells many admiring anecdotes of Hepburn's loyal devotion: Kate kneeling at Spence's feet and leaping up to make fresh coffee when the old was still hot but he said it was cold, Kate scrubbing the floor of Spence's dressing room, Kate sleeping outside his locked hotel-room door as Spence drank himself sick over a period of days, waiting for the chance to get inside to clean him off. And he observes with official, glitter-eyed cheeriness how Kate "never felt bereft or sidetracked" when Spence went off to spend time with his wife at their home, The Hill, since Kate herself so appreciated the value of family, as demonstrated by her own frequent visits to her mother and dad.

Her brother Bob tried to make sense of her behavior by suggesting that Tracy "was sort of a younger edition of her father, in her mind." It's true that she spoke of her father, adoringly, as an "over-male" male. For all his liberal philosophy, Dr. Hepburn was an authoritarian in his domestic demands and in his harsh (some in the family said overharsh) corporal punishment of the children. And she spoke of Tracy, just as adoringly, as "a throwback to an age of rugged heroism." This was, of course, Tracy's stock-in-trade on-screen, part of his image as the all-American, not too threateningly handsome, gruff but decent man. Yet Tracy's actual "small life"—as he himself described it—was anything but rugged; rather, it was bounded by the studios and The Hill and various Hollywood bars and restaurants. Even his highly cinematic acting style seems to depend on expending the least effort possible. By the time Hepburn published her autobiography, in 1991, she had come to see Tracy in a very different light, but she sustained herself for decades on what appears to have been a set of furiously willed illusions: that fiction could be transformed into fact by the intensity of belief, that her lover's frequent cruelties were a sign of heroic masculinity, and that she could save him.

In the late forties, Tracy was drinking heavily and rumored to be chasing other women. Hepburn was hemmed in and worn out when *Adam's Rib* finally established the intimate, home-movie interplay and beloved status of the partnership—in 1949, the year that Ingrid Bergman was run out of American movies for being an adulteress. The "Tracy and Hepburn" routine was already pat in its mixture of feistiness and comfort, and the pair exemplified what later feminists would gratefully view as "an ideal relationship celebrating the most happily integrated emancipated woman of the era." At the time, however, the woman was in need of emancipation from nothing so much as the relationship itself.

For the next few years, Hepburn took on every job she could. Real life resembled the old movies played backward: the hero disappeared from the frame and the heroine was suddenly brash and striving again. She spent months coaching her voice in order to play Rosalind in the New York Theatre Guild's *As You Like It*, in 1950. The reviews were not encouraging, but it pleased her greatly that her mother got to see her perform Shakespeare; Katharine Houghton Hepburn died the following year. Hepburn's fame secured a four-month Broadway run, and after a summer break in California with Tracy, a national tour kept her away for another half year. Then in April 1951—just a month after her mother's death—she set sail for England and Africa on a new adventure.

Rosie Sayer, the "psalm-singing skinny old maid" of *The African Queen*, is probably the heroine most responsible for carving Hepburn's chin-up, indomitable image into our cinematic equivalent of Mount Rushmore. In a breezy little book she wrote years later—*The Making of "The African Queen," or How I Went to Africa with Bogart, Bacall and Huston and Almost Lost My Mind*—Hepburn tells how, after the first few scenes, John Huston walked into her hut to say that she was approaching the part all wrong and to offer a suggestion: play it like Mrs. Roosevelt, who felt that she was ugly and always put on a smile to cover the ugliness or the worry about the ugliness, and to keep herself going. Hepburn calls this the most brilliant bit of direction she ever received.

The effect isn't much apparent in her early prim and bothered scenes, which any number of actresses could have played. But when Rosie is freed from her inhibitions by the hazarding of dangers and lets out a hell-for-leather Jo March baritonal "Hip hip hooray!" accompanied by snorts of laughter, then her smile becomes a face-splitting dissolution into radiance, and something in Hepburn (at her most irremediably Hepburn) does evoke Mrs. Roosevelt—something that is clearly not a feint but a great compensatory gift for self-forgetting, for hands-on-the-world exuberance, which the actress in all her first-time Technicolor beauty would seem to bear no right to, and which makes her appear the happiest woman alive.

The movie took five exciting, exhausting, self-forgetful months to complete. When she returned home, she found that her father had remarried and that the entire record of her mother's lifework in the suffrage and birth-control movements had been destroyed. No point in looking back. As for Tracy, he'd been making his softest pictures yet; at fifty, with *Father of the Bride*, he'd begun to move into papa-bear roles. Back in Hollywood, Hepburn fulfilled her last MGM commitment with him in *Pat and Mike*, a sports-division trifle by the loyal team—Cukor directing, Kanin and Ruth Gordon writing—and did not renew her contract. Instead, as Tracy began filming *The Plymouth Adventure*, she went off to prepare for Shaw's *The Millionairess* onstage in London. In the summer of 1952, she was playing there to rave reviews when Tracy arrived for a visit, accompanied by his new co-star and latest paramour, the thirty-one-year-old Gene Tierney.

There were separate hotels and gossip and near-brushes at dinner. Tierney told people that Tracy was in love with her; Tierney's mother told people that he was the most tormented man she'd ever met. Night after night, Hepburn's performances became so agitated and ranting that close observers worried for her health, while the *Times* commended "her ability to be violent in about twenty-five different ways." The play was scheduled to move to New York, and she wrote to the head of the Theatre Guild, her old friend Lawrence Langner, that she thought she might be "cracking up." It is apparent that by August a full-scale nervous breakdown was passing as a tour de force.

In September, Tracy went back to Hollywood and Hepburn spent several weeks recovering at Fenwick, but severe vocal problems— which she described as a sense of being strangled when she spoke— persisted through the play's disastrous New York run that fall. At her lowest point, she checked into Presbyterian Hospital, whether to regain her voice or her emotional control isn't clear, and there may not have been a real distinction.

After this, she cut a wider arc than ever around Hollywood, al- though she and Tracy were never out of touch. It was three years— and a different era—before she made another movie. The glorious strength of Rosie Sayer had survived a trip down a crocodile-infested river and a German gunboat attack, but no amount of pluck could see Hepburn through the American fifties with her dignity intact. The lush and rudely punishing *Summertime*, made in Venice in 1954, in- augurated a series of films that might be called Hepburn's Spinster Cycle, in all of which an intelligent, middle-aged, and previously inde- pendent woman is reduced to desperation by her lack of a man; the old tacked-on endings were now the main event. The massive domes- tic reengineering project of postwar America, shifting millions of women out of factories and offices and back to the kitchen, was still making full use of movies as propaganda. For all the wistfully Jamesian aura of *Summertime*, Hepburn's new persona was a coup in the counter- revolution, a clear depiction of what flouting the rules would get you now: loneliness, a boring job, a few stolen moments with someone else's husband, public humiliation, and a hairdo with little bows. It is a mark of how fine Hepburn's performance is in *Summertime* that one can hardly bear to watch her.

From Venice she moved on to Australia, where she toured Shake- speare with the Old Vic Theatre Company. She was playing her first real Kate the Shrew when she got word that Tracy had become so drunk and unreasonable on his latest picture that he'd been fired. Clearly, he was unable to manage without her. And so, in late 1955, she returned to his side in Hollywood, and they took up much where they had left off; some say they were never closer. His career was soon flourishing again, and she took on films when his schedule allowed. Approaching fifty, she played two more plaintive spinsters, in *The Rainmaker* (1956) and *Desk Set* (1957)—the latter a near-complete inversion of *Woman of the Year*—and one all-devouring mother (*Suddenly, Last Summer*), after which she reputedly spat in the producer's eye and shut down her movie career. She kept on with Shakespeare at three hundred and fifty dollars a week in Stratford, Connecticut, drawing large crowds and mixed reviews, living alone on the river and hoping Tracy would join her. She cooed to the press over what a great Macbeth he would be, since he was, after all, America's presiding actor of genius. By 1960, her public activities were confined to sitting in on Tracy's sets, calling out his praises and knitting.

She made a single exception when she was offered the role of Mary Tyrone, O'Neill's magnificently tormented portrait of his mother, in Sidney Lumet's film of *Long Day's Journey into Night*. (She tried to persuade Tracy to play opposite her, as the brilliant wreck of a drunken actor James Tyrone, but he said the fee was too small.) In the fall of 1961, she came to New York for three weeks of rehearsal and thirty-seven days of shooting, to make what many consider to be the crowning achievement of her career and a few dissenting voices call a travesty.

Lumet's film is choppy and strained and the actors rarely mesh, but in the circa-1912, hair-piled-high style of Mary, Hepburn is almost painfully ravishing. She really did become more beautiful as she aged, and her looks and her history here take on a kind of allegorical force. The elegant bones that were once the latest in chic now appear a Gothic cage, a reliquary for the martyred spirit staring out. The familiar voice is harder to accept, but even her most actressy intonations may be taken for Mary's attempt to hide her secrets behind girlish affectation. While it may justly be complained, as always, that Hepburn is too much Hepburn, by now that very fact adds to our emotion. When the sickled curve of her mouth or the lift of her head brings Jo March or Rosie Sayer or Alice Adams flashingly before our eyes, we register with fresh surprise the way that movies capture time. For we can actually see, in a person we have only just met—Mary Tyrone, a trusting girl who fell in love one spring and became a wraith of a wife—shades of bloom and loss not present even in O'Neill's exhaustive text.

Nothing was important enough to draw her to the screen again for five more years. Both her father and Tracy became ill during the filming of *Long Day's Journey*, and when her father died, in November 1962, she devoted herself to Tracy as a full-time aide, nurse, friend, lover, and nearly a wife—but for the presence of Louise. A tell-all *Look* feature in early 1962 seems not to have altered the situation. When Tracy suffered a pulmonary crisis in 1963, the two women took shifts at his hospital bedside, and Louise told reporters gathered out front that she expected her husband to be coming home any day. What bothered Hepburn most was that she seemed to believe it.

When Tracy returned home, to the cottage on Cukor's estate where he had lived for years, Hepburn threw all her energies into his recovery. She said that she was completely happy then; she was needed, she was keeping him alive. By 1966, when Stanley Kramer came up with *Guess Who's Coming to Dinner?* as a vehicle for them both, Tracy's health was so poor that he couldn't be insured, and Kramer and Hepburn put their salaries in escrow, to repay costs if Tracy couldn't finish the picture. A trouper, he lasted for fifteen days after the final shoot. He died in the early morning, in his cottage, and although he did not permit Hepburn to sleep in the room with him—she kept herself tethered nearby, with a cord attached to a bedside buzzer—she heard him walk to the kitchen, and then the crash of a cup, and then a thud. She was through the door in a flash, crouching down to take him in her arms, and there is a sense in her telling of this story in which the forty-six years of life between Tom's death and this moment seems no more than a brief passage between an early and a late Pietà.

She moved her possessions out and then—annoyed with herself—back in again, before Louise arrived later that day. Face to face, the women bickered over which suit he would wear in the casket. The official fairy tale went into production two days after the funeral, when the *Los Angeles Times* called the Tracy-Hepburn films "a remarkable legacy of an association as beautiful and dignified as any this town has ever known." Later that year, *Guess Who's Coming to Dinner?* got reviews that excused themselves from being reviews: there was no criticism possible anymore for these two, we were so glad just to be in their presence again. Hepburn won her second Oscar for this film, thirty-four years after her first, and she went on to win two more, the all-time record so far: for *The Lion in Winter* (1968) and *On Golden Pond* (1981), a final movie in the Tracy-Hepburn style, with Henry Fonda filling in as the old curmudgeon and Hepburn succeeding to the role of the saintly wife.

For the rest of her life, Hepburn spoke of Tracy as reverentially as she did of her mother and father. She frequently recalled their "twenty-seven years together in what was to me absolute bliss." There was no other great love. Highly disconcerting, though, is her account of a flirtation, after Tracy's death, with the screenwriter of *Guess Who's Coming to Dinner?*, William Rose, in which she elevates this handsome but childish and destructive man (to judge by her own transcribed conversations) to the status of a god among writers, a suffering giant of an artist beside whose talent she is a mere mouse, and thus meant to serve. The thoughts are familiar; only the name of the hero has changed. Hepburn herself came to write in regard to Tracy and his problems: "one builds one's own jail." In looking back—and possibly all along, from the part of her that required someone to save—she recognized him as a soul "in misery with life." He was such a natural actor, she wrote in 1991, because he couldn't bear living in himself. And there was "no one able to help him, really." She concluded that she had never known him; she wasn't entirely sure there was anyone to know.

After Tracy's death, she set herself back to work, with the same relentless energy she'd put into keeping him alive. Until well into her seventies, she took on role after role, indefatigable, a pronounced wobble just slipping in among her other fondly noted mannerisms. When movie projects were scarce, there were Broadway shows—she learned to sing, in a manner of speaking, for *Coco*—and grueling national tours that no other star of her stature would have considered. There is a generation that knows her from a remake of *The Corn Is Green*, or as Warren Beatty's aunt in a second remake of *Love Affair*—her last screen appearance, in 1994—or simply as a majestic but suspiciously lonely television talk-show guest, addressing her public just a bit more directly than she ever had in what may qualify as her finest late performances, with no story line and no director and no part left even to pretend to play but Katharine Hepburn.

The old question about whether she could act may not only not have an answer; it may not be the right question. "She does not enter into the leading character: she substitutes herself for it," Shaw wrote of Sarah Bernhardt. And, if Hepburn showed us how Jo March and Eleanor of Aquitaine took their turns at playing Katharine Hepburn, the exchange seemed to involve no loss of scale or interest. Hepburn claimed that she was too content with herself as a person to be among the really great actors, too much the strong and happily unreflective product of her parents. There is some truth in this: the engine of the Hepburn machinery seems to have been a survival instinct in permanent overdrive, which is visible in the almost unhinged force that broke through the mediocrity of her early material, and which carried her through her uniquely Lazarus-like career. She overcame every obstacle—horror, failure, love, the endings of most of her movies—to provide us with a continually renewed image of the strength that such overcoming required. We held her close not because she could act but because of the insistent life that hummed through every taut and peremptory inch of her, a life that we imagined to be as natural as breathing or winning for someone so easily, imperiously free. It was in making us believe in this that she may have been our greatest actress of all.

THE PLAYER KINGS

ORSON WELLES
AND
LAURENCE OLIVIER

Laurence Olivier as Hamlet, 1948

After appearing in Paris, Hamburg, and the British military post at the remains of the concentration camp at Belsen, the Old Vic Theatre Company arrived in New York in April 1946, on a victory tour for a battered but triumphant Western culture. Ticket prices were high, but lines at the box office were long and the atmosphere was frenzied with anticipation. The company opened with Shakespeare—*Henry IV*, Parts 1 and 2—and continued with Chekhov and a double bill of Sophocles and Sheridan: six weeks of repertory, fifty classically trained British actors, even a small orchestra in the pit. Although top billing was shared by the company's two leading actors, Ralph Richardson and Laurence Olivier, there was no doubt who the star really was. Playing valiant Hotspur on opening night, Olivier employed a nervous stutter that made the exalted (and possibly intimidating) language startlingly real. The following night, in Part 2, he was unrecognizable in the minor role of ancient Justice Shallow, whom he played as a fixated beekeeper—an occupation that Shakespeare had failed to mention—upstaging Richardson, in the larger role of Falstaff, by continually swatting at imaginary bees. More brazenly virtuosic was the contrast between Sophocles' Oedipus and the giddy eighteenth-century dandy Mr. Puff, in Sheridan's *The Critic*: Olivier left the stage with his eye sockets streaming blood and returned, after a brief intermission, prancing in lace and a powdered wig. The *Times*, speaking for the conquered city, noted, "The spring seems to be given over to Laurence Olivier."

This was not the spring that Orson Welles had planned. In March, just before the Old Vic's impending visit made the news, he had announced the rebirth of the famous Mercury Theatre, starting with a musical extravaganza based on *Around the World in Eighty Days*. But it wasn't long before tales of disaster started drifting in from out-of-town tryouts. Forty-five tons of sets, a sixteen-hundred-pound mechanized elephant, and a Japanese circus were making for an epic level of chaos: on the eve of the show's Broadway opening, the *Times* compared the backstage scene, perhaps inevitably, to Charles Foster Kane's warehouse. Several critics appreciated Welles's old-fashioned showmanship; he promised a reporter that he was equally prepared to "act Hamlet and do a roller-skating act" to sell the show. Nevertheless, *Around the World* closed in less time than its hero took to circle the globe. Welles, saddled with enormous debts and thousands of souvenir books, spoke nostalgically of 1937, when there was widespread hope that he would single-handedly create an American national theater: "I was the Laurence Olivier of that year."

The twentieth century's two greatest dramatic illusionists had more in common and, ultimately, more effect on each other's work— as friendly if occasionally cutthroat competitors; as reinventors of Shakespeare for a modern audience—than has been noted even in the mountain of books that each has inspired. By 1946, comparison was unavoidable, and not just because Welles and Olivier were occupying theaters a few blocks apart. Growing up an ocean apart, they had emerged independently, in the mid-thirties, as the biggest theater personalities and Shakespeare revolutionaries of the age. Barely out of his teens, Welles directed a sensational all-black *Macbeth*, at the Lafayette Theater in Harlem; Olivier—eight years Welles's senior— was twenty-seven when he gave a performance of Romeo so painfully, youthfully awkward that London critics accused him of not knowing how to speak verse. To the wider public, they were, moreover, Mr. Rochester and Heathcliff: their film portrayals of the Brontë heartthrobs had turned them into full-fledged movie stars. And each was now paired with a matching screen goddess: Olivier was married to Vivien Leigh (who very noticeably accompanied him to New York)

Orson Welles as Macbeth, 1948

and Welles to Rita Hayworth (who just as noticeably stayed home). Yet neither was instinctively or even happily a movie actor. Taking an approach rare in the post-Stanislavsky age, each lived in professional thrall to the infinite possibilities of false noses, padding, wigs, and generally disguising or (better yet) disfiguring makeup. Welles called it "camouflage," suggesting more profound similarities between the men, since these physical transformations allowed the actor, as Olivier later explained, "to avoid anything so embarrassing as self-representation."

This theatrical ideal had already got them both into trouble. Despite the swooning female audience, Welles's flamboyant portrayal of Mr. Rochester, in the 1943 film *Jane Eyre*, had earned him reviews that he complained were "the worst accorded to an American actor since John Wilkes Booth." He had agreed to take a mere acting job only after his career as Hollywood's wunderkind—at twenty-five, he had co-written, produced, directed, and starred in *Citizen Kane*— came to an unhappy end, with his failure to prove that art could turn a profit. Still, he remained a fearsome presence. The unassuming director of *Jane Eyre*, Robert Stevenson, was too intimidated to bully Welles the way William Wyler had bullied Olivier when, at the start of work on *Wuthering Heights*, in 1938, the cocky British stage star offered the same sort of grandstanding performance. Olivier had rebuffed Wyler's corrections by informing him that his chosen medium was "too anemic to take great acting." But Wyler persisted, and Olivier credited him for the rest of his life with teaching him how to act in films. And more: with teaching him to respect the medium, assuring him that there was nothing in literature, not even Shakespeare, that a film could not encompass.

The most difficult role for Olivier during his early years onstage was Henry V. Its problems were the opposite of those he had with film. Shakespeare's blazing soldier-king was too unhesitatingly bold, his speeches too fervently jingoistic ("God for Harry, England, and Saint George!") to suit the young actor's comfort. Olivier later explained that he had been "frightened of the heroism" at the heart of *Henry V* because the feeling throughout England during the thirties was against heroics, inclining instead toward the languid elegance of the immensely popular Noël Coward. Then came the war. And Olivier, performing a one-man show for British troops, discovered that Henry's clarion calls to arms had a powerful effect on real and unquestionably heroic soldiers. He went on to read Henry's speeches on national radio, and by 1943 he had a motion picture in the works. Seeking a director, he had asked Wyler, who passed him to John Ford, who found the idea that he might direct Shakespeare very funny. When other candidates fell through, Olivier himself took on the job, becoming the director, producer, and star of the most important English movie yet made—which, if not what he'd intended all along, soon produced in him a state of pure exhilaration.

The problem with converting Shakespeare to the movies has always been the disparity between the language and modern reality. Max Reinhardt's spectacular film of *A Midsummer Night's Dream* (1935) and George Cukor's equally lavish *Romeo and Juliet* (1936) were the most expensive Shakespeare films made after the advent of sound; designed to seduce viewers with their visual luxuriance, they had both been box-office flops. Olivier, to prepare his audience for the linguistic shock, begins *Henry V* with a performance of the play in the Globe Playhouse, circa 1600, with a cast of heavily rouged and floridly versifying actors (including Olivier, playing the actor playing Henry) working a rapt if obstreperous crowd: the mere mention of Falstaff raises a cheer; a reminder that the king has banished the old rogue brings a roar of outrage. The contemporary audience gets to see Shakespeare taken down from his pedestal, even while it adjusts to highly wrought Elizabethan speech as entirely natural for an Elizabethan theater. And then, just as we are feeling comfortable, Olivier's camera leaves the theater behind and, almost imperceptibly at first, moves out into the world. As real breezes begin to blow, the actors disappear into their characters, their flighty vocal lines dissolve into meaning—"Now sits the wind fair," Olivier softly breathes—and the story is being told directly to us.

Yet Olivier also ensures that the rest of the film is too unnaturally beautiful ever to be confused with mere reality. *Henry V* is a storybook pageant shot in the saturated artificialities of Technicolor; even the climactic battle at Agincourt is beautiful, with its knights in silver armor, its deep-blue sky, its bright-green grass. The only color notably absent from the battle is red: despite the reported thousands of enemy dead, there is little sign of bloodshed. For, in addition to finding a visual poetry equivalent to Shakespeare's language, Olivier's intention was to turn the play's political meaning upside down. By judiciously cutting, for example, Henry's order to kill all prisoners of war, and his threat to see his soldiers rape the daughters of a besieged enemy town, he masked the English king's brutality and, with it, Shakespeare's ironies about the ways of power.

Furthering this agenda, Olivier devised a way to effectively film Henry's big vocal climaxes without displaying his tonsils or forcing himself to underplay. During a speech, slowly and steadily, he pulls the camera ever farther back, to reveal, in the most famous instance, a field of soldiers gazing up toward the king astride a white horse that rears magnificently and tears away ("God for Harry, England, and Saint George!") on his last echoing syllable. And when, on the eve of battle, Henry reflects on the burdens of his crown, Olivier's troubled face is shot very close, his lips unmoving; heard in voice-over, his speech seems to take us deep into the mind of Shakespeare's "warlike Harry," where no audience had been before. This was the king and the picture that England required in 1943, a picture dedicated "To the Commandos and Airborne Troops of Great Britain."

Henry V opened in New York in the spring of 1946, just days after the Old Vic run had closed to sold-out crowds. The film had been a success in London, and, despite warnings about the taste of "the great unwashed," Olivier's loyal backers refused to cut it for American consumption. And, washed or dirty, the Americans came, and they kept on coming, not only in New York but in twenty cities across the country. Whether spurred by an admiration for British wartime courage, or by a *Time* cover story titled "Masterpiece," or by a creeping rumor that the film mixed familiar duty with actual pleasure, they turned *Henry V* into a box-office phenomenon. It broke the language barrier, the class barrier, the culture barrier: the opening scene of a broad audience comfortably enjoying its greatest literature looked—thanks to the film itself—a little like us.

To Welles, the great roller-skating, Hamlet-reciting democrat of the American theater, *Henry V* was a mine of possibility and provocation. He had first met Olivier at a party in New York in the mid-thirties, when both were performing on Broadway; they were engrossed in conversation when, as Welles recalled, the hostess came up to say, "Mr. Olivier, you must stop boring Mr. Welles"; or, as Olivier recalled, "Mr. Welles, you must stop boring Mr. Olivier." No accord on this was ever reached. They had performed together once, in a weekly radio drama, in 1939. By the time of *Henry V*, Welles had made his stunning professional ascent and an equally precipitous decline, and was struggling with a reputation as a film director incapable of commercial success (*Citizen Kane*) or, worse, incapable of finishing his films. *The Magnificent Ambersons*, fully shot but not edited before he went to Brazil to make *It's All True*, had been released in a version butchered by the studio; *It's All True*, in its turn, was canceled by the studio in mid-production and never released at all. But Welles, despite his reversals, appears to have viewed Olivier with warmth, as perhaps his only equal.

Most important, the pair were comrades in arms against the plummy British style of playing Shakespeare that prevailed in New York in the performances of Maurice Evans (Welles once claimed that he went to Hollywood to escape from Evans) and in London with John Gielgud. Although Olivier was only a few years younger than Gielgud, he seemed to represent a new generation, consciously opposing the old-fashioned style of "singing" verse with a direct and even dangerous power that tended to put critics in mind of various handsome jungle beasts. Welles remained undaunted. In fact, he had not been overawed by *Henry V*, beyond the fact of its success. He later remarked that the battle of Agincourt looked as though it were taking place on a golf course—which is to say that the film was too prettified and safe, and failed to make a connection between its characters and the outside world. He was sure that he could do better. To prove it, he started shooting *Macbeth* the following spring.

Welles saw Shakespeare as something of an American. He was still in his teens when, in 1934, he collaborated with his former schoolmaster Roger Hill—one of the important father figures in his life—on an edition of the plays titled *Everybody's Shakespeare*, which was designed to shake off the dust of the classroom and get readers to put on the plays in their local gymnasiums, dance halls, or backyards. Shakespeare belonged to us as much as to anyone: the playwright's England, like present-day America, was "a kid of a country,"

Welles wrote in his introduction, "bounding blithely into the sunny, early morning of modern times."

The blithely bounding George Orson Welles was born in Kenosha, Wisconsin, in 1915, and had been performing Shakespeare ever since he commandeered the theater department of Hill's Illinois boarding school, which provided the only formal education that he ever had. It was also his only steady home. Welles's parents had separated when he was four, after his artistically ambitious mother took up with the family physician—who, as the official discoverer of Welles's "genius," was the other significant father figure in his life. By his own account, Welles was too busy fulfilling this genius to waste time being a child. In Chicago, where his family (and the good doctor) had moved, he became the star of his mother's musical salon, while his father, whose tastes ran more to vaudeville and magic shows, descended into drunkenness. At a very young age, the boy had made his choice between them. His mother died after a lingering illness when Orson was nine, but he remained very close to the man known as his guardian. His weak but adoring father, with whom he had broken completely, died of drink six years later. For much of his life, Welles firmly believed that his rejection of his father's affections had killed him.

He was playing Tybalt in Katharine Cornell's polite and predominantly British production of *Romeo and Juliet*, on Broadway, in 1934, when a would-be impresario in the audience, John Houseman, felt the earth shake on the entrance of the furiously energetic young man, whose rich mahogany voice "tore like a high wind through the genteel, modulated voices of the well-trained professionals around him." Houseman eagerly hitched his fortunes to the unknown nineteen-year-old actor, becoming Welles's producer, promoter, factotum, confidant, and general caretaker through a series of productions that made New York theater history. Although Welles starred in several of these shows, his greatest gift proved to be for directing—and for making the director the star. After the Harlem *Macbeth* and Marc Blitzstein's socialist saga *The Cradle Will Rock*, Welles and Houseman founded the Mercury Theatre in 1937, in the commercial heart of Broadway. Their opening production, *Julius Caesar*, with its cast dressed in Fascist uniforms and lit with piercing shafts of "Nuremberg" lights, turned Shakespeare into the hottest political dramatist of the thirties.

Tall and boyishly good-looking, Welles cut an ideally princely fig-ure. Yet, when it came to Shakespeare's *Henry* plays, he already felt a deep affinity for the fat old comic knight Sir John Falstaff, rather than for the more physically suitable Prince Hal. And so, at twenty-three, he padded himself out grotesquely, as Falstaff, for the Mercury's big-gest production ever: *Five Kings*, a mosaic that Welles pieced together from several of the history plays into a single five-hour Henriad. Biogra-phers have been quick to note the relevance of the filial drama in these plays to Welles's life: Prince Hal, torn between two fathers—the calculating usurper Henry IV, the loving scalawag Falstaff—banishes Falstaff upon taking the throne, as Henry V, causing the old man's heart literally to break. Welles himself called this "triangle" the greatest story Shakespeare ever told.

But the vast requirements of *Five Kings* underscored the difficul-ties in the way that Welles achieved his goals: distracted and disorga-nized, working half the night and partying the other half, keeping his spirits up with vast quantities of food and brandy—his most percep-tive biographer, Simon Callow, calls Welles's theater "a temple of adrenaline"—teetering on the brink of failure and then soaring upward on a last-minute stroke of what everyone wearily agreed to call genius. At times, though, the chaos proved beyond redemption. Houseman observed that even a minor reversal sent Welles to his bed, where he lay for days "like a sick child, convinced that he was going to die." (In fact, Welles suffered terribly from asthma, along with a host of other ailments that were to keep him out of the military draft.) *Five Kings* proved to be a major reversal: a shapeless catastro-phe that closed in Philadelphia in March 1939, taking the Mercury Theatre with it. Welles kept the scenery in storage when he went to Hollywood. It was going to be just a quick trip to the fleshpots to earn the money to get his Falstaff back onstage.

"I wouldn't be surprised if Orson Welles is the biggest menace that's come to Hollywood for years," F. Scott Fitzgerald wrote in a short story of 1940, titled "Pat Hobby and Orson Welles," in which Fitzgerald's down-and-out screenwriter hero resentfully compares himself with the wildly successful new arrival. Everyone knew about Welles (or, to be precise, ninety-one percent of the population knew about him, according to a contemporary Gallup poll) and about the astounding contract that he had made with RKO to write, produce, direct, and act in one movie per year. He was also responsible for the final edit—a degree of control previously awarded only to Charlie Chaplin, who, unlike Welles, did not require a studio-assigned teacher to instruct him in the uses of a movie camera. Welles, after considering several different subjects for his first effort, hit on a story about William Randolph Hearst and his newspaper empire, a project that he and the screenwriter Herbert Mankiewicz (with whom Welles shared a much disputed credit) turned into a script initially titled, very simply, *American*.

Fitzgerald's hero jealously warns a local mogul that Welles will force the studios to "start all over again," as they did with sound. The real impact of *Citizen Kane*—not quite that of sound, but nevertheless profound—came well after its release, in 1941. Welles's film is renowned as much for the way its story is told as for the story itself: multiple points of view, overlapping dialogue, and, the most famed of its innovations, deep-focus photography, by means of which figures in the background are rendered as clear as those close up. Welles's cinematographer, Gregg Toland, had been striving to perfect the technique for years, and the result was a diamond-pointed black-and-white—the effect was almost impossible on color stock—that revealed complex relationships at a glance: while young Kane's mother signs the agreement that will send her son away forever, the unsuspecting boy is seen through a distant window, playing in the snow. (Three-quarters of a century later, Steven Spielberg described the excitement of the film's visual ambition: "You're going to see from one inch to infinity in every shot!")

But the core of Welles's revolution (and an idea all his own) was to set the camera free, physically and dramatically. Gazing up at a suddenly towering figure, or rushing eagerly down a corridor toward a door that has just slammed shut—almost pruriently interested in what is going on behind it—the camera becomes a seemingly subjective intelligence, part of the story that it tells. (In his earliest Hollywood days, Welles had hoped to make a film of *Heart of Darkness* in which the camera represents a narrator who is never seen.) Although this formal excitement was eventually to have enormous repercussions, none of the era's big directors, not even the ones who subsequently worked with Toland (William Wyler, Howard Hawks, George Cukor) seemed to regard Welles's achievement as a serious model. The only exception, working far from Hollywood, was Laurence Olivier.

On New Year's Day 1947, Olivier resolved to take on what he called "the big one": to direct, produce, and star in *Hamlet*. He cut the play himself: individual lines, subplots, characters—Rosencrantz and Guildenstern, Fortinbras—all were omitted for the sake of a clear story line and a running time of two and a half hours. He abandoned the use of Technicolor because, he later explained, "I thought it would be rather fun to do a black-and-white . . . and really show them some things in the way of focus"—that is, Welles and Toland's deep focus. "I could create distances between characters, giving an effect of alienation, or of yearning for past pleasure," he wrote, "as when Hamlet sees Ophelia an eternity away down the long corridor . . . sitting on a solid wooden chair—in focus—with love clearly in her eyes." This has been called the longest-distance love scene ever filmed.

But the more arresting love scenes for most viewers occurred between Hamlet and his mother: lingering kisses, a confrontation played across Gertrude's marital bed. (Aside from predictably "phallic" interpretations of various towers, pillars, and knives, one critic compared Gertrude's bed to "a giant vagina.") The Oedipal interpretation derived from Olivier's first stage performance of the role, in 1937, when the director Tyrone Guthrie took him to meet with the Freudian analyst Ernest Jones, the author of "The Oedipus-Complex as an Explanation of Hamlet's Mystery." Even before that, however, it had been part of John Barrymore's *Hamlet*, which electrified Olivier as a seventeen-year-old drama student in 1925. Nevertheless, biographers have not had to look very hard for Olivier's own Oedipal motivations—no harder than for Welles's motivations in his obsession with Falstaff—since Olivier claimed that his first childhood memory was of his mother's breasts "in a black lace sort of thing," and that his father had disliked him from the moment he was born.

A poor Anglican clergyman, Gerard Olivier had found the birth of Laurence, his third child, in 1907, an undue expense. Although in his youth Olivier considered his father's miserliness a perpetual torment, it was the grand ritual of church that established his love for theater, and almost compensated for his life at home. His early delight in performing was encouraged by his mother—"my heaven, my hope, my entire world, my own worshipped Mummy"—who died when he was twelve years old and away at school. Even Vivien Leigh believed that, in *Hamlet*, he was confronting this insupportable loss. (On the paternal side, Olivier's beady-eyed, cagey Justice Shallow was said to have been a dead ringer for Gerard, and to have sent his stepmother weeping from the stalls.)

In theatrical terms, the Freudian interpretation—which posited that Hamlet hesitated to kill Claudius because he identified with the man who shared his mother's bed—allowed the prince to be shown as a strong, if tortured, man, rather than as the sensitive weakling that the Victorians had popularized, and that Gielgud still played to perfection. (Olivier called this the "castrated" tradition.) The truly shocking aspect of Olivier's stage performance was his daunting physical power. This, too, came out of Barrymore's emphatically American, swashbuckling Hamlet, which Olivier said had "put the balls back" in the role, although he outdid Barrymore in virility and athletic risk. Critics had announced that Olivier was tremendously exciting, if "entirely without melancholy," and entirely wrong.

This criticism may account for the fact that his film offers an extremely melancholy Dane. His acrobatic strength is still occasionally visible, as when he makes a perilous fourteen-foot dive onto Claudius while finally carrying out his revenge. (Olivier shot this scene last, in case he seriously hurt himself; as it happened, he was fine, although he knocked out the front teeth of the professional stuntman who doubled for Claudius.) But such feats do not comport with the Gielgudian wistfulness of the performance. In his grander moments, moreover, Olivier has a Victorian staginess unlike anything else he did on film. His frequent use of voice-over in the soliloquies, so effective as contrast in *Henry V*, reduces the lengthy workings of Hamlet's mind to murmuring monotony. (Is this what thought is really like?) The performance suggests that playing weakness was Olivier's greatest weakness.

The true star of this *Hamlet* is the camera. The film is shot as though it were a forties mystery—what the French were just beginning to call film noir—edged in darkness and soaked in paranoia. At times, the camera seems nearly sick with emotion as it leads us through the narrative maze. "I saw the camera seeing most things through Hamlet's eyes," Olivier explained, sounding distinctly like Welles in his early Hollywood days, "wandering, or running, through the empty corridors, piercing the vast shadows of Elsinore's great rooms of state for some joy or the sight of some familiar object." This visual language tightly binds the drama, as does the scene of Hamlet's funeral procession, which Olivier claimed came to him suddenly (in fact, he lifted it from Barrymore's production) and gave him "the whole conception of the film." Glimpsed at the opening, the full procession brings the film to a thunderingly romantic end: the prince's body, laid on a bier, is carried up a twisting staircase to the turret; we get just a glimpse of his face, upside down as the bier moves past. And as the brass in William Walton's score begin to shriek, and the cannon boom their salute, the mournful little cortege emerges into the open air and stands in silhouette against a glowing sky.

Welles knew that Olivier was filming *Hamlet* when he began to shoot *Macbeth*, in June 1947. He also knew that he was lucky to get the job. He was still famous for the radio broadcast that had scared a good part of the population into thinking they were being invaded by Martians, he was a recognized movie actor, and he had become a radio personality known for his political stands (he worshipped FDR). But it was only thanks to the success of *Henry V* that he was able to get a contract to direct *Macbeth*. His deal this time was not with RKO or any other major studio but with a cowboy-picture outfit, Republic Pictures, which was willing to take a chance on his ability to turn out a "superior product" on a budget so low that, no matter how superior it turned out to be, it could not fail. Like Olivier, Welles adapted the script—cutting Shakespeare's shortest tragedy to under two hours—and signed on to produce, direct, and star. *Hamlet* took six months to film; Welles, however, shot *Macbeth* in twenty-three days.

If *Hamlet* approaches film noir, *Macbeth* resembles a cheap sci-fi or horror film. The papier-mâché sets were painted to resemble barren rock and to mirror Macbeth's soul, providing the metaphysical unity that Welles had felt was lacking in *Henry V*. Welles is a somewhat dazed Macbeth; the trap of the murmuring voice-over catches him, too. Sitting on his high-chair throne like a petulant child, he seems more Ubu Roi than the Scottish king. And despite the historical setting,

Lady Macbeth—a serpentlike performance by Jeanette Nolan—is introduced wearing a forties gown. Reality is not remotely a consideration. Welles wanted above all to create a world where the witches might be real, and here they are pagan priestesses hurling their spells against a sea of Celtic crosses, in a theological battle that he wrested from the text by scavenging lines to produce a whole new character, personifying the Church. With equal willfulness, Welles had the actors speak in a Scottish burr, chiefly to avoid both the British accent that he dismissed as "BBC" and the regional accents of his American cast; it also gave the words a lilting strangeness ("so right," Welles told Peter Bogdanovich, "for all that gooseflesh and grue"). The result is a film at once embarrassingly bad yet undeniably powerful. The viewer may laugh, but nervously: *Macbeth* is unrelenting—one long, intensifying shriek.

Welles managed to bring *Macbeth* in on budget and on time. Officials at Republic were thrilled until, as editing began, he ran away. Recalling Houseman's tales about Welles's hysteria at the scent of failure, one can only conclude that he was far less thrilled than his B-picture backers with what he had achieved. "Some of the individual scenes are the best things I've done," he told a friend that summer, "but when they are stuck together, the picture may be a complete flop." Although Welles had already started shooting *Othello*, in Europe, executives at Republic managed to cajole him into completing their film. In September 1948, *Macbeth* was proudly entered in the Venice International Film Festival—and immediately withdrawn when Welles realized that Olivier's *Hamlet* was in competition, too.

"Welles has failed utterly to live up to the standard set by Laurence Olivier's *Hamlet*," *Newsweek* announced when the films were released, and there was hardly a major journal that saw the comparison any other way. (*Hamlet* indeed went on to win the Venice prize for best foreign film, as Welles had feared.) Although several European critics displayed an enthusiasm and even a preference for Welles's work, in the English-speaking world he was taken for a bumbler unable to appreciate the Bard. Olivier, on the other hand, now Sir Laurence—he had been knighted during the filming of *Hamlet*—was Shakespeare's representative on earth. Republic Pictures, its expectations crushed, recalled *Macbeth* for radical reconstruction, during which Welles himself redubbed the film without the Scottish accents and cut out two reels, or nearly one-quarter of its length. ("I thought they shouldn't have been cut out, but I'm the one that cut it. Not some idiot back at home.") Republic added an introduction, spoken in voice-over and unfurled in writing on the screen, in an attempt to relieve the incoherence created by the cuts, and to emulate Olivier's use of the same opening device. By the time Olivier was collecting Oscars for *Hamlet*—Best Picture, Best Actor—Welles had decided that the only way to continue working was to leave America.

A dark man's face is seen very close, and disconcertingly upside down. His body is slowly revealed to be lying on a bier, which is carried from interior gloom into blinding sun. The only sound, a drum like a heartbeat, expands to a grief-stricken chant as a procession of monks following the bier is joined by a second procession—it cuts across the frame much closer to us, its leading churchman as startlingly huge as a saint in a medieval painting—bearing a young woman whose ivory pallor is set off by a black gossamer shroud. The funeral of Othello and Desdemona, unremarked by Shakespeare, winds along windswept battlements for four minutes before Welles launches the story of how they lived and died. A breathtaking tour de force, set to Francesco Lavagnino's "hair-raising" (Welles's word) score, the scene grew out of the funeral of a simple fisherman that Welles had shot for the never-finished *It's All True*, in the early forties, mixed with elements of the funeral procession Olivier devised for *Hamlet*. Opening *Othello* in the same imaginative key in which Olivier closed his celebrated film—but with a procession even more expressively grand—Welles was unmistakably throwing down the gauntlet. Most remarkable, however, the lyric intensity of this wordless passage carries through his entire film.

It is true that one comes away from *Othello* heady with the imagery more than with the verse, which may be the primary difference between the films of Welles and Olivier. Welles's rather light-skinned Othello is almost as muted as his Macbeth (one suspects him of struggling against his tendency to be a "hambone"), but his restraint acquires nobility beside the prissy Iago of Micheál MacLiammóir and the Venetian angel of a Desdemona played by Suzanne Cloutier, her gold hair strewn with pearls. If these are not virtuoso performances, there is among them not a note of declamation, or a moment's sense of transposed theater. The faces, the language, the velvety darks of Venetian streets, the wheeling gulls over Cyprus—all merge in a work that seems as independent, in its way, as Verdi's opera, by which Welles was reportedly inspired.

But his real inspiration seems to have come from the French directors who had taken in the exile as one of their own. *Othello* often looks so much like a work of the French poetic tradition that one is surprised to hear its characters speaking English: like Cocteau's *Beauty and the Beast*, in its fairy-tale air and its black-and-pewter tones; like Marcel Carné's *Children of Paradise*, whose production designer, Alexandre Trauner, Welles had managed to steal away. (Welles and Trauner also planned a never-executed film of *The Odyssey* and another—just imagine!—of *A Thousand and One Nights*.) Trauner based his designs on the sixteenth-century Venetian painter Carpaccio, but Welles contrived to capture not so much the look of the paintings as the immediate, gleaming life from which the painter drew.

It seems a wonder that Welles finished the film at all. He financed it entirely himself and adapted constantly as he went along. When constructing sets turned out to be too expensive, he filmed in various locations in Italy, Portugal, and Morocco. In one famous instance, when costumes did not arrive, he reset the scene of Roderigo's murder in a Turkish bath. The process took nearly four years, from 1948 to 1952, during which Welles continually interrupted shooting to take on acting roles in other films. Even *The Third Man* was done only to earn the money to resume *Othello*. Because the filming often took place outdoors, it was impossible to capture sound, so dubbing—with all its synchronization problems—was required. Actors came and went. The whole extraordinarily flowing film was painstakingly pieced together from shots made years and countries apart. "Roderigo kicks Cassio in Massaga," Welles enjoyed explaining, "and gets punched back in Orgete, a thousand miles away."

He was still editing *Othello* when Olivier, who was making forays into theatrical producing, invited him to direct and/or star in a play in London, in the fall of 1951. Welles chose to do both, in *Othello*. ("On the *stage*?" John Gielgud asked, aghast. "In *London*?") This was the first time the men had worked together since the radio play of

1939, and Welles was cautious, perhaps even intimidated. He later confided to his biographer Barbara Leaming, "I wanted to do as much of an English *Othello* as I could."

Olivier by then had played every major Shakespeare hero except Othello, a role he regarded as "pretty well unplayable" and inevitably upstaged by Iago. (Welles could not resist telling Olivier that he should never play the role, since he lacked the requisite bass voice.) Nevertheless, by Welles's admission, Olivier freely advised him on interpretation. And there is some evidence that Welles, departing from his film performance, approached Olivier's later rendering of the role: he wore very dark makeup and a vain man's big gold earrings; his dominant effect was of a rising, dangerous rage. Rehearsals were typically disorganized, the only certainty being the enormous lunch hamper that was delivered every day from the best restaurant in London. In the end, though, reviews were largely favorable, despite snide references to Welles's infamous radio broadcast ("some dark monster invading us from Mars") or, worse, to "Citizen Coon." Olivier, however, was unimpressed, feeling that Welles might have achieved real greatness if he had trained for the role and studied breath control. Instead, he had squandered his formidable gifts through a lack of discipline.

In May 1952, Welles's film of *Othello* won the Palme d'Or at Cannes. He was now the darling of the French critics, who had first seen *Citizen Kane*, as they had seen all contemporary American films, only after the war; for them, the thrill of freedom clung especially to Welles's highly personal and expressive style. He found himself the guiding spirit of a new movement in which the director was credited as the sole author of a film, an "auteur" in the same sense as Sartre or Camus. English critics, however, remained unmoved. MR. WELLES MURDERS SHAKESPEARE IN THE DARK, read the headline of one London review. In America, where distributors were nervous about even an Elizabethan interracial romance, the film wasn't released until three years later. Its box-office receipts amounted to forty thousand dollars.

After this crushing failure, things went rapidly downhill, as Welles's weight went wildly up. A modern-dress film of *Julius Caesar* was canceled before it was begun. He appeared in a mini-version of *King Lear*, on American television, in 1953, but TV's favorite Shakespearean

actor turned out to be Welles's old nemesis Maurice Evans, who
sounded the way Americans still thought Shakespeare was supposed
to sound. In late 1955, caught in the coils of a privately financed and
largely bungled film that he'd been shooting in Spain, *Mr. Arkadin*,
Welles returned to America. He was forty years old, and it seemed time
to make good on his long-ago promise of an American classical theater,
in New York. He started with *King Lear*. On opening night, in January
1956, he received an ovation as soon as he stepped onstage, which he
claimed unnerved him and ruined his performance. ("I knew I couldn't
possibly do justice to that," he explained.) He had already broken one
ankle—his weight was approaching three hundred pounds—and before the night was out he injured the other; he played the rest of the
run in a wheelchair. The reviews were devastating, and all thoughts of
future productions were scotched. He never appeared on a legitimate
stage in the United States again.

As for Olivier, the mid-fifties merely settled his crown. In 1954
he agreed to film one of his most celebrated stage roles, Richard III,
the supreme Shakespearean monster, whom he had managed to make
wittily ingratiating, with a nose like the Big Bad Wolf and a troublingly
sexual charm. As the film's star, he had no problems; as its director,
though, he worried that he had exhausted his ideas. It's true that
Richard III has none of the shaping conceits of his earlier films, relying instead on a charged theatricality: exaggerated makeup, elaborate
costumes, and the pleasure of virtuoso acting in and for itself. The following year, at Stratford-upon-Avon, he took on *Macbeth* for the first
time since his early Old Vic days; half a million ticket orders were
received before the season opened.

Orson Welles was in Las Vegas when, in March 1956, the film of
Richard III had its American premiere. He had moved there with his
family—third wife, third daughter—and was at last enjoying a big success, with an act at the Riviera Hotel in which he mixed magic tricks
with recitations from *Julius Caesar* and *King Lear*. Under the terms of
a unique agreement, *Richard III* opened in movie theaters, in vividly
colored wide-screen VistaVision, the same day it appeared on national
TV. Tens of millions of people watched the NBC broadcast that Sunday afternoon, more than had seen *Richard III* during all the previous
centuries combined. The following month, Welles moved back to

Hollywood, where he appeared in an episode of *I Love Lucy*. The story revolved around his having agreed to perform his Vegas act for a benefit at Ricky Ricardo's nightclub. Lucy, of course, wants to perform Shakespeare with him, and she attempts to win him over. "I think you're the greatest Shakespearean actor in the whole world," she gushes. "I think you're better than John Gielgud. I think you're better than Maurice Evans. I think you're better than Sir Ralph Richardson!" To which Welles responds, after a slight pause, "You left out Laurence Olivier." The studio audience howled with laughter.

There is a photograph of the two of them backstage in a Dublin theater, in 1960. Olivier had come to see Welles's play *Chimes at Midnight*, a reshaped and mercifully pared-down version of *Five Kings*, which retained the essential story of Falstaff and Prince Hal. Neatly correct in a suit and a tie, Olivier stands with one arm stiffly draped around Welles's shoulders. Welles, in costume as Falstaff, returns a crinkly grin and gazes into Olivier's eyes, as though seeking something there. In fact, Welles was hoping that *Chimes* would move on to London, and there was little that Olivier could not have made happen if he chose. But Olivier asked Welles to come to London only to direct his own first venture as an actor into the avant-garde, in Ionesco's *Rhinoceros*. Even then, as Welles tells the story, Olivier took over the directing himself, after informing the cast that Welles had been doing everything wrong and sending him away, humiliated, a few days before the opening. (Austin Pendleton has written an ingenious play, *Orson's Shadow*, about the *Rhinoceros* fiasco.) "He had to destroy me," Welles explained, with an oddly inverted ring of respect. "He doesn't want anybody else up there. He's like Chaplin, you know. He's a real fighting star."

The establishment of Britain's National Theatre was announced in 1962. Although impeded for fifteen years by budgeting failures, the project had grown out of a recognition of the national importance of the great theatrical productions of the war years—for morale, for pride, for communal strength. In an acknowledgment of his near-Churchillian stature, Olivier was named director, and his debut as Othello, in April 1964, was the big event of the first season. He had trained like a prizefighter to expand his lung power and, working with a voice teacher for six months, had managed to lower his vocal range by nearly an octave. His first appearance as a coal-black African lord caused a wave of shock; his makeup took nearly three hours to apply and included gentian violet on the inside of his mouth, a pinkish coloring on his palms and the soles of his feet, and drops in his eyes to increase the white sheen. Playing a creature of swaggering vanity, sexuality, and pride, who is quickly reduced to a howling, nearly naked slave, he gave a towering performance that offered something to offend everyone.

A filmed record of the production was made the following summer. Olivier approached the project apprehensively, and was not pleased with the result. (Many have found his performance far too broad for the camera; Welles happily claimed that Olivier reminded him of Sammy Davis, Jr.) Most of all, Olivier regretted that a "full-blown Shakespeare film" could not be made, because there was no money to make it. Despite *Richard III*'s phenomenal premiere—or precisely because of the coup of the television showing—the film had failed at the box office, not even making back its costs. As a result, the gates thrown open by *Henry V* were shut; no one would take a chance on Shakespeare, not even with Olivier. He had already tried to raise money to film *Macbeth*, for which he had plenty of ideas, as his best biographer, Anthony Holden, has pointed out. (For one, it would have been shot in Scotland with—hats off to Welles—Scottish accents.) But Olivier did not have Welles's Falstaffian stomach for begging, tricks, and impoverished stumbling through. *Richard III* was the last "full-blown Shakespeare film" that he directed or appeared in.

No one ever accused Olivier of playing himself, or presumed even to know who that person was. ("Scratch an actor," Olivier said, "and underneath you will find another actor.") Range and continual change were all. The only major roles in which he displayed no interest were the morbidly unheroic Richard II, who was temperamentally the property of Gielgud, and Falstaff—whom Welles had been drawn to for decades, even before the tragic clown took him over body and soul. In 1964, Welles talked a Spanish producer into financing *Chimes at Midnight*, a movie so pressingly personal that it hardly seems surprising when Jeanne Moreau, playing Doll Tearsheet, blithely addresses

Welles's Falstaff as "Orson." (This is what a French accent does to the Shakespearean epithet "whoreson.")

The result was sometimes as fractured as the process of getting the film made. Welles hired Gielgud to play the imperiously cold Henry IV, but he could pay him for only two weeks of work, and used a double for the rest; at times, all the major actors (except Welles) were doubles, and there were the usual problems with dubbing and synching. But, shooting in black and white, Welles managed to impart an astoundingly rich physical texture to every scene: the wintry air, the glow of a fire in Justice Shallow's hut, the fullness of the surrounding life appear so natural—the showy camerawork of his youth is mostly gone—that he seems merely to have photographed a world miraculously found. Yet we know how exactingly he built it, burning incense even out of doors to diffuse the light. Although one would hardly guess it from the look of the two films, Welles's goal was not so different from Olivier's in *Henry V*. "It mustn't seem perfectly real," he warned. "It doesn't mean anything unless it makes poetry possible."

In other ways, Welles's late masterpiece is the deliberate inverse of *Henry V*. The divergence is clearest in the set-piece battle of Shrewsbury, where Henry IV consolidates his powers, and Prince Hal proves himself his royal son. Welles allows us the marvelous sight of knights lowered out of trees onto their horses, by winches, a sight he derived from the similar hoisting of a pompously stiff French knight at Olivier's Agincourt, although Welles ups the joke by having the immensely fat Falstaff crash rattlingly to the ground. Once the battle has begun, however, both comedy and chivalry give way to unflinching barbarism: swinging maces, shrieks of pain, the clang of armor and the squish of mud as corpses pile high, and even the horses fall to agonized death. It is a scene less Agincourt than Guernica. (The film scholar Dale Silviria points to the influence of Eisenstein's wintry battle in *Alexander Nevsky*, where the heavily armored knights fall through the ice and drown.) Peace is restored at extraordinary cost, yet the soul-divided Hal, succeeding to the throne as Henry V, promptly follows his father's advice to "busy giddy minds with foreign quarrels," and—Shakespeare having no illusions about mankind— declares war on France. When Keith Baxter, who plays Hal with unforced charm, told Welles that he wanted to go on to play Henry V in full some day, Welles responded, "Why would you want to do that? He's a most awful shit."

In opposition to all this power-mongering and war stands (or falls) Falstaff. Welles is at his best when, wearing a saucepan crown, he mocks the old king—wickedly imitating Gielgud's fluty tremolo—and when, at Hal's coronation, he kneels before his beloved boy's callous but politically necessary rebuke: "I know thee not, old man." Welles expands on the play to let us know, through the pain in the young king's eyes, that he understands what he is losing by this renunciation. The look that Welles returns, mixing paternal pride and stunned sorrow, makes this exchange of glances one of Shakespeare's greatest moments, even if Shakespeare never wrote it.

In America about this time, the French veneration of Welles was finally having an impact. In 1961, the Museum of Modern Art held a major Welles retrospective, curated by Peter Bogdanovich. The following year, the critic Andrew Sarris introduced the "auteur theory" to these shores, and Welles was securely installed in the pantheon of the new academic discipline of film. None of which meant that *Chimes at Midnight* made any money, or even that anyone got to see it. It opened and closed in New York almost simultaneously, in 1967, after the *Times* complained that the soundtrack was incomprehensible. Although commercial failure seemed only to increase Welles's highbrow status, when asked to comment on "the art of cinema," he confessed, "I'd rather be caught without my pants in the middle of Times Square."

Olivier was by now an upstanding paterfamilias, both to the National Theatre, where he worked tirelessly as an actor and administrator, and to his new wife, Joan Plowright, and their young children. But as he approached his sixties his body seemed to give way. Flu, prostate cancer, and pneumonia struck him in succession; he suffered from a rare and often agonizing muscle disease for the last fifteen years of his life. And yet it is possible that more people saw him act in these years than ever before, owing to the film and television roles that he took on, ostensibly because he needed the money for his family, but also because the work kept him alive. In 1983, at seventy-five, lacking the strength to appear onstage, he played King Lear in a television production. Pale and disturbingly gaunt—Cordelia, dead in his arms, had to be suspended on wires—he was at once ethereal and majestic, and he seemed to feel that at last he was playing himself: "When you get to my age, you are Lear, in every nerve of your body." He managed to complete two versions of his memoirs; looking back on the success of *Henry V*, the first thing he recalled was that some people had said it was "the best first film since *Citizen Kane*."

Olivier endured long past expectations, and when he died, in 1989, the memorial service, at Westminster Abbey, was fit for one of the kings he had played. In a grand processional, Paul Scofield bore a silver model of the National Theatre, Derek Jacobi the crown Olivier had worn as Richard III, and Dorothy Tutin the crown he had worn as Lear. The most revered theatrical relic, though, was a sword that had belonged to Edmund Kean. It had been passed down through generations of actors, and the unfailingly generous and admiring Gielgud had given it to Olivier years before. Olivier, however, had refused to pass it any further, insisting simply, "It's mine." The high point of the ceremony was Olivier's own voice resounding in the battle speech from *Henry V*. He was buried in the abbey very near the monarch himself.

But in the art of acting, yesterday's realism is today's mannerism. Just as Olivier rebelled against Gielgud's way of "singing" verse, Kenneth Branagh has rebelled against the "oratorical, rhetorical style" of Olivier's Henry V (as Branagh put it) and his "self-conscious" Hamlet, and has remade Shakespeare for another era, brightly polished and wholly conventional. More daring films, such as Baz Luhrmann's *Romeo+Juliet* and Michael Almereyda's *Hamlet*, have turned the disjunction between Elizabethan speech and the modern age into the central ironic point: Denmark is the name of a corporation; ecstasy is a drug. This new method of meeting the same old goals has proved a huge success with an audience that no longer expects its world, on or off the screen, to be coherent.

The rise of this looser aesthetic has been a boon to Welles's reputation. In the eighties, *Macbeth* was restored to his original version; and in the following decade, *Othello* was restored to a version superior to the original, in terms of sound—just when many English-speaking critics were coming around to the idea that technical flaws were part of his works' "raffish" charm. A digitized restoration of *Chimes at Mid-*

night, visually sharpened and verbally synchronized (more or less), appeared to acclaim at New York's Film Forum in 2015. Yet, while books and seminars on Welles abound, the audience for his Shakespeare trilogy remains small. Although all three films are available on variably produced DVDs, a combination of legal and technical problems have kept them from receiving the deluxe treatment awarded to Olivier's Shakespeare films, to *Citizen Kane*, or, for that matter, to Welles's unfinished botch of a film, *Mr. Arkadin*. Welles, who considered *Chimes* his finest work ("If I wanted to get into heaven on the basis of one movie, that's the one I would offer up"), ruefully told of a Hollywood producer who, during Welles's later years, asked if he had ever thought of playing Falstaff.

By then, he was famous for being grotesquely fat, for appearing on talk shows, for selling cheap wine on TV. But he was famous most of all as the man who had got everything he wanted and then—as a reporter says of Charles Foster Kane—lost it. The more often *Citizen Kane* showed up on lists as the best movie ever made, the steeper his descent appeared. Welles's monumental failure has become as ingrained in the notion of who he was as the sound of his voice, even though *Othello* and *Chimes at Midnight* are more humanly rich achievements than *Kane*, and among the greatest Shakespeare movies ever made. Welles admitted to "thousands" of regrets, but he did not offer blame for the way things turned out: he did not care to look back at all. The real masterpiece was always the movie waiting to be made. Like Olivier, Welles was indefatigable to the end. He died of a heart attack, at seventy, in 1985, apparently in his sleep. He had drifted off while revising a script; by one report, he was found by his driver the next morning with a typewriter balanced on his belly. He had been working on his latest project, a video version of *Julius Caesar* in which he was to play every role. His plans for filming *King Lear* were also well under way.

METHOD MAN

MARLON BRANDO

Marlon Brando during the filming of *A Streetcar Named Desire*, 1951

I n the midst of Broadway's "victory season," in March 1946, an outraged ad denouncing the critics appeared in *The New York Times*. Signed by the production team of Elia Kazan and Harold Clurman, the ad failed to save their drama about returning vets, *Truckline Café*, from closing after a mere thirteen performances. But the play has gone down in history, thanks to a five-minute speech made by a little-known actor in a secondary role. Marlon Brando, at twenty-one, played an ex-G.I. who comes home to find that his wife has been unfaithful; in his final scene, he entered exhausted and wringing wet, and confessed that he had killed her and carried her body out to sea. Karl Malden, who played another minor role, reported that the rest of the cast sometimes had to wait for nearly two minutes after Brando's exit while the audience screamed and stamped its feet. The performance was as remarkable for what Brando didn't do as for what he did. Pauline Kael, very young herself and years away from a career as a critic, happened to come late to the play one evening and recalled that she averted her eyes, in embarrassment, from what appeared to be a man having a seizure onstage. It wasn't until her companion "grabbed my arm and said 'Watch this guy!' that I realized he was *acting*."

The dismal fate of *Truckline Café* inspired Kazan to form the Actors Studio the following year. Of the entire cast, only Brando and

Malden had given the kind of performance that he and Clurman wanted: natural and psychologically acute, as contemporary American plays required. Their ideal of acting derived from their days in the Group Theatre, which had flourished in the thirties with brashly vernacular and politically conscious plays—Clifford Odets's *Waiting for Lefty* was its first big hit—in which ordinary people were portrayed in a startlingly realistic style. Group actors were so determinedly authentic that it was sometimes difficult to understand what they were saying.

This revolution in American acting had in fact begun with performances by the touring Moscow Art Theatre, which had stunned New York back in 1923, and from accounts by the troupe's director, Konstantin Stanislavsky, of how the actors had achieved their remarkable honesty onstage. (Stanislavsky himself told an interviewer that all the praise his troupe earned in New York merely showed "at what an embryonic stage art is here.") In the Group, Stanislavsky's approach—eventually known simply as the Method—replaced traditional theatrical training with exercises designed to stir up personal memories, refine powers of observation, and free the imagination through improvisation. The larger goal was an anti-Broadway, anti-commercial theater of power and relevance. For the actors, however, the Method presented a paradox: real emotion, produced on cue.

Although the Group had disbanded by the time Brando arrived in New York, in 1943, he soon began taking classes at the New School with a charter member, Stella Adler, who had actually studied with Stanislavsky, and whom Brando credited as his teacher to the end of his life. ("She taught me to be real," he wrote, "and not to try to act out an emotion I didn't personally experience during a performance.") Adler seems to have taken less than a week to decide that the brooding nineteen-year-old in the torn blue jeans and the dirty T-shirt was going to become "America's finest actor," but she always denied that she had taught him a thing. As his fellow student Elaine Stritch later remarked, "Marlon's going to class to learn the Method was like sending a tiger to jungle school."

Yet Brando's early rehearsals for *Truckline Café* had been disastrous. He mumbled his lines and could not be heard past the fifth row. Kazan, who was producing, worried that Adler (who was, not incidentally, married to Clurman, who was directing) had made claims that her protégé could not fulfill. The playwright, Maxwell Anderson, wanted Brando fired. But Clurman sensed that the young actor was nearly choked with feeling and pushed him with harsh and relentless physical demands—Brando had to shout his way through his speech while climbing a rope—until he got him to explode. Exhaustion, frustration, and fury produced the performance that became the centerpiece of the play. As it turned out, that Broadway season was the first portent of a momentous transition in the art, if not the business, of acting: *Variety's* annual poll named Laurence Olivier Best Actor for playing Shakespeare and Sophocles on tour with England's Old Vic; Brando won Most Promising Young Actor and was out of work as soon as *Truckline Café* closed.

But he had learned from all his early mentors that even in America, deprived of Shakespeare and Sophocles, theater was a morally serious enterprise that treated life's important themes. Or that it should be. And so, after an awkward stint in Shaw's *Candida*, the Most Promising Young Actor turned down Noël Coward's *Present Laughter*, imperiously asking England's star playwright, "Don't you know there are people starving in Europe?" He turned down a seven-year contract at three thousand dollars a week with MGM. Instead, in the fall of 1946, he chose to do a play that Ben Hecht had devised to raise money for transporting Jewish refugees from Europe to Palestine, during which he shouted at the cowering audience, "Where were you when the killing was going on? When the six million were burned and buried alive in the lime pits, where were you? Where was your voice crying out against the slaughter?" The play may not have been art, but a lot of people filled out the donation forms inserted in their programs.

Brando was no one's first choice when, the following summer, a great American play finally came along. Tennessee Williams's *A Streetcar Named Desire* was the story of a highly sexed and poorly spoken middle-aged Polish American man named Stanley Kowalski—another vet with a violent streak—who rapes an emotionally fragile and aristocratic woman, Blanche DuBois. The play's cautionary theme was described by Williams, who strongly identified with Blanche, as "the apes will inherit the earth." Kazan was scheduled to direct, Irene Mayer

Selznick to produce, and all agreed that John Garfield, a movie star and a street-talking graduate of the Group Theatre, was the right choice for their antihero. It was only when Garfield made impossible demands that Kazan, scanning his "beginners" class at the brand-new Actors Studio, decided to take a risk on Brando, even though he was too young for the role. Auditioning for Williams, Brando got about thirty seconds into the script (by Williams's report) when Williams interrupted to say he had the part.

Not only did he have the sexual power the play required; he provided the key to redressing what Williams had worried was the too-easy moral imbalance of his work. Precisely because he was so young—barely twenty-three—Brando humanized the vengeful Stanley, reducing his willful destructiveness to what Williams excitedly described as "the brutality or callousness of youth." Good and evil were now more subtly matched: it would not be so easy to take sides. Brando was not as sure as Williams that he was a "God-sent Stanley." He worked slowly and seemed to find it difficult to learn his lines. Selznick repeatedly complained that she couldn't hear him. But Kazan had faith, and so did Williams, whose opening-night telegram to Brando predicted, "From the greasy Polack you will someday arrive at the gloomy Dane."

By then Kazan was almost rueful that the play, which Williams had built around the character of Blanche, was looking like "the Marlon Brando Show." Without changing a word, the actor seemed to have expanded the role and nearly reversed Williams's original intent. Jessica Tandy, the British actress who played Blanche, was furious that the audience laughed along with Stanley's jokes at her expense, as though he were a regular guy putting an uppity woman in her place; she was stunned that people openly extended their sympathies more to the executioner than to his victim. The reason was not just Brando's youth: it was the comic innocence that fueled the gibes, the baffled tenderness beneath the toughness. The face above the heavily muscled body was angelic; the pain he showed when he broke down and wailed for his wife was searing, elemental. And his intensity was almost unbearable. One critic wrote that "Brando seems always on the verge of tearing down the proscenium with his bare hands." *Streetcar* was an enormous hit, and Tandy received excellent notices, but it was

Brando the audiences loved. More, theater people recognized him as the long-promised revolution in the flesh. In Kazan's view, others were giving fine performances but Brando was "living onstage"—with the result that he longed to escape the play after only a few weeks. How many times, on schedule, can one rip oneself apart?

He had a contract, however, which kept him smashing dishes and wailing his soul out for a year and a half, during which his performance varied tremendously from night to night. Free at last, in late 1949, he ended up in Hollywood, where he cheerfully antagonized the local monarchs (Louella Parsons wrote that he had "the gall of a Kinsey researcher") and announced that he would soon be returning to the stage. He was nevertheless excited about his first film, *The Men*, an uplifting Stanley Kramer production about a paralyzed veteran whose faithful fiancée draws him out of despair and into life. Although the film did not do well—the subject of wounded veterans lost its fascination as the Korean War began—Brando's reviews tended toward ecstatic variations on the word "real." And he became known for a correspondingly real if peculiar way of working: publicity stressed that he had spent three weeks living in a veterans' hospital among paraplegics, learning how they moved and what they felt. (Brando himself had been exempt from service because of knee injuries acquired while playing football in high school.) On the set, the slow perfectionism of his endless retakes caused a co-star to grumble about "New York acting," which was exactly what Kazan wanted when, in 1950, he began filming *Streetcar*.

With the exception of Vivien Leigh, as Blanche, all of the film's major cast members had been part of the Broadway production. And Leigh had played Blanche onstage in London, where the play was a huge success despite being denounced in Parliament as "low and repugnant." The actors hardly needed to do more than get reacquainted with their roles. Kazan, however, disliked repeating himself as much as Brando did, and he seized on Leigh's sublime fragility as a way to turn the play around again, and to restore something like Williams's original moral balance. Brando, who had always thought that Tandy was miscast, felt that Leigh was truly Williams's "wounded butterfly," and reacted with an emotional and sexual charge that was beyond anything he had shown onstage. Seen against this tragically sympathetic

Blanche, though, Stanley's brutality was harder to tolerate. If he was not a villain, he was an extremely charming monster, and the audience was uncomfortably implicated in Blanche's destruction by its laughter and its deep attraction to him. Brando was nominated for an Academy Award (and so was Leigh, who won). Yet, the uncanny life he put into the slouching, scratching, sweating Stanley, along with his tabloid antics, and probably some public confusion about the much publicized Method—did it mean an actor was just playing himself?— led him to be widely described as what he resentfully called "a blue-jeaned slobbermouth," and dubbed by the press "the Neanderthal man."

This was not the only reason that Brando hated Stanley, whom he spoke of with a disgust not unlike that felt by Blanche DuBois. In his next film, *Viva Zapata!*, a politically ambitious effort (directed by Kazan, with a screenplay by John Steinbeck) about the legendary Mexican revolutionary, he did his best to disappear into the role. Playing a noble idealist of mixed Spanish and Native American ancestry, Brando darkened his skin and used invisible tape to pull back his nostrils and his eyes. The look, the sound, the mentality: nothing could have been further from Stanley. Although this display of range won him another Academy Award nomination, the movie had limited appeal and did nothing to alter his image. The announcement that he was going to play Mark Antony in *Julius Caesar* was greeted most joyously by the nation's comedians, who lost no time declaiming "Friends, Romans, countrymen" in a nasal, Kowalskian bleat.

Brando himself was worried about appearing a fool. Although he was an avid reader and memorizer of Shakespeare, his performing experience had been confined to an acting-school production of *Twelfth Night* and, more recently, to taunting Vivien Leigh (then Mrs. Laurence Olivier) with a nastily precise imitation of Olivier's Agincourt speech from *Henry V.* But he went at the project eagerly. Early on, the film's director, Joseph Mankiewicz, came upon his star studying tapes of speeches by Olivier, John Barrymore, and Maurice Evans, and complained that the genteel result made him sound like June Allyson. Brando later explained that the most daunting aspect of playing Shakespeare was relying on the written text, since he had learned to search around and under words—in pauses, in gestures, in grunts and mumbles, even in silence—for a sense of truth.

Once on the *Caesar* set, in 1952, he asked John Gielgud, who was playing Cassius, to make him a recording of Antony's speeches, presumably as a model of diction and prosodic stress. Brando admired Gielgud, but there is not a trace of the British actor's stylized and vibrato-laden music in the young American's stark and driven reading. To accord with the rest of the cast, Brando adopted a mildly British accent, but the way he inflected his lines was so unexpected and so commonsensical that the most familiar phrases took on a credible urgency ("*Lend* me your ears!") and much of the rest seemed nearly made up on the spot, as when the hint of a stutter causes him to falter in his plea: "Bear with me; my heart is in the coffin there with Caesar, and I must p-pause till it come back to me." None of this came as easily or "naturally" as it seemed. The film's producer, John Houseman, who had also produced Orson Welles's groundbreaking *Julius Caesar* at the Mercury Theatre, recalled Brando slowly working his way into the Forum scene, sharing his excitement in each discovery about how to play the text. The scene took a week to film because Mankiewicz wanted many different kinds of camera shots, and Brando went through it again and again, without losing energy or concentration. When he performed Antony's great funeral speech for the final time, the crew burst into applause.

Reviewers, too, were thrilled, and took open pride in the thought that an American Olivier might be at hand. Indeed, the film was given the kind of deluxe opening treatment that Olivier's *Henry V* had received seven years earlier, playing in a Broadway theater for just two reserved shows a day. Brando was praised not only for his heat and passion but for his diction; the *Times*, noting that his speech in previous films had been "guttural and slurred," was now ready to declare "a major talent has emerged." In Mankiewicz's private opinion, he was "better than Orson, better than Burton," and the director also pointed out that, unlike Olivier, Brando did not rely on makeup; his phenomenal skill was in "just *becoming*." Brando was nominated for yet another Academy Award, and, in a truly startling vote of confidence, won the British Academy of Film's award for Best Foreign Actor of 1953. Gielgud was sufficiently impressed to ask his would-be pupil to participate in a theater season he was directing in England, where Brando could fulfill Tennessee Williams's prediction and play Hamlet.

Brando turned him down. He seems to have been the only person who did not believe that he was up to the test. Perhaps all the early jokes about his performance got to him more than he let on. Even years later, in his memoir, he wrote, "For me to walk onto a movie set and play Mark Antony without more experience was asinine." But it was impossible to gain more experience outside the spotlight. And for a man whose enormous talent meant that almost everything came easy, and whose satisfactions in the work he got were few, Brando's forfeit of the entire classical repertory after this single venture seems a sad mistake, a loss of challenges and rewards that might have ultimately changed his regard for his profession, if not for himself.

Instead of *Hamlet*, he did a biker movie. It was meant to be another socially conscious film, based on an incident that had taken place in 1947, when a motorcycle gang terrorized a California town. Brando said he hoped that the film would explore the reasons that young people were resorting to antisocial behavior. In fact, juvenile delinquency had become such a huge concern that a Senate subcommittee was investigating its causes. *The Wild One*, released in December 1953, did not so much explore the causes as define the era's terms of opposition: jive-talking hipsters versus squares, leather jackets versus button-down shirts and ties, easy-riding freedom versus the straight and narrow. Youth versus age. A mediocre film, it was just enough ahead of its time to strike a nerve. Jack Kerouac was struggling to publish a book about his adventures on the road (he later begged Brando to make the movie); Elvis was a year away from appearing on national TV and being labeled "a guitar-playing Marlon Brando." Brando's Johnny, the leader of the pack, was the antidote to that other mythic figure of the fifties, the Man in the Gray Flannel Suit, trapped on the corporate treadmill. Once again, though, as with Stanley Kowalski, the actor seemed indistinguishable from the role, and Brando himself came to embody the rebel. The script gave a hint of the pain behind Johnny's steely cool, but his anger and dissatisfaction were unrelenting. Unlike the tough-guy heroes of the forties, with their ulterior noble causes (say, Bogart in *Casablanca*), Johnny has no idea what he really wants. In the film's most quoted line, someone asks, "Hey, Johnny, what are you rebelling against?" And Brando answers, deadpan, "Whaddya got?"

•

W hat was real about the realest actor of them all? What did he draw on during those improvisations or rehearsals when, by training and by instinct, to go further he had to go within? "The torment that underlay Brando's art is the subject of this book," Stefan Kanfer writes in *Somebody: The Reckless Life and Remarkable Career of Marlon Brando*—the first biography to appear after Brando's death, at eighty, in 2004—because, as Kanfer explains, "the man's internal anguish was what drove him on to the heights of his vocation." Examining a career that spanned more than five decades and thirty-eight films, Kanfer maintains that Brando, unique among actors, "worked without a mask." While other actors preserve boundary lines between their private lives and their performances, "no such boundary existed between Brando the actor and Brando the man," both of whom apparently suffered from what Kanfer, assisted by several psychiatrists, labels "oppositional defiant disorder," "narcissistic personality disorder," and an "oral fixation." This is not entirely news: long ago Harold Clurman wrote that Brando's acting had "its source in suffering," and Peter Manso, the author of a previous biography, consulted his own set of psychiatrists to diagnose the actor's "dissociated personality," "manic-depressive mood swings," and "anxieties over sexual identity," among other afflictions. (Brando appears to have slept with an uncertain number of men and a staggering number of women.) But nothing has approached Kanfer's assertion that the "Rosebud in Brando's life" was "the mental illness that had dogged him for decades," an illness that made his achievements all the more a marvel and his failures no surprise.

Brando might have agreed. In his later years, he published his story and freely explained its impact, starting with the fact that he was born in 1924 in Omaha, Nebraska, to a mother who "abandoned me for a bottle when I was little more than an infant," and who proceeded to drink his childhood away. His father was an alcoholic, too, and a very angry man, although the larger problem was his failure to show his son any affection or approval; to his friends, Brando also confided that his father had beaten him. His two older sisters provided some support, and a young nursemaid gave him something like love, but she left one day without saying goodbye: he had been abandoned twice over, and, he wrote, "my world collapsed." He flunked kindergarten and did little better in school as the years progressed. He stammered badly, and he seems to have been dyslexic, so that reading out loud in class was an agony. Some who knew him at the time suggested, in interviews with Manso, that this was the source of the famous pauses and obscuring mumble. Always the class bad boy, he was thrown out of the military school that was supposed to teach him discipline. Aside from sports, and despite his early speech problems, drama was the only subject in which he excelled.

Acting, which might have provided an escape for someone of a different temperament, was for him a way of sounding out his depths; he described his work with Stella Adler as "psychotherapeutic," teaching him not only about theater but about himself. He'd been in New York only about a year when his mother left his father and came to live with him and his two sisters, who were also making their careers there, in a huge apartment she rented for them all. Despite the years of neglect, Marlon adored her; she was an amateur actress and a poetical soul, very vulnerable, something of a Blanche DuBois. Although the siblings had a lot of trouble looking after her, desperately trying to control her drinking and often hunting her down in bars, when she returned to their father Brando confessed that he had a nervous breakdown. By the time he was in *Streetcar*, the panic attacks had got so bad, and he was so afraid that in his rage he might kill someone, that he began to see a psychiatrist recommended by Kazan. Five years later, in 1953, he told Kazan that the only reason he had agreed to do *On the Waterfront* was that the New Jersey location allowed him to be near his psychiatrist. If this was just a jibe, his contract did include the right to leave early every afternoon to make his session.

Brando had initially refused to appear in *On the Waterfront*, out of shock and disappointment that Kazan had testified as a "friendly" witness before the House Un-American Activities Committee, not only confessing his former membership in the Communist Party but betraying old Group Theatre friends. Kazan's testimony had hit the papers in the summer of 1952, while Brando was filming *Julius Caesar*, and Mankiewicz reported that he was crushed by the news; up until then, Kazan had been like a god to Brando, or a father. It had required a great deal of wrangling to get him to take the role of the naive ex-boxer Terry Malloy, who slowly realizes that it is his moral duty to inform on his gangster friends before a government commission. For Terry, informing is a courageous act that makes him a man and a hero. Kazan later admitted that the movie had been an attempt to excuse and even glorify his actions—or, as Brando put it, an attempt to justify "finking" on his friends. It is doubtful that many viewers saw a connection between mobsters and Communists, but the film's emotional grip and its unprecedented visual authenticity made it a triumph.

Shot on the Hoboken piers during a freezing winter, with a cast drawn almost entirely from the Actors Studio, and backed by a population of authentically rough-hewn longshoremen, *On the Waterfront* signaled a new sort of anti-Hollywood, neorealistic style of filmmaking. Much like the revolutionary painters across the Hudson, Kazan and company could have been called the New York School. But the film's success was also due to Brando, who, by all reports, invented Terry as much as played him, freely altering words and scenes with an infallible sense of what the gentle, tortured boy would do. Kazan, who called this performance the best ever given by a man in American film, spoke of the importance of Brando's having been able to draw on his own "pain," "self-doubt," and "inner conflict," but he also wrote of the actor's professionalism and exceptional talent, without which no amount of anguish could have done the job. As for Brando, he said it was "so cold out there that you couldn't overact."

On the Waterfront won eight Academy Awards, including Oscars for Brando and Kazan, yet it proved not the start of something but the end. No independent school of film developed from it, and the crassness of Hollywood only seemed to worsen as the studios struggled against the new menace of television, wooing audiences through CinemaScope and spectacle. Brando, who had let down his guard enough to sign a two-picture deal with Twentieth Century–Fox, was assigned to a bloated historical epic titled *The Egyptian*, which he fled as shooting began. Hightailing it on a train east, hiding out at friends' apartments in New York, he sent the studio a note from his psychiatrist claiming that he was too sick to work for at least ten weeks—exactly the shooting schedule of *The Egyptian*. The studio responded by suing him for two million dollars. He was officially released from the picture only after his mother died suddenly, in March 1954, and, too emotionally wrecked to go on fighting, he agreed to play Napoleon, no less, in another historical turkey, *Désirée*.

Although Brando finished this film, his behavior made the poor director, a hack named Henry Koster, wish that he hadn't. Brando's anger at being stuck in the role was exacerbated by the fact that Kazan—a fallen god but still a god to him—was then filming *East of Eden* with James Dean on the Warner Bros. lot across town, and the word was that the new kid was very good. In regard to his own performance, Brando seemed to pay more attention to perfecting his false nose than to anything else. (Perhaps that's why Olivier had particular praise for Brando in this role: "He wouldn't like to be called a technician but he was one, a very great one.") On the film's release, Brando announced that he had let his makeup play the part.

In October 1954, *Time* ran a cover story that featured Brando in full Napoleonic drag, but the article focused less on the new film than on questions arising from its utter and all-too-predictable mediocrity: If Brando cared about acting as an art, what was there for him in Hollywood? Yet returning to the stage was no more promising, since Broadway rarely produced first-rate work, and "there is no U.S. repertory theater in which a young actor can try the great roles for size." Compared with the careers of his European counterparts (Olivier, of course, and Jean-Louis Barrault in France), even the roles he had already played were sadly limited, so many being "variations on the Kowalski theme." These questions recurred with every film that Brando made for the next eighteen years. Here at last was the great American actor: not a copy of a British actor or a mere matinee idol but someone original, contemporary, and uniquely representative of the culture. But what could the culture produce for him to do?

The answer was *Guys and Dolls*, *The Teahouse of the August Moon*, *Sayonara*, *The Young Lions*, *The Fugitive Kind*, *One-Eyed Jacks*, and *Mutiny on the Bounty*, just to bring his career into the sixties. One can hardly doubt his desire to break away from the "Kowalski theme." He played an elegant gangster who sang (a little), a Japanese servant, an American officer, a Nazi officer, a Southern stud, a frontier bandit, and an aristocratic British fop. He even tried directing, in the case of *One-Eyed Jacks*, a bizarrely Oedipal western that seems almost an illustration of Kanfer's thesis: a villain named Dad betrays the hero (Brando as Rio the Kid, inevitably called the Kid), prompting a consuming desire for revenge; although Dad further punishes the Kid with a vicious whipping, the Kid ultimately succeeds and shoots Dad dead. It was the first film made by Brando's company, Pennebaker Productions, established in 1955 under his mother's maiden name, and with his father as chief employee, sitting around and watching every scene.

Although this kind of company was a standard Hollywood tax shelter, Brando dedicated Pennebaker to making "important" films of "social value." If it produced very few films during its existence, these intentions pervaded Brando's work, and he now had the power to have scripts rewritten and characters refashioned to make his points. At his insistence, the Nazi of *The Young Lions* sees the error of his ways and rises to ethical enlightenment, not because Brando didn't want to play a villain but because he wished to show that no nation of people is all good or all evil. The American soldier of *Sayonara* overcomes society's racism and, reversing the story's original *Madame Butterfly* ending, marries the Japanese woman he loves. Through the immeasurably influential fantasy of movies, Brando believed that he might help improve reality.

With such lofty goals, however, every project was sooner or later a disappointment. In response to his frustrations, he made trouble on the set, he refused to learn his lines, he ate so compulsively that he had to be fitted with new costumes in ever-larger sizes—as with Orson Welles, the line between self-indulgence and self-contempt becomes difficult to locate. And he cost the studios a fortune, as movie after movie failed. Yet the face on the screen was so compelling that the question of what to do with his talent remained a kind of national burden. Truman Capote, in a scathing profile from the late fifties, portrayed the actor as a bore and a poseur, yet pressed him earnestly about when he would return to play the "Mount Everest roles in stage literature." By the late sixties, Pauline Kael, her hopes for his career seriously battered, noted that "his greatness is in a range that is too disturbing to be encompassed by regular movies." But what other kind was there?

Brando had good reasons for choosing many of his films in these bleak years. *The Ugly American* and *Burn!* revolved around serious political issues; there was an accomplished young director, Arthur Penn, behind *The Chase*, and a legendary director, Charlie Chaplin, behind *A Countess from Hong Kong*. *Reflections in a Golden Eye* offered the image-shattering role of a stiffly repressed homosexual army officer, a role that few other male stars would have taken on. His performances ranged from as good as possible in deadly circumstances (*The Chase, A Countess from Hong Kong*) to brilliant (*Golden Eye*), but no other career so clearly illustrates how complex a work of art a movie really is, and how many forces it requires—of whatever genius— to make it right.

Even when his pictures were plainly bad, he strained to hold on to some higher purpose, as when he fought against the usual Indian stereotypes in the cowboy movie *The Appaloosa*. But his sense of accomplishment no longer had much to do with his work, outside of earning the money required to support two ex-wives, a third wife who had been his Tahitian co-star in *Mutiny on the Bounty*, and a growing number of children. Inspired, he said, by hearing a speech by Martin Luther King, Jr., he supported civil rights as early as 1960; the following year, he began his involvement with rights for Native Americans. In 1963, he helped set up a scholarship for Medgar Evers's children, flew to Alabama to join a demonstration by the Congress of Racial Equality, picketed against discriminatory housing practices in Torrance, California, and joined the March on Washington.

Immediately after the march, Brando appeared in a televised discussion with a small group of other celebrities committed to the cause: Harry Belafonte, Charlton Heston, Joseph Mankiewicz, Sidney Poitier, and James Baldwin, who was an old friend from his New School days. Brando seemed nervous, as if he needed to show that he wasn't out of his depth. But he knew what he wanted to say, offering a broadly idealistic perspective shored up by a slightly self-conscious recital of historical information. As he saw it, the essential problem was the intractability of human hatred. The movement, if successful, would benefit all minorities ("Jews, Filipinos, Chinese, Negroes, Hindustani, Koreans, all people") and ensure that "Indians will be given some of their land back." It would also, most importantly, bring us "one step closer to trying to understand the human heart," or whatever it is that allows us to make excuses for "burning children with cattle prods."

His racial politics became more extreme as the decade progressed, and he went on to support the Black Panthers. Bobby Seale, it turned out, was a big fan of *The Wild One*, and Brando not only gave Seale money to bail out members of his group but accompanied him to court when Seale was charged with possession of illegal weapons. In 1968, Brando spoke at the funeral of Bobby Hutton, the seventeen-year-old Panthers treasurer who was killed by Oakland police. He spoke modestly—"That could have been my son"—and there weren't many other white faces present; he was sued by the Oakland police after saying on television that they had murdered Hutton. It's been claimed that Brando really didn't understand the Panthers' full political intentions. Indeed, he turned against them when their advocacy of violence was spelled out by the far-less-starstruck and more hostile Eldridge Cleaver, after which he returned to raising Hollywood-sized quantities of cash for nonviolent groups associated with King. It's worth emphasizing how much he contributed to the cause—in time as well as money—even if he has also justifiably been called a political dilettante. He could not always deliver on the expectations that he raised; his personal necessities lay elsewhere. He was, after all, a movie star. Among many in the movement, he was criticized for being distracted, for a lack of follow-through, and for disappearing to a private atoll he had purchased in Tahiti.

There is no doubt, however, that he was deeply affected when King was shot, in 1968, and he probably meant it when he announced that he was quitting film entirely to work for civil rights. But by then it was more accurate to say that the movies were quitting him. *Burn!*, a film about a nineteenth-century Caribbean slave uprising, was exactly the kind of work Brando felt he should do; Gillo Pontecorvo was a director he admired. Indeed, late in his life he said that he thought this film contained the best acting he'd ever done. At the time, however, Brando was so incensed about virtually everything to do with the actual process of filming—the script, the number of takes, the set on a blistering hot island off the coast of Colombia, the bad and often spoiled food—that his behavior was hardly better than it had been on *Désirée*. To hear Brando tell it, he'd cared too much about this role, rather than too little. With the failure of *Burn!* at the box office, in 1969, he rounded off a full decade of commercial flops. He was, in his own words, "washed up and unemployable." And then Mario Puzo called.

•

Puzo had Brando in mind all the while he was writing *The Godfather*, which had been optioned by Paramount before he finished the book. Only Brando, he said, could bring the "quiet force and irony" that he wanted to Don Corleone, family patriarch and honorable killer. Although studio executives refused to consider him, the young director they hired in 1970 for what they thought of as a low-budget gangster film, Francis Ford Coppola, had grander things in mind and argued that the Don ought to be played by one of the two greatest actors alive: Olivier or Brando. (Orson Welles later said, "I would have sold my soul to play in *The Godfather*, but I never get any of those parts.") Since Olivier, at sixty-three, was too ill to work, Coppola conspired with Brando to overcome Paramount's qualms. Brando even agreed to do a screen test, mostly to show that, at forty-seven, he was capable of aging the required twenty years. He stuffed his cheeks to create jowls ("the face of a bull dog," he said with satisfaction, "mean-looking, but warm underneath") and devised a light, unthreatening voice based on tapes of the mobster Frank Costello; power makes people lean in to listen. He wanted the role very much, in part because he believed the film offered a lesson in the sins of American capitalism, and in part because he was nearly broke.

And yet, once shooting was under way, he could not or would not remember his lines. He wrote them on his cuffs, he kept cue cards stuck all over the set. When questioned by Coppola, he claimed that this was necessary for his spontaneity: "Real people don't know what they're going to say. Their words often come as a surprise to them. That's the way it should be in a movie." Whether or not this was the reason, it worked. Although Coppola says that Brando never asked for changes in the dialogue, the recent book *Brando's Smile*, by Susan L. Mizruchi, who had access to the actor's annotated scripts, suggests substantial differences between some of his scripted lines and what he actually said. (He struck out the clichéd phrase "with bitter tears" with a simply marked "Ugh.") Coppola generally encouraged spontaneity by putting props—for example, a cat—on the set near Brando, knowing that he would use them but not knowing (or suggesting) how. In fact, Brando's improvisatory touches are among the most memorable aspects of the character: stopping to smell a rose as he denies being a murderer, suddenly slapping a whining younger man, molding an orange peel into a set of fangs when the Don plays with his grandchild in a summer garden. None of this was in the script but simply happened when the cameras rolled.

The Godfather was not only Brando's redemption but Hollywood's, proving that a big commercial movie could be a work of beauty and significance. It was an American epic, and, for a time, at least, it took the oxymoronic sting out of the term "mass culture." Everyone agreed that it was the kind of film Brando should have been making all along. At the other end of the spectrum, so was his next picture, *Last Tango in Paris*, a European art film that used simulated sex and a veneer of existential chic to do for porn what *The Godfather* did for cops and robbers. The director, Bernardo Bertolucci, crafted the role just for Brando. Or, rather, he asked Brando to craft the role: "He wanted me to play myself, to improvise completely and portray Paul"—an American expatriate in Paris, who falls into an intense affair with a beautiful girl—"as if he were an autobiographical mirror of me." Brando was more than willing to oblige. So when Paul tells the girl, "My father was a drunk, tough, whore-fucker, bar fighter" and "my mother was very, very poetic and also a drunk," the life Brando was exposing was at least partly his own, and he seems to have arrived at a literal crossing between acting and psychotherapy. The result, made all the more exciting by having been banned for obscenity in Italy, was greeted as a distinctly modern masterpiece. Pauline Kael compared its premiere to that of Stravinsky's *Rite of Spring*, and declared Brando's performance the fulfillment of his non-acting acting in *Truckline Café*, twenty-six years before. "Paul feels so 'real' and the character is brought so close," she wrote, "that a new dimension in screen acting has been reached."

The Godfather was released in the spring of 1972; the premiere of *Last Tango* took place at the New York Film Festival that fall. It was a double tour de force, the deadly Italian grandpa followed by the art-house stud, and Brando brought the old intensity and a mournful new dignity to both. Perhaps he should have stopped there; for a while, it seemed that he would. He not only rejected his Academy Award for *The Godfather* but had an Apache woman go to the stage in his place and give a speech about Hollywood's mistreatment of Native

Americans; the moral confrontation recalls his speech about the slaughter of six million back in 1946. He talked of making a movie about Native American history, but it never went anywhere, and when he returned to what Kael had called "regular" films—bad scripts, no scripts, nothing to control him—some final link of faith and discipline was gone.

He was getting enormous fees, but his performance in the incoherent *Missouri Breaks* was campy, edged with contempt. By the time of *Apocalypse Now*, in 1979, he had gained so much weight that Tennessee Williams suggested that he was being paid by the pound. The emotional delving of *Last Tango* had been so devastating, Brando later wrote, that "in subsequent pictures I stopped trying to experience the emotions of my characters" and began "simply to act the part in a technical way." He was certain that "the audience doesn't know the difference." It is impossible to say if he was trying to explain or merely to justify what he had become. In 1980, playing a fat old oil tycoon in *The Formula*, he wore a radio transmitter disguised as a hearing aid; past even the bother of using cue cards, he now had his lines read directly into his ear.

For the rest of the decade, Brando played only one small role in a single film, *A Dry White Season*, about South African apartheid. He did it for scale: roughly four thousand dollars. The rest of the time he was, he said, "content doing other things: traveling, searching, exploring, seeking." Brando took his education seriously; he was a prodigious reader, with a library of thousands of closely marked-up books. But nothing ever seemed to cohere. At home in Beverly Hills, he saw a psychiatrist several times a week, slowly learning to "be the child I never had a chance to be." At the same time, divorced again and the father of nine (by his own count; the actual number is uncertain), he was trying "to get to know my children better." The efforts involved in these two ventures—becoming a child, becoming a father—were rarely compatible, and destined to fail. Brando's oldest son, Christian, had been hooked on drugs and alcohol since his teens and had dropped out of high school. In his new attempt at closeness, Brando proposed that they get their high-school degrees together (Brando was sixty-three, Christian twenty-eight), but Brando could not keep up and he let the project go. A similar fate attended all the utopian projects he dreamed up for his Tahiti paradise: it was going to be a gathering place for artists and intellectuals; there would be ecological experiments leading to breakthroughs in solar and wind power; hired scientists would find a way to process algae into a protein supplement for third world nations. Instead, he watched his expensive equipment rust and his plans crumble. Discussing poetry with an interviewer there one day—"The Love Song of J. Alfred Prufrock" had come up—he remarked, "If the mermaids can't sing for me here, Christ, they never will."

In 1990, Christian Brando shot his half-sister Cheyenne's boyfriend in the head, from behind, in the den of his father's Beverly Hills house. Cheyenne was pregnant at the time. The trial hypnotized the press, and some (including the father of the dead boy) considered Papa Brando's performance on the witness stand one of the best he ever gave: sobbing, dazed, and often incoherent, he was wretchedly apologetic for what he swore had been a terrible accident. The child of Brando's third wife, Cheyenne had grown up in Tahiti and had not seen much of her father until he brought her and her boyfriend to L.A. to have the baby. Like Christian, she had dropped out of high school and had trouble with drugs; a beautiful girl, she'd had a modeling career until she crashed Christian's car, when he was visiting Tahiti, and injured her face. (Brando had flown her to L.A. then, too, for reconstructive surgery.) After that, she'd struggled with depression and showed signs of being mentally unstable. She had told Christian that her boyfriend was beating her, and he'd believed her. As the trial got under way, she attempted suicide, and Brando sent her back to Tahiti to keep her from having to testify, both for her sake and for Christian's. In and out of mental hospitals for the next several years, Cheyenne ultimately hanged herself, at the age of twenty-five, in her bedroom in the family's compound. Brando never returned to Tahiti again.

At the trial, Christian pleaded guilty to voluntary manslaughter and received a ten-year sentence. And his father, saddled with enormous legal bills, went to work on an autobiography. The fee was reportedly five million dollars. Brando's first stipulation was that the book should contain nothing about his films (not important enough) or his marriages and children. Although he was prevailed upon to discuss the films, the central irrepressible subject of *Songs My Mother Taught*

Me, which appeared in 1994, is his childhood and what might be called the psychiatric life that followed from it. Sadly, even his best impulses are reduced to the language of the couch: "Frustrated in my attempts to take care of my mother, I suppose that instead I tried to help Indians, blacks and Jews." His comments about acting are striking, however, whether for the scant respect he pays his own accomplishments, or his dismissal of Hollywood's domination of international film and television as "a tragedy." But, beyond the seventy-year-old unloved child's self-denigration, it is worth considering Brando's argument that, in some sense, his entire career was a mistake.

"Generally actors don't realize how deeply affected the technique of acting was by the fact that Stella went to Russia and studied with Stanislavsky," Brando writes about his beloved teacher, Stella Adler, a half century after he studied with her in New York. And he adds, modestly, "Virtually all acting in motion pictures today stems from her." Of course, most actors would say that it stems from Brando: the man who brought those slightly incredible theories about realism and honesty and a new kind of art to the screen. And none of the awful films besides the glorious six or eight that are his primary legacy have done any damage to his example or his reputation. Whether one calls it Method or, as Brando preferred, "instinctive," the tradition he began extends from James Dean ("Mr. Dean appears to be wearing my last year's wardrobe," Brando said on the release of *East of Eden*, in 1955, "and using my last year's talent") to Robert De Niro and Al Pacino and beyond. Jack Nicholson, speaking for American actors, said, "He gave us our freedom."

But Brando's thoughts on his heritage continue: "This school of acting served the American theater and motion pictures well, but it was restricting." For all the gains, something essential had been lost, or, rather, was never given a chance to develop: an American capacity "to present Shakespeare or classical drama of any kind satisfactorily." The single contemporary performance that Brando discusses with rapt admiration is Kenneth Branagh's Henry V. "In America we are unable to approach such refinements," he writes. "We simply do not have the style, the regard for language, or the cultural disposition." And we are probably further from it after Brando than we were before. Stella Adler, speaking late in life about the roles her former protégé had *not* played, replied to a question about whether Brando was indeed a great actor, "We'll never know."

Yet there was a way in which the contrasting styles were in accord, a deeper and more satisfying truth about truth in acting. "If you're not good at improv you're not an actor," Brando insisted in his last major interview, with *Rolling Stone*, in 2002, just two years before his death. He had been teaching an acting workshop—with assistance from Leonardo DiCaprio and Sean Penn—to a select group that included the tightrope walker Philippe Petit, one of Michael Jackson's bodyguards, several local acting students, and a man he'd found rummaging through the trash outside the studio. He was putting the group through a lot of improvisations, and, for the first time in years, he was enjoying his work. Still talking about improv, he informed the interviewer of another source for the tradition that he had unwittingly founded.

"There's a speech from *Hamlet* that applies to all artists," he explained, "but it certainly applies to actors: 'To hold as 'twere the mirror up to nature.' To be natural." Didn't this sum up the lessons he was trying to pass on? And then, against every expectation about who he was and what he stood for, Brando backed up a few lines and launched into Hamlet's soliloquy—act 3, scene 2—from memory: "'Let your own discretion be your tutor. Suit the action to the word, the word to the action, with this special observance, that you o'erstep not the modesty of nature: for anything so o'erdone is from the purpose of playing, whose end, both at the first and now, was and is, to hold as 'twere the mirror up to nature.'" "And it goes on," Brando told the guy from *Rolling Stone*. "It says it all."

ANOTHER COUNTRY
JAMES BALDWIN

James Baldwin at his home in Saint-Paul-de-Vence, France, 1979

Feeling more than usually restless, James Baldwin flew from New York to Paris in the late summer of 1961, and from there to Israel. Then, rather than proceed, as he had planned, to Africa—a part of the world he was not ready to confront—he decided to visit a friend in Istanbul. Baldwin's arrival at his Turkish friend's door, in the midst of a party, was, as the friend recalled, a great surprise: two rings of the bell, and there stood a small and bedraggled black man with a battered suitcase and enormous eyes. Engin Cezzar was a Turkish actor who had worked with Baldwin in New York, and he excitedly introduced "Jimmy Baldwin, of literary fame, the famous black American novelist" to the roomful of intellectuals and artists. Baldwin, in his element, eventually fell asleep in an actress's lap.

It soon became clear that Baldwin was in terrible shape: exhausted, in poor health, worried that he was losing sight of his aims both as a writer and as a man. He desperately needed to be taken care of, Cezzar said; or, in the more dramatic terms that Baldwin used throughout his life, to be saved. His suitcase contained the manuscript of a long and ambitious novel that he had been working on for years, and that had already brought him to the brink of suicide. Of the many things that the wandering writer hoped to find—friends, rest, peace of mind—his single overwhelming need, his only real hope of salvation, was to finish the book.

Baldwin had been fleeing from place to place for much of his adult life. He was barely out of his teens when he left his Harlem home for Greenwich Village, in the early forties, and he had escaped altogether at twenty-four, in 1948, buying a one-way ticket to Paris, with no intention of coming back. His father was dead by then, and his mother had eight younger children whom it tortured him to be deserting; he didn't have the courage to tell her he was going until the afternoon he left. There was, of course, no shortage of reasons for a young black man to leave the country in 1948. Devastation was all around: his contemporaries, out on Lenox Avenue, were steadily going to jail or else were on "the needle." His father, a factory worker and a preacher—"he was righteous in the pulpit," Baldwin said, "and a monster in the house"—had died insane, tormented by racial bitterness. Baldwin had also sought refuge in the church, becoming a boy preacher when he was fourteen, but had soon realized that he was hiding from everything he wanted and feared he could never achieve. He began his first novel around the time he left the church, at seventeen; its young protagonist planned to kill his preacher father by adding poison to the Communion chalice. Within a few years, he was publishing regularly in magazines—book reviews, mostly, but finally an essay and even a short story. Still, who really believed that he could make it as a writer? In America?

The answer to both questions came from Richard Wright. Although Baldwin seemed a natural heir to the Harlem Renaissance—he was born right there, in 1924, and Countee Cullen was one of his schoolteachers—the bittersweet poetry of writers like Cullen and Langston Hughes held no appeal for him. It was Wright's unabating fury that hit him hard. Reading *Native Son*, Wright's novel about a Negro rapist and murderer, Baldwin was stunned to recognize the world that he saw around him. He knew those far-from-bittersweet tenements, he knew the rats inside the walls. Equally striking for a young writer, it seems, was Wright's success: *Native Son*, published in 1940, had been greeted as a revelation about the cruelties of a racist culture and its vicious human costs. In the swell of national self-congratulation over the fact that such a book could be published, it became a big bestseller. Wright was the most successful black author in history when Baldwin—twenty years old, hungry and scared—got himself invited to Wright's Brooklyn home, where, over a generously proffered bottle of bourbon, he explained the novel that he was trying to write. Wright, sixteen years Baldwin's senior, was more than sympathetic. He read Baldwin's pages, found him a publisher, and got him a fellowship to give him time to write. Although the publisher ultimately turned the book down, Wright gave Baldwin the confidence to continue and the wisdom to do it somewhere else.

Wright moved to Paris in 1947 and, the following year, greeted Baldwin at the café Les Deux Magots on the day he arrived, introducing him then and there to editors of a new publication, called *Zero*, who were eager for his contributions. Baldwin had forty dollars, spoke no French, and knew hardly anyone else. Wright helped him find a room, and while it is true that the two writers were not close friends—Baldwin later noted the difference in their ages, and the fact that he had never even visited the brutal American South where Wright was formed—one can appreciate Wright's shock when Baldwin's first article for *Zero* was an attack on "the protest novel," and, in particular, on *Native Son*. The central problem with the book, as Baldwin saw it, was that Wright's criminal hero, Bigger Thomas, was "defined by his hatred and his fear" and represented not a man but a social category; as a literary figure, he was no better than Harriet Beecher Stowe's Uncle Tom. And, because he raped and murdered a white woman, he was more dangerous, perpetuating the "monstrous legend" of the black man that Wright had meant to destroy. Wright blew up at Baldwin when they ran into each other at the Brasserie Lipp, but Baldwin did not back down. His article, reprinted later that year in *Partisan Review*, marked the start of his reputation in New York. He went on to publish even harsher attacks, arguing that Wright's work was gratuitously violent, that it ignored the traditions of Negro life, and that Wright had become a spokesman rather than an artist. In denigrating his mentor's example, Baldwin was struggling to formulate everything that he wanted his own work to be.

He knew very well the hatred and fear that Wright described. Crucial to his development, he said, was the notion that he was a "bastard of the West," without any natural claim to "Shakespeare, Bach, Rembrandt, to the stones of Paris, to the cathedral at Chartres": to all the things that, as a budding artist and a Western citizen, he treasured most. As a result, he was forced to admit, "I hated and feared white people," which did not mean that he loved blacks: "On the contrary, I despised them, possibly because they failed to produce Rembrandt." He had been encouraged by white teachers, though, ever since he was in grade school. It was a white teacher who took him to see Orson Welles's all-black production of *Macbeth*, which aroused his passion for the theater and stayed with him all his life. (As an aspiring playwright, Baldwin later studied acting at the New School, where one of his fellow students and immediate friends was Marlon Brando.) With his enormous intellectual promise recognized in these early years, he had attended the prestigious De Witt Clinton High School, in the Bronx, where he worked on the literary magazine alongside his white and mainly Jewish friends. And so the cultural hatred that he felt for whites remained a fairly abstract notion, and he assumed that he would never feel his father's rage.

Then one day, in 1942, not too long after graduation, he was turned away from a New Jersey diner with the phrase "We don't serve Negroes here." Ironically, he was working for the army in a defense-related job nearby; more ironic still, the place that turned him away was called the American Diner. It was a new experience even for a young man raised on the injustices of Harlem, and it left him stunned. In a kind of trance, he deliberately entered a glittering, obviously whites-only restaurant, and sat down. This time, when the waitress refused to serve him, he pretended not to hear in order to draw her closer: "I wanted her to come close enough for me to get her neck between my hands." He finally hurled a mug of water at her and ran, realizing only when he had come to his senses that he had been ready to murder another human being. In some ways, *Native Son* may have come too close.

The terrifying experience in the restaurant—terrifying not because of the evil done to him but because of the evil he suddenly felt able to do—helped give Baldwin his first real understanding of his father, who had grown up in the South, the son of a slave, and who had, like Wright, been witness to unnameable horrors before escaping to the mundane humiliations of the North. Baldwin knew by then that the man whom he called his father was actually his stepfather, who had married his mother when James was two years old; but, if this seemed to explain the extra measure of harshness that had been meted out to him, the greater tragedy of the man's embittered life and death remained. On the day of his funeral, in 1943, Baldwin recognized the need to fight this dreadful legacy, if he, too, were not to be consumed. He was far from any awareness of the stirrings of a civil rights movement. The Congress of Racial Equality, founded in Chicago the year before, had sponsored its first sit-in at a local restaurant just that spring. Facing his crisis alone, the only way he could conceive this fight was from within. "It now had been laid to my charge," he wrote, "to keep my own heart free of hatred and despair."

It takes a fire-breathing religion to blunt the hatred and despair in *Go Tell It on the Mountain* (1953), the autobiographical coming-of-age novel that Baldwin wrote and rewrote for a decade, centering on the battle for the soul of young John Grimes, on the occasion of his fourteenth birthday, in a shouting and swaying Harlem storefront church. Baldwin reshaped the melodrama of his early poisoning plot into something far more subtle, as he turned his young protagonist's thoughts from revenge to escape. For the boy, now, being saved is a way of winning the love of his preacher father, a goal he learns that he will never reach. Still, part of the nobility of this remarkable book derives from Baldwin's reluctance to stain religious faith with too much psychological knowingness. More of the nobility lies in its language, which is touched with the grandeur of the sermons that Baldwin had heard so often in his youth. Then, too, after arriving in Paris, he had become immersed in the works of Henry James and, reading Joyce's *Portrait of the Artist as a Young Man*, he had strongly identified with its self-creating hero. "He would not be like his father or his father's fathers," John Grimes swears. "He would have another life." Baldwin, led by these towering authorial guides, to whom he felt a perfectly natural claim, set out to turn his shabby Harlem streets and churches into literature. There is still a startling freshness in the language he found to carry out his task. Although Baldwin's people speak a simple and irregular "black" grammar, their easy use of "ain't" and "I reckon" flows without strain into prose of Jamesian complexity, of biblical resonance, as he penetrates their minds.

Baldwin wrote about the strictures of Harlem piety while living the bohemian life in Paris, hanging out in cafés and jazz clubs and gay bars; after having affairs with both men and women in New York, he had slowly come to accept that his desires were exclusively for men. His often frantic social schedule was one reason that the writing of *Go Tell It on the Mountain* dragged on and on. It seems as though he somehow used places up and had to move to others, at least temporarily, in order to write. In the winter of 1951, he had packed the unruly manuscript and gone to stay with his current lover in a small Swiss village, where he completed it in three months, listening to Bessie Smith records to get the native sounds back in his ears. Published two years later, the book was a critical success. Baldwin claimed to have missed out on the National Book Award only because Ralph Ellison had won it for *Invisible Man* the year before, and two Negroes in a row was just too much.

But it was Wright whom he still took for the monster he had to slay—or, perhaps, as he sometimes worried, for his father—and the book of essays that Baldwin published in 1955, which included two that were vehemently anti-Wright, was titled, in direct challenge, *Notes of a Native Son*. It was not, by intent, a political book. In its first few pages, Baldwin explained that race was something he had to address in order to be free to write about other subjects: the writer's only real task was "to recreate out of the disorder of life that order which is art." The best of these essays are indeed personal, but invariably open to a political awareness that endows them with both order and weight. Baldwin's great strength, in fact, is in the intertwining of the personal and the political, so that it becomes impossible to distinguish between these aspects of a life. His art, however, is in the closeness and power of the voice that makes this life important to us. The story of his father's funeral is also the story of a riot that broke out in Harlem that day, in the summer of 1943, when a white policeman shot a black soldier and set off a rampage in which white businesses were looted and smashed. "For Harlem had needed something to smash," Baldwin wrote: "To smash something is the ghetto's chronic need." If it had not been so late in the evening and the stores had not been closed, he warned, a lot more blood might have been shed.

Baldwin was notably articulate about the emotions that had been bred to require an outlet in violence:

> And there is, I should think, no Negro living in America who has not felt, briefly or for long periods, with anguish sharp or dull, in varying

degrees and to varying effect, simple, naked and unanswerable hatred; who has not wanted to smash any white face he may encounter in a day, to violate, out of motives of the cruelest vengeance, their women, to break the bodies of all white people and bring them low, as low as that dust into which he himself has been and is being trampled; no Negro, finally, who has not had to make his own precarious adjustment to the "nigger" who surrounds him and to the "nigger" in himself.

Yet this explanation—so scrupulously analytic, so delicately nuanced on the subject of murderous hatred—was the beginning of his argument, not the end. If Baldwin's bitter warning drew attention, it was overshadowed by the gentler yet more startling statements that made his work unique. For there was a larger lesson to be drawn from the hard-won wisdom, offered from his father's grave, and it was that hatred "never failed to destroy the man who hated and this was an immutable law." It was his charge now to free a great many hearts from hatred and despair.

Many of these essays were originally published in white liberal magazines and, addressing a predominantly white audience, Baldwin sounds a confidingly sympathetic tone. Living abroad, he explained, had made him realize how irrevocably he was an American. He confessed that he felt a closer kinship with the white Americans he saw in Paris than with the African blacks, whose culture and experiences he had never shared. The races' mutual obsession, in America, and their long if hidden history of physical commingling had finally made them something like a family. For these reasons, Baldwin revoked the threat of violence—the great retributional threat that caused so many white people to read Baldwin in the first place—with an astonishingly broad reassurance: American Negroes, he claimed, have no desire for vengeance. The relationship of blacks and whites is, after all, "a blood relationship, perhaps the most profound reality of the American experience," and cannot be understood until we recognize how much it contains of "the force and anguish and terror of love."

When Rosa Parks refused to give up her seat to a white man on a Montgomery bus, in December 1955, Baldwin was absorbed with the publication of his second novel, *Giovanni's Room*; he watched from Paris as the civil rights movement gathered force the following spring. His new book had a Paris setting, no black characters, and not a word

about race. From its opening paragraph—"My reflection is tall, perhaps rather like an arrow, my blond hair gleams"—Baldwin announced his refusal to repeat his past accomplishments or to shackle
his imagination. More boldly still, the novel is about homosexual
love—or, rather, about the inability of a privileged young American
man to come to terms with his sexuality and ultimately to feel any
love at all. Baldwin is effortless in his conjuring of a Paris of gay bars
and low cafés, and pitiless in his exploration of emotional cowardice.
Yet the book founders on a melodramatic plot that feels distinctly secondhand and, worse, a tone that tends to the portentous. But this was
clearly a novel that he had to write. His agent advised him to burn the
manuscript, and his previous publisher refused to consider it. (This
was strictly due to its controversial subject; the book is not in the least
pornographic; in fact, it contains no sex scenes at all.) Baldwin refused to back down. When *Giovanni's Room* was published, by Dial
Press, in 1956, it received generally good reviews. (According to the
Times, Baldwin treated his subject with "dignity and intensity.") It
sold six thousand copies in the first six weeks and went into a second
printing. As a writer, he had won the freedom he desired. His decision to live abroad seemed fully vindicated.

By the end of that year, however, he was no longer feeling quite so
content in Paris. The Algerian war had made it difficult to ignore
France's own racial problems. If Baldwin was spared the continual humiliations of life in America, he realized, this was because, absurdly
enough, he was American; black Algerians were not treated nearly so
well. Moreover, newspaper headlines in the kiosks outside the cafés
made it impossible not to fixate on the troubles back home. And so,
the following summer, Baldwin embarked on his most adventurous
trip, to the land that some in Harlem still called the Old Country: the
American South.

He was genuinely afraid. Looking down from the plane as it cir-
cled the red earth of Georgia, he could not help thinking that it
"had acquired its color from the blood that had dripped down from
these trees." It was September 1957. With assignments (and funding)
from both *Partisan Review* and *Harper's Magazine*, he was arriving just

as the small number of black children who were entering all-white schools were being harassed by jeering mobs, spat upon, and threatened with much worse. In Charlotte, North Carolina, he interviewed one of these children, a proudly stoic straight-A student, and his mother. ("I wonder sometimes," she says, "what makes white folks so mean.") He also spoke with the principal of the boy's new school, a white man who had dutifully escorted the boy past a blockade of students but announced that he did not accept the idea of racial integration, because it was "contrary to everything he had ever seen or believed." Baldwin, who is elsewhere stingingly eloquent about the effects of segregation, confronts this individual with the scope of his sympathies remarkably intact. Viewing him as the victim of a sorry heritage, he does not argue but instead commiserates, with a kind of higher moral cunning, about the difficulty of having to mistreat an innocent child. And at these words, Baldwin reports, "a veil fell, and I found myself staring at a man in anguish."

This evidence of dawning white conscience, as it appeared to Baldwin, accorded with the optimistic faith that he found in Atlanta, where he met the twenty-eight-year-old Martin Luther King, Jr., and heard him preach. Baldwin was deeply struck by King's description of bigotry as a disease most harmful to the bigots, and by his belief that, in Baldwin's words, "these people could only be saved by love." This idealistic notion, shared by the two preachers' sons, was a basic tenet, and a basic strength, of the early civil rights movement. Baldwin went on to visit Birmingham ("a doomed city"), Little Rock, Tuskegee, Montgomery, and Nashville; in 1960, he covered the sit-in movement in Tallahassee. His second volume of essays, *Nobody Knows My Name*, published in 1961, was once again welcomed by white readers as something of a guidebook to the uncharted racial landscape. Although Baldwin laid the so-called Negro problem squarely at white America's door, viewing racism as a species of pathology, he nevertheless offered the consoling possibility of redemption through mutual love— no other writer would have described the historic relation of the races in America as "a wedding." And he avowed an enduring belief in "the vitality of the so transgressed Western ideals." When the book hit the bestseller list, Baldwin found himself suddenly, as much as Richard Wright had ever been, a spokesman for his race.

The role was a great temptation and a greater danger. Given his ambitions, this was not the sort of success that he most wanted, and the previous few years had been plagued with disappointment at failing to achieve the successes he craved. A play he had adapted from *Giovanni's Room*, for the Actors Studio, in New York, had yielded nothing except a friendship with the young Turkish actor, Engin Cezzar, whom Baldwin had chosen to play Giovanni. Baldwin had hoped to get his old pal Marlon Brando to play Giovanni's conflicted American lover, and to move the play to Broadway, or even Hollywood, but this was not to be. *Giovanni's Room* never made it past a workshop trial.

Meanwhile, his new novel, *Another Country*, was hopelessly stalled; the characters, he said, refused to talk to him, and the "unpublishable" manuscript was ruining his life. He was drinking too much, getting hardly any sleep, and his love affairs had all gone sour. He wrote about having reached "the point at which many artists lose their minds, or commit suicide, or throw themselves into good works, or try to enter politics." To fend off all these possibilities, it seems, he accepted a magazine assignment to travel to Israel and Africa, then, out of weariness and fear, took up Cezzar's long-standing invitation, and found himself at the party in Istanbul. It was a wise move. In this distant city, no one wanted to interview him, no one was pressing him for social prophecy. He knew few people. He couldn't speak the language. There was time to work. He stayed for two months, and he was at another party—Baldwin would always find another party—calmly writing at a kitchen counter covered with glasses and papers and hors d'oeuvres, when he put down the final words of *Another Country*. The book was dated, with a flourish, "Istanbul, Dec. 10, 1961."

It is an incongruous image, the black American writer in Istanbul, but Baldwin returned to the city many times during the next ten years, making it a second or third not-quite-home. Divided between Europe and Asia, with a highly cosmopolitan Muslim population, Istanbul was unlike any place he had been before. Whatever Turkey's history of prejudice, divisions there did not have an automatic black/white racial cast. And on the sexual front, Istanbul had long been so notorious that some Americans snidely assumed that Baldwin went there for the baths. As it happened, during his first days in the city, he was nearly giddy at the sight of men in the street openly holding hands and could not accept Cezzar's explanation that this was a custom without sexual import. In fact, the culture hardly proved to be lacking in the usual prejudices, even in Baldwin's immediate and certainly liberal circle. In *James Baldwin's Turkish Decade*, Magdalena J. Zaborowska cites interviews with some of Baldwin's closest Turkish friends: one makes free use of what Zaborowska calls "the n-word" and another offers the laudatory comment "Jimmy was not a typical 'gay.' He was a real human being." Given that Baldwin never wrote about Istanbul, it is difficult to know what deeper effects—if any—the city had on him. All that seems certain is that it provided a refuge in which to write, a refuge that was ever more necessary as the sixties wore on.

Another Country turned out to be his most ambitious work so far, and a big bestseller. A sprawling book that brought together Baldwin's longtime concerns about race and sex, it contains an array of daring themes—black rage, interracial sex, homosexuality, white guilt, urban malaise—that, unfortunately, have greater substance than the characters who illustrate them. The story revolves around the suicide of a black jazz musician, a furiously broken man who, having more than a little in common with Wright's wretched hero, Bigger Thomas, beats his white girlfriend brutally; it's part of Baldwin's twist on the subject of black rage that this man finally takes his own life rather than hers. His death, however, some eighty pages in, leaves the bulk of the book to the meandering lives and reflections of those who knew him: a mostly white group of New York hipsters who do and do not finish writing novels, move in and out of each other's beds, and seem to live in ever-narrowing circles of interest. This very long book reveals, more than anything, Baldwin's immense will and dogged professionalism. Like the contemporary bestsellers *Ship of Fools* and *The Group*, it suggests a fine-tuned talent pushed past its narrative limits in pursuit of the "big" work. Baldwin claimed to have been inspired by the sound of jazz musicians, but aside from some lingo on the order of "Some cat turned her on, and then he split," the writing is too often careless and stale—"The train rushed into the blackness with a phallic abandon"—compared both with his earlier works and with the burnished eloquence of his next book, which riveted the country on its publication, in early 1963.

The Fire Next Time, Baldwin's most celebrated work, is a pair of essays totaling little more than a hundred pages. Some of these pages were written in Istanbul, but more significant is the fact that Baldwin had finally visited Africa—Senegal, Ghana, Sierra Leone—on a writing assignment for *The New Yorker*. And after years of worry that the Africans would look down on him or, worse, that he would look down on them, he had been accepted and impressed. One can perhaps date a new and full-throated confidence about black historical culture from this time, although Africa itself remained so essentially foreign that he found he could not write about it after all, any more than he could write about Istanbul. What Baldwin's book most reveals is his intensely renewed closeness with his family, whose support had come to counterbalance both his public performances and his private loneliness. Eagerly making up for his desertion, he became a munificent son and brother and a doting uncle, glorying in his ability to hold them all together at last. His brother David was his chief counselor and aide; his sister Gloria managed his money; he bought a large house in Manhattan, well outside Harlem, for his mother and the rest of the clan to share. To hear him tell it, this is what he had intended ever since he'd left.

A new and protective pride is evident in the book's brief introductory essay, "Letter to My Nephew," in which he assures the boy, his brother Wilmer's son James, that he descends from "some of the greatest poets since Homer," and quotes the words of a Negro spiritual. This pride is present, too, in the longer essay, "Down at the Cross"— which he published in *The New Yorker* in place of the promised essay on Africa—when he portrays the Southern black children who had faced down angry white mobs as "the only genuine aristocrats this country has produced." Although Baldwin writes once again of his childhood, his father, and his church, the essay's central and very political subject is the Black Muslim movement then terrifying white America.

With the fire of the title blazing ever nearer, Baldwin praised the truthfulness of Malcolm X but rejected the separatism and violence of the movement he led. He offered pity rather than hatred—pity in order to avoid hatred—to the white racists who, he firmly believed, despised in blacks the very things they feared in themselves. And, seeking dignity as much as freedom, he counseled black people to desist from doing to others as had been done to them. Most important, Baldwin once again promised a way out: "If we—and now I mean the relatively conscious whites and the relatively conscious blacks, who must, like lovers, insist on, or create, the consciousness of the others—do not falter in our duty now, we may be able, handful that we are, to end the racial nightmare, and achieve our country, and change the history of the world."

When did he stop believing it? No matter how many months he hid away in Istanbul or Paris, the sixties were inescapably Baldwin's American decade. In May 1963, thanks to his current and entirely unconventional bestseller, he appeared on the cover of *Time*. Although he insisted that he was a writer and not a public spokesman, he had recently undertaken a lecture tour of the South for the Congress of Racial Equality, at a time when civil rights demonstrators were being brutally mistreated and thrown in jail. That same May, he attended a meeting in New York with Attorney General Robert Kennedy, and brought with him, at Kennedy's request, a group of "Negroes that other Negroes will listen to." Harry Belafonte, Lena Horne, and Lorraine Hansberry, as well as Jerome Smith, a Freedom Rider who had been beaten half to death in Mississippi, were among the people who came to help Kennedy understand how to defuse the racial situation. (Baldwin also chose to include a white ally, the actor Rip Torn.) The meeting did not go well. RFK refused the group's request to have President Kennedy escort an African American child into a Southern school, and there was an argument about patriotism and military service—Smith declared that he could never fight for his country overseas—that showed how far apart the two sides stood. In the end, the entire group got up and followed Hansberry when she politely shook Kennedy's hand and walked out.

One month later, and just a day after President Kennedy made a televised speech about the moral imperative of civil rights, the murder of Baldwin's good friend Medgar Evers, head of the NAACP in Mississippi, made Baldwin begin to voice doubts about the efficacy of nonviolence. Such doubts, however, even then, had to be put aside. In August, he flew back from Paris to take part in the March on Washington. He had expected to be among the speakers that afternoon but, as we know from documents revealed years later, King questioned his stature as a civil rights leader and considered him, as a well-known homosexual, to be a potential hindrance to the movement. Later in the day, Baldwin took his place with a group of five other "entertainers and artists" who had joined the march, and had their say about it in a discussion on TV. In a dialogue that included several old friends— Marlon Brando and Sidney Poitier, as well as Belafonte—Baldwin was devastatingly direct ("If we do not achieve this dream we will have no future at all") but insistently optimistic, stressing the importance of this "demonstration to free *Americans*," of all colors. When asked if he believed that King's dream would be achieved, he replied, "I certainly believe it." And, unlike Belafonte, he felt sure that it would happen without violence.

It was the bombing just two weeks later, on September 15, of an African American church in Birmingham—the Sixteenth Street Baptist Church, a meeting place for civil rights leaders—and the death of four young schoolgirls there that brought a new toughness to his writing: a new willingness to deal in white stereotypes, and a new regard for hate. ("You're going to make yourself sick with hatred," someone warns a young man in Baldwin's 1964 play, *Blues for Mister Charlie*. "No, I'm not," he replies. "I'm going to make myself well.") It is ironic that Baldwin was dismissed by the new radical activists and attacked by Eldridge Cleaver as this change was taking place. In an essay published in 1966, titled "Notes on a Native Son"—a near duplication of Baldwin's old essay title "Notes of a Native Son"—Cleaver did to Baldwin something like what Baldwin had done to Richard Wright, condemning him as a sycophant to whites and a traitor to his people. The new macho militants openly derided Baldwin's homosexuality, even referring to him as Martin Luther Queen. But the end point for Baldwin was the murder of King, in 1968. After that, he confessed, "something has altered in me, something has gone away."

In the era of the Black Panthers, he was politically obsolete. By the early seventies, when the very young Henry Louis Gates, Jr., suggested an article about Baldwin for *Time*, he found the magazine no longer interested. Far worse for Baldwin, he was also seen as artistically exhausted. It is difficult for even the most fervent advocate to defend *Tell Me How Long the Train's Been Gone*, an oddly unconvincing novel about a famous black actor, which, on its publication, in 1968, appeared to finish Baldwin as a novelist in the minds of everyone but Baldwin, whose ambitions seemed only to grow.

There are some vivid and powerful pages in Baldwin's later books, although these segments can be hard to find. There are also pages where he seems to have lost his way, along with his hope: his concessions to despair and self-hatred make for painful reading. *No Name in the Street*, a deeply troubled but erratically brilliant book-length essay, written at the end of the decade, was described by Baldwin as being about "the life and death of what we call the civil rights movement"—which he had now come to call a "slave rebellion." Unable to believe anymore that he or anyone else could "reach the conscience of a nation," he embraced the Panthers as folk heroes, while resignedly turning the other cheek to Cleaver, whom he mildly excused for confusing him with "all those faggots, punks, and sissies, the sight and sound of whom, in prison, must have made him vomit."

No Name in the Street is a disorderly book, both chronologically and emotionally chaotic. At its core, Baldwin details his long and fruitless attempt to get a falsely accused friend out of prison. He looks back at the Southern experiences that he had reported on so coolly years before, and exposes the agony that he had actually felt. At the same time, he wants us to know how far he has come: there is ample mention of the Cadillac limousine and the cook-chauffeur and the private pool; he assures us that the sufferings of the world make even the Beverly Hills Hotel, for him, "another circle of Hell." And he is undoubtedly suffering. He does his best to denounce Western culture in the terms of the day, as a "mask for power," and insists that to be rid of Texaco and Coca-Cola one should be prepared to jettison Balzac and Shakespeare. Then, as though he had finally gone too far, he adds, "later, of course, one may welcome them back," a loss of nerve that he immediately feels he has to justify: "Whoever is part of whatever civilization helplessly loves some aspects of it and some of the people in it."

Struggling to finish the book, Baldwin left Istanbul for good in 1971. The city was now as overfilled with distractions as Paris or New York. His increased income had allowed him to rent a big house that he called the Pasha's Library, where he'd entertained lavishly, and wonderfully diverting friends had been dropping by from all over the world. (Marlon Brando traveled around in Cezzar's little car while a decoy limousine lured the press and other would-be followers off the scent.) So he started over again. Seeking peace and solitude, he bought a house in the South of France, where he settled down to write. The book's concluding dateline, a glaring mixture of restlessness and pride, reads "New York, San Francisco, Hollywood, London, Istanbul, St. Paul de Vence, 1967–1971."

Still, Baldwin's fiction was the work that he deemed most important. His next two novels, largely about family love, are heartfelt but mixed achievements. *If Beale Street Could Talk* (1974), the brief and affecting story of an unjustly imprisoned Harlem youth, is told from the surprising perspective of his pregnant teenage girlfriend (who only occasionally sounds like James Baldwin). *Just Above My Head* (1979), a multigenerational saga, contains one unforgettable segment, nearly four hundred pages in, about a trio of young black men traveling through the South. There were still signs of the exceptional gift. But the intensity, the coruscating language, the tight coherence of the first novel and the early essays—where had they gone? The answers to this often-asked question have varied: he had stayed away too long and become detached from his essential subject; he had been corrupted by fame, and the booze didn't help; or, maybe, he could really write only about himself. Baldwin's biographer and close friend David Leeming suggested to Baldwin, in the mid-sixties, that "the anarchic aspect" of his daily existence was interfering with his work. But the most widely credited accusation is that his political commitments had deprived him of the necessary concentration and cost him his creative life.

The case is presented by another of Baldwin's biographers, James Campbell, who states that in 1963 Baldwin "exchanged art for politics, the patient scrutiny for the hasty judgment, *le mot juste* for *le mot fort*," and that as a result he "died a little death." But isn't it as likely that Baldwin's dedication to the movement, starting back in the late fifties, allowed him to accomplish as much as he did? That the hope it occasioned helped him push back a lifetime's hatred and despair and made it possible for him to write at all? It is worth noting that the flaws of the later books are evident in *Another Country*, and even in *Giovanni's Room*, both completed before he had marched a step. As for the roads not taken, among black writers who had similar choices: Richard Wright did not return to the United States and continued writing novels, in France, until his death, in 1960, yet his later books have been dismissed as major disappointments; Ralph Ellison took no part in the civil rights movement yet did not publish another novel after *Invisible Man*. Every talent has its terms, and, while Baldwin was in no ordinary sense a political writer, something in him required that he rise above himself. "How, indeed, would I be able to keep on working," he worried, "if I could never be released from the prison of my egocentricity?" As Baldwin noted about his childhood, it may be that the things that helped him and the things that hurt him cannot be divorced.

The final years were often bitter. Campbell recalls Baldwin, in 1984, reading aloud from an essay about Harlem that he'd written in the forties, crying out after every catalogued indignity, "Nothing has changed!" He was already in failing health, and tremendously overworked. He had begun to teach in the late seventies—the conviviality and uplift seem to have filled the place of politics—returning to the States for a few months every year until he turned sixty-two, in 1986. He traveled constantly, for conferences and speaking engagements: New York, London, Moscow. He published articles and his first book of poetry. He saw no need to cut back on alcohol or cigarettes. Baldwin was only sixty-three when he underwent surgery for esophageal cancer, in April 1987; he died that autumn, after a Thanksgiving celebration at his house in France.

He was in the midst of several projects: a novel that would have been, in part, about Istanbul; a triple biography of "Medgar, Malcolm, and Martin"; and introductions to paperback editions of two novels by Richard Wright. But Baldwin's final book was *The Price of the Ticket*, a thick volume of his collected essays, summing up nearly forty years, in which his faith in human possibility burns like a candle in the historical dark. The concluding essay, about American myths of masculinity (originally published in, of all places, *Playboy*) offers a plea for the recognition that "each of us, helplessly and forever, contains the other—male in female, female in male, white in black and black in white."

It is shocking to realize that as early as 1951, and based on no evidence whatever, Baldwin saw that our "fantastic racial history" might ultimately be for the good. "Out of what has been our greatest shame," he wrote, in an essay titled "The Negro at Home and Abroad," "we may be able to create one day our greatest opportunity." He would have been eighty-four had he lived to see Barack Obama elected president. It is an event to which he surely contributed, through his essays and novels, his teaching and preaching, the outsized faith and energy that he spent so freely in so many ways. Obama himself has listed Baldwin among the writers who helped to shape his sense of racial identity. Yet Baldwin knew—again, shockingly early—that even such an election would not be an answer, in itself, to the country's entrenched history. In a 1961 speech at a forum hosted by the Liberation Committee for Africa, in New York, he responded to Robert Kennedy's assurance that there would someday be an African American president (Kennedy predicted it would take thirty years) with little more than a shrug about one more "Negro 'first.'" This was not an issue that occupied his thoughts. "What I am really curious about," Baldwin said, "is just what kind of country he'll be President of."

This statement has been quoted often during President Obama's second term, and it is one of many that have brought a resurgence of interest in Baldwin in these years, when he has repeatedly been called a "prophet" with both admiration and regret. The country today would have offered him few surprises. In place of the outrage of Selma, we have the outrage of Ferguson, and a long list of names of black men, women, and children added to the deadly roll call that drove Baldwin to despair. He wrote about the black population in our prisons, about the difficulties whites confront in giving up their fears, about a society bent on convincing a black boy that he is "a worthless human being." During his wanderings, Baldwin warned a friend who had urged him to settle down that "the place in which I'll fit will not exist until I make it." There was not enough time, of course. He died far from the promised land, as prophets usually do. But he worked with all his strength "to make the kingdom new, to make it honorable and worthy of life," looking always to the day when he could come home.

A RAISED VOICE
NINA SIMONE

Nina Simone, circa 1970

"My skin is black," the first woman's story begins, "my arms are long." And, to a slow and steady beat, "my hair is woolly, my back is strong." Singing in a club in Holland, in 1965, Nina Simone introduced a song she had written about what she called "four Negro women" to a young, homogenously white and transfixed crowd. "And one of the women's hair," she instructed, brushing her hand lightly across her own woolly Afro, "is like mine." Every performance of "Four Women" caught on film or disk is different. Sometimes Simone coolly chants the first three women's parts—the effect is of resigned weariness—and at other times, as on this particular night, she gives each woman an individual, sharply dramatized voice. All four have names. Aunt Sarah is old, and her strong back has allowed her only "to take the pain inflicted again and again." Safronia's yellow skin and long hair are the result of her rich white father having raped her mother—"Between two worlds I do belong"—and Sweet Thing, a prostitute, has tan skin and a smiling bravado that seduced at least some of the eager Dutch audience into the mistake of smiling, too. And then Simone hit them with the last and most resolutely up-to-date of the women, improbably named Peaches. "My skin is brown," she growled ferociously, "my manner is tough. I'll kill the first mother I see. 'Cause my life has been rough." (One has to wonder what the Dutch made of killing that "mother.") If Simone's song suggests a history of black women in America, it is also a history of long-suppressed and finally uncontainable anger.

A lot of black women have been openly angry over a new movie about Simone, a biopic titled *Nina*—not to be confused with the successful Netflix documentary, *What Happened, Miss Simone?*—and they began mounting protests even before the filming was complete. The issue for these women is color, and what it meant to Simone to be not only categorically African American but specifically African in her features and her very dark skin. Is it possible to separate Simone's physical characteristics, and what they cost her in this country, from the woman she became? Can she be played by an actress with less distinctively African features, or a lighter skin tone? *Should* she be played by such an actress? The casting of Zoe Saldana, a movie star of mixed Puerto Rican and Dominican descent, and a light-skinned beauty along European lines, has caused these questions—rarely phrased as questions—to dog the production of *Nina*, from the moment Saldana's casting was announced to the completed film's debut at Cannes, in May 2014, in a screening confined to possible distributors. The film's director, Cynthia Mort, remained stalwart in her defense of Saldana's rightness for the role, citing not only the obvious relevance of acting skills but Simone's inclusion of a range of colors among her own "Four Women"—which is a fair point. None of the women in Simone's most personal and searing song escape the damage and degradation accorded their race.

Ironically, "Four Women" was charged with being insulting to black women and was banned on a couple of radio stations in New York and Philadelphia soon after the recording was released, in 1966. The ban was lifted, however, when it produced more outrage than the song. Simone's husband, Andrew Stroud, who was also her manager, worried about the dangers that the controversy might have for her career, although this was hardly a new problem. Simone had been singing out loud and clear about civil rights since 1963—well after the heroic stand of figures like Harry Belafonte and Dick Gregory, yet still at a time when many black performers felt trapped between the rules of commercial success and the increasing pressure for racial confrontation. At Motown, in the early sixties, the wildly popular performers of a stream of crossover hits became models of black achievement, but had virtually no contact with the movement at all.

Simone herself had been hesitant at first. Known for her sophisticated pianism, her imperious attitude, and her velvety rendition of
"I Loves You, Porgy" (which, like Billie Holiday before her, she performed without the demeaningly ungrammatical "s" on "loves"), she
had arrived in New York in late 1958, establishing her reputation not
in Harlem but in the clubs of hip and relatively interracial Greenwich
Village. Her repertoire of jazz and folk and show tunes, often played
with a classical touch, made her impossible to classify. In these early
years, she performed African songs and also Hebrew songs, and wove
a Bach fugue through a rapid-fire version of "Love Me or Leave Me."
She tossed off the thirties bauble "My Baby Just Cares for Me" with
airy insouciance, and wrung the heart out of the lullaby "Brown
Baby"—newly written by Oscar Brown, Jr., about a parent's hopes for
a child born into a better racial order—erupting in a hair-raising wail
on the word "freedom," as though expressing all the longing of the
generations that had never known it. For a while, "Brown Baby" was as
close to a protest song as Simone got. She believed it was enough.

And then her friend Lorraine Hansberry set her straight. It speaks
to Simone's intelligence and restless force that, in her twenties, she
attracted some of African American culture's finest minds. Both Langston Hughes and James Baldwin elected themselves mentors: Simone,
appearing on the scene just as Holiday died, seemed to evoke their
most exuberant hopes and most protective instincts. But Hansberry
offered her a special bond. A young woman also dealing with a startling early success, Hansberry was twenty-eight when *A Raisin in the
Sun* won the New York Drama Critics' Circle Award, in 1959; she
had a strongly cultivated black pride and a pedagogical bent. "We
never talked about men or clothes," Simone wrote in her memoir, decades later. "It was always Marx, Lenin and revolution—real girls'
talk." A milestone in Simone's career was a solo concert at Carnegie
Hall—a happy chance to show off her pianism—on April 12, 1963,
which happened also to be the day that Martin Luther King, Jr., was
arrested with other protesters in Birmingham, Alabama, and locked
up in the local jail. The discrepancy between the events was pointed
out by Hansberry, who telephoned Simone after the concert, although
not to offer praise.

Two months later, Simone played a benefit for the NAACP. In
early August, she sang "Brown Baby" before a crowd gathered in the

football stadium of a black college outside Birmingham—the first integrated concert ever given in the area—while guards with guns and dogs prowled the field. But Hansberry only started a process that events in America quickly accelerated. Later that August, Simone watched the March on Washington on television while she was preparing for performances at the club that had become her base, the Village Gate. She was rehearsing at home for another date when, on September 15, news came of the bombing of Birmingham's Sixteenth Street Baptist Church and the death of four young African American girls who had just got out of Bible class—the same horrific news that shook Baldwin and so many others from their commitment to nonviolence. Simone's first impulsive act, she recalled, was to try to make a zip gun with tools from her garage. "I had it in my mind to kill someone," she wrote. "I didn't yet know who, but someone I could identify as being in the way of my people, and getting some justice for the first time in three hundred years."

This urge to violence was not a wholly new impulse but something that had been brewing on a national scale, however tamped down by cooler heads and political pragmatists. At the Washington march, John Lewis, then a leader of the Student Nonviolent Coordinating Committee, was forced to cut the word "revolution" from his speech and to omit the threat that, absent immediate progress, the marchers would go through the South "the way Sherman did" and "burn Jim Crow to the ground." James Baldwin, in a televised discussion after the bombing, noted that throughout American history "the only time that nonviolence has been admired is when the Negroes practice it." But the center held. Simone's husband, a smart businessman, told her to forget the gun and put her rage into her music.

It took her an hour to write "Mississippi Goddam." A freewheeling cri de coeur based on the place names of oppression, the song's jaunty tune makes an ironic contrast with words—"Alabama's got me so upset, / Tennessee made me lose my rest"—that arose from injustices so familiar they hardly needed to be stated: "And everybody knows about Mississippi, goddam!" Still, Simone spelled them out. She mocked stereotypical insults ("Too damn lazy!"), government promises ("Desegregation / Mass participation"), and, above all, the continuing admonition of public leaders to "Go slow," a line that prompted her backup musicians to call out repeatedly, as punctuation, "Too slow!" It wasn't "We Shall Overcome" or "Blowin' in the Wind": Simone had little feeling for the biblically inflected uplift that defined the anthems of the era. It's a song about a movement nearly out of patience—you can hear this in King's "Letter from a Birmingham Jail"—by a woman who never had very much to begin with, and who had no great hope for the American future. "Oh but this whole country is full of lies," she sang. "You're all gonna die and die like flies."

She introduced the song in her set at a Los Angeles club the following week. And she sang it when she returned to Carnegie Hall, in March 1964, brazenly flinging "You're all gonna die" at a mostly white audience. That historic night, she performed several protest songs that she had taken a hand in writing, including the defiantly jazzy ditty "Old Jim Crow." She also performed the quietly haunting "Images," about a black woman's inability to see her own beauty ("She thinks her brown body has no glory")—a wistful predecessor to "Four Women" that she had composed to words by the Harlem Renaissance poet Waring Cuney. At the time, Simone herself was still wearing her hair in a harshly straightened fifties-style bob; sometimes the small personal freedoms are harder to speak up for than the larger political ones. And, clearly, it wasn't time yet for such specifically female injuries to take their place in the racial picture. "Mississippi Goddam" was the song of the moment: bold and urgent and easy to sing, it was adopted by embattled protesters in the cursed state itself just months after Simone's concert, during what they called the Mississippi Summer Project, or Freedom Summer, and what President Johnson called "the summer of our discontent."

There was no looking back by the time she performed the song outside Montgomery, Alabama, in March 1965, when some three thousand marchers were making their way along the fifty-four-mile route from Selma. Two weeks earlier, protesters making the same attempt had been driven back by state troopers with clubs, whips, and tear gas. The triumphant concert on the fourth night of the march was organized by the indefatigable Belafonte, at the request of King, and took place on a makeshift stage built atop stacks of empty coffins lent by local funeral homes, and in front of an audience that had swelled with twenty-five thousand additional people, drawn either by the cause or by a lineup of stars that ranged from Tony Bennett and Johnny Mathis to Joan Baez. Simone, accompanied only by her long-time guitarist, Al Schackman, drew cheers on the interpolated line "Selma made me lose my rest." In the course of events that night, she was introduced to King, and Schackman remembered that she stuck her hand out and warned him, "I'm not nonviolent!" It was only when King replied, gently, "Not to worry, sister," that she calmed down.

Simone's explosiveness was well known. In concert, she was quick to call out anyone she noticed talking, to stop and glare or to hurl a few insults or even leave the stage. Yet her performances, richly improvised, were also confidingly intimate—she *needed* the unbroken connection with her audience—and often riveting. Even in her best years, Simone never put many records on the charts, but people flocked to her shows. In 1966, the critic for *The Philadelphia Tribune*, an African American newspaper, explained that to hear Simone sing "is to be brought into abrasive contact with the black heart and to feel the power and beauty which for centuries have beat there." She was proclaimed the voice of the movement not by Martin Luther King but by Stokely Carmichael and H. Rap Brown, whose Black Power philosophy answered to her own experience and inclinations. As the sixties progressed, the feelings she displayed—pain, lacerating anger, the desire to burn down whole cities in revenge—made her seem at times emotionally disturbed and at other times simply the most honest black woman in America.

While attending a speech given by Carmichael about Black Power, in July 1966—just a month after he had alarmed a large part of the nation by introducing the phrase to public discourse—Simone told the audience, assembled in a Philadelphia church, that she'd been "thinking of some of the things I have heard tonight since I was three years old." This seems to have been a slight exaggeration; in her memoir, she recalls that racial anger first arose in her when she was eleven. Born Eunice Waymon, in 1933, she was the sixth of eight children of John and Kate Waymon, who were descendants of slaves and pillars of the small black community of Tryon, North Carolina. Her mother was a Methodist preacher, a severely religious woman who made extra money by cleaning house for a white Tryon family; her father, who had started off as an entertainer, worked at whatever the circumstances required. Even during the Depression, the Waymons made a good home. Simone's earliest memories were of her mother singing hymns, and both the house and the church were so filled with music that no one noticed little Eunice climbing up to the organ bench until, at the age of two and a half, she played "God Be with You till We Meet Again" straight through.

This is a familiar sort of revelation in the history of a musical prodigy, similar to the story of the untrained George Gershwin tossing off a pop tune at his family's new piano—although Gershwin was twelve years old, not two and a half. Yet, as unexpected as the little girl's musical gift is the way that, in that time and place, the gift was encouraged. She began playing for her mother's sermons before her feet could reach the pedals, and was soon accompanying the church choir and Sunday services. Playing for visiting revivalists was a special pleasure throughout her childhood, because of the raptures she discovered that she could loose in an audience with music. But she was introduced to another musical world when she was five years old and the woman for whom her mother cleaned house offered to pay for lessons with a local piano teacher, Muriel Mazzanovich. The British-born Miz Mazzy, as Eunice called her—and also, later on, "my white momma"—inspired her lifelong love of Bach and her plans to become a great and famous classical pianist. Giving a recital in the local library, at eleven, Eunice saw her parents being removed from their front-row seats to make room for a white couple. She had been schooled by Miz Mazzy in proper deportment, but she nevertheless stood up and announced that if anyone wanted to hear her play they'd better let her parents sit back down in the front row. There were some laughs, but her parents were returned to their seats. The next day, she later wrote, she felt "as if I had been flayed, and every slight, real or imagined, cut me raw. But, the skin grew back a little tougher, a little less innocent, and a little more black."

Her skin was very black, and she was made fully aware of that as she grew up, along with the fact that her nose was too broad and her lips too full. The aesthetics of race—and the loathing and self-loathing inflicted on those who vary from accepted standards of beauty—is one of the most pervasive aspects of racism, yet it is not often discussed. The standards, especially punishing for women, have been enforced by blacks as well as whites. Even Harry Belafonte wrote, in his memoir, about his mother's well-intentioned counsel to "marry a woman with good hair," and he added, in unnecessary clarification, "good hair meant straight hair." (Reader, he married her.) But Nina Simone, strong and fierce and proud Nina Simone? *"I can't be white* and I'm the kind of colored girl who looks like everything white people despise or have been taught to despise," she wrote in a note to herself, not during her adolescence but in the years when she was already a successful performer. "If I were a boy, it wouldn't matter so much, but I'm a girl and in front of the public all the time wide open for them to jeer and approve of or disapprove of."

Countering the charge of physical inferiority, in her youth, was the talent that her mother assured her was God-given. Music was her salvation, her identity. Thanks to a fund established by a pair of generous white patrons in Tryon, she was sent to board at a private high school, where she practiced piano five hours a day and graduated as valedictorian. The remainder of the money allowed her to go off to a summer course at Juilliard, with the unwavering aim of getting into the Curtis Institute of Music, in Philadelphia, where tuition was free. Her destiny seemed so assured that her parents moved to Philadelphia before she took the Curtis exam. But Curtis was also terrifically competitive. The school rejected her, and while it's impossible to know exactly why—there were seventy-three applicants for three places in piano studies that year—her belief that her race was the cause was a source of unending bitterness. But the rejection was also a turning point. In the summer of 1954, in need of money, Eunice Waymon took a job playing cocktail piano in an Atlantic City dive; there was sawdust on the floor and a little room for drunks to sleep it off, and the owner demanded that she also sing. Hoping to keep the news of this unholy employment from her mother, she turned herself into Nina Simone, feeling every right to the anger that Nina Simone displayed forever after.

At times, it seemed that she could outdistance her worst feelings. In 1961, after a brief marriage to a white hanger-on at the Atlantic City club, she married Andrew Stroud, a tough police detective on the Harlem beat whom she initially sized up as "a light-skinned man," "well built," and "very sure of himself." The following year, she gave birth to a daughter, Lisa Celeste, and Stroud left his job to manage Simone's career. They lived in a large house in the leafy Westchester suburb of Mount Vernon, complete with a gardener and a maid. Although she complained of working too hard and touring too much—of being desperately exhausted—her life was not the stuff of the blues. And then, before a concert in early 1967, Stroud found her in her dressing room putting makeup in her hair. She didn't know who he was; she didn't quite know who she was. She later remembered that she had been trying to get her hair to match her skin: "I had visions of laser beams and heaven, with skin—always skin—involved in there somewhere."

The full medical facts of Simone's mental illness became public only after her death, in 2003, thanks to two British fan-club founders and friends of Simone's, Sylvia Hampton and David Nathan, whose account of the singer's career was aptly titled, after one of Simone's songs, *Nina Simone: Break Down and Let It All Out* (2004). Subsequent biographies—the warmly overdramatizing *Nina Simone*, by David Brun-Lambert (2009), and the coolly meticulous *Princess Noire*, by Nadine Cohodas (2010)—have filled in terrible details of depression and violence and long-sought but uncertain diagnoses: "bipolar disorder" appears to be the best contemporary explanation. Excerpts from Simone's diaries and letters of the sixties, published by Joe Hagan (who got them from Andrew Stroud) in *The Believer*, in 2010, added the news that Simone's personal hell was compounded by regular beatings from Stroud. Her letters to him display a fervent mix of love ("I pray we'll be together until death") and, unsurprisingly, hatred. And while the diary contains some alarming signs that Simone at times felt she deserved to be beaten—"Andrew hit me last night (swollen lip) of course it was what I need after so many days of depression"—the letters make it clear just how desperately the beatings affected her, and show her trying to make Stroud understand. "For some reason, they destroy everything within me—my confidence, my warmth and my spirit! And when that happens I just feel that I must kill or be killed—you know how I just about lost my mind the last time." The marriage dissolved in 1970, but it was many more years before she received any helpful medication for the pain within.

All the more remarkable, then, the strength that Simone projected through the sixties. As the decade wore on, she began to favor bright African gowns and toweringly braided African hairstyles. She became the High Priestess of Soul, and though the title was no more than a record company's PR gambit—Aretha Franklin was soon crowned the Queen of Soul—she bore it with conviction. In 1965, she recorded "Strange Fruit," the classic anti-lynching ballad, which had been more or less the property of Billie Holiday since she'd introduced it in 1939. Simone's account is as distinctively personal as Holiday's: less rapt and quiveringly introspective—her voice, darker and fuller than Holiday's, has virtually no vibrato—more forthright and accusing. ("That is about the ugliest song I've ever heard," Simone said of "Strange Fruit." "Ugly in the sense that it is violent and tears at the guts of what white people have done to my people in this country.") But Simone could give even unexpected songs an edge of racial protest: listen to her harrowing version of the Brecht-Weill "Pirate Jenny," which Al Schackman re-called had once sent parents holding their crying children fleeing from the theater.

It would be wrong, however, to give the impression that her songs were mostly about civil rights. Stroud, with his eye on the bottom line, was always there to keep her from going too far in that direction. In concert, she even pulled back on "Mississippi Goddam," singing the rather more democratically inclusive "We're all gonna die, and die like flies" in place of the gleefully threatening "You're all gonna die." Yet she herself had a vast and often surprising musical appetite. A great part of her repertoire consisted of romantic nightclub standards by Rodgers and Hart, Charles Aznavour, and Jacques Brel, which she sang with simple beauty. In the late sixties, she was so concerned with falling behind the times that she expanded her range to include Bob Dylan, Leonard Cohen, and, covering all bases, the Bee Gees. One of her biggest hits of the era was the joyously innocuous "Ain't Got No/I Got Life," a medley from the musical *Hair*—which, in her hands, became a classic freedom song.

But womanly strength was in everything she sang: in the cavern-ous depths of her voice—some people think Simone sounds like a man—in her intensity, her drama, her determination. It's there in the crazy love song "I Put a Spell on You," in which she recasts the crip-pling needs of love ("Because you're *mine*!") as an erotically unhinged command. It's there in the ten-minute gospel tour de force "Sinner-man," when she cries out "Power!" like a Southern preacher and her musicians shout back, "Power to the Lord!" and especially when she takes the disapproving voice of the Lord upon herself: "Where were you, when you oughta been praying?" If you'd never before thought of the Lord as a black woman, you did now.

The civil rights songs were nevertheless what she called "the important ones." And the movement is where she gained her strength. It's also where her private anger took on public dimensions, in the years when patience gave way entirely and the rage in many black communities could no longer be tamped down. Onstage in Detroit, on August 13, 1967—two weeks after a five-day riot had left forty-three people dead, hundreds injured, and the city in ruins—Simone, singing "Just in Time," added a message to the crowd: "Detroit, you did it . . . I love you, Detroit—you did it!" She was met with roars of approval, which one Detroit critic said he presumed had come from "the arsonists, looters and snipers in the audience." Another critic, however, wrote that her show let white people know what they had to learn, and learn fast. Was she the voice of national tragedy or of the next American revolution?

And then King was shot, on April 4, 1968. Sections of Washington, Chicago, Baltimore, and more than one hundred smaller cities went berserk. Despite her rhetoric, Simone was profoundly shaken. At a concert in Westbury, Long Island, just a few days afterward, her tone of quietly bewildered heartbreak was as striking as the fury that quickly spiraled out of it. Unsurprisingly, her views of what might be accomplished in this country became only more bleak. And at an outdoor concert in Harlem, the following summer—it's available on YouTube—she went for broke.

Majestically bedecked *à l'africaine*, she opened with "Four Women," singing now before a crowd where an Afro was the norm. After several other stirring, politically focused songs—"Revolution," "Backlash Blues"—she closed with something so new that she had not had time to learn it, a poem by David Nelson, who was then part of a group called the Last Poets and is now among the revered begetters of rap. She read the words from a sheet of paper, stalking the stage and repeatedly exhorting the crowd to answer the question "Are

you ready, black people? . . . Are you ready to do what is necessary?"
The crowd responded to this rather vague injunction with a mild
cheer, prompted by the bongos behind her and the demand in her
voice. And then: "Are you ready to kill, if necessary?" Now a bigger if
somewhat incongruous cheer rose from the smiling crowd filled with
little kids dancing to the rhythm on a sunny afternoon. It had been
five years since the Harlem riot of 1964, the granddaddy of sixties
riots; New York had largely escaped the ruinations of both 1967
and 1968. "Are you ready to smash white things, to burn buildings,
are you ready?" she cried. "Are you ready to build black things?"

Despite her best efforts, Simone failed to incite a riot in Harlem
that day in 1969. The crowd received the poem as it had received her
songs: with noisy affirmation, but merely as part of a performance.
People applauded and went on their way. There are many possible
reasons: no brutal incident of the kind that frequently set off riots,
massive weariness, the knowledge of people elsewhere trapped in riot-
devastated ruins, maybe even hope. Simone had her unlikeliest hit
that year with a simple hymn of promise, "To Be Young, Gifted and
Black," based on the title of a play that had been put together from
Lorraine Hansberry's uncollected writings. Hansberry, who died in
1965, had used the phrase in a speech to prize-winning black students, and Simone asked a fellow musician, Weldon Irvine, to come
up with lyrics that "will make black children all over the world feel
good about themselves forever." Indeed, it is a children's song (or it
was, until Aretha took it over). Simone's most moving performance
may have been on *Sesame Street*, where she sat on the set's tenement
steps wearing an African gown and lip-synched her recording to four
enchanting if slightly mystified black children, who raised their arms
in victory toward the end.

It was not a victory she could believe in or a mood she could sustain.
By the end of the sixties, both Simone's career and her marriage
were in serious trouble. Pop-rock did not really suit her, and the jazz
and folk markets had radically shrunk. The all-exhausting concert
stage still assured her income and her stature. And if the collapse of
her marriage was in some ways a liberation, she was also now without

the person who had managed her finances and her schedule, who had been able to keep her calm before she went onstage (by forbidding her alcohol, among other means), and who got her offstage quickly when the calm failed. She was left to govern herself in a world that suddenly had no rules and, just as frightening, was emptied of its larger, steadying purpose. "Andy was gone and the movement had walked out on me too," she wrote, "leaving me like a seduced schoolgirl, lost."

Looking back on the historic protests and legislative victories of the sixties, one may find it easy to assume a course of inevitable if often halting racial progress, but this was anything but apparent as the decade closed. When, in 1970, James Baldwin set out to write about "the life and death of what we call the Civil Rights movement," in *No Name in the Street*, its failure seemed to him beyond contention. As for the black leaders who had "walked out" on Simone, they were in cemeteries (Malcolm X, Medgar Evers, King, Fred Hampton), in jail (Huey Newton, Bobby Seale), or in Africa (Stokely Carmichael), or else had "run for cover," as she put it, "in community or academic programs." White liberals had diverted their efforts to Vietnam; this was now the war being fought on televisions in living rooms every night. According to Simone, "The days when revolution had seemed possible were gone forever."

She left the country in 1974. Traveling to Liberia with her twelve-year-old daughter, Lisa, she stayed for two years, during which she performed hardly at all. Her own account of this period dwells on consuming love affairs and exhilarating social freedoms, but Simone was always an erratic mother, and Lisa has revealed that, in these years, she became something much worse. Speaking in an interview for the recent documentary film *What Happened, Miss Simone?*, directed by Liz Garbus, Lisa says that during their first year in Liberia she lived with a local family and only rarely saw her mother. After that, Simone bought a house on the beach and brought Lisa to live with her, and it was then that "she went from being my comfort to the monster in my life." There were frequent beatings, as though Simone were reacting to the brutality of her marital past, but "now she was the person that was doing the beating," Lisa says. "And she was beating me." The objective seemed to be to make her daughter cry, and Lisa recalls reaching "the point where I thought about committing suicide." At the end of the year, mother and daughter moved to Switzerland, with the plan of Lisa enrolling in school there. Instead, at fourteen, she got on a plane to visit her father in New York, and never came back. She did not see her mother again for nearly a decade.

Eventually, Simone moved to France, alone. And there she stayed. She returned to performing at the Montreux Jazz Festival in 1976, and a film of the event leaves no doubt that something was radically wrong: she is dead-eyed, confused, rambling. Still, she slowly resumed her career. It seems to have been only the recurrent need for money that spurred her to perform again in the United States, although she took great pride in an honorary doctorate that she received from Amherst, in 1977, and insisted ever after on being called "Doctor Nina Simone." But her engagements were few, as her concerts tended increasingly toward disaster.

There's a lovely photograph of her onstage with James Baldwin at the Village Gate, in 1979. She's seated at the piano and he's standing behind her, leaning over to hold her shoulders in a tight embrace, and both are smiling broadly; you can almost hear the laughter. Cohodas's biography tells the story: Simone had just interrupted a performance of "Porgy" to rail about unchanging racial conditions in the United States—"We are still used here like black and brown horses!"—and had got into an argument with a white man in the audience. Baldwin, who happened to be there, went up onstage to ease the tension and encourage her to sing; at one point, they danced together as the audience clapped. It worked. She finished the show without incident. But no one could save her on a nightly basis, and there was no place where she felt at home. As she now sang in "Mississippi Goddam," "the whole damn world's made me lose my rest."

The remainder of her life, some twenty-five years, is a tale of escalating misery. At the worst, she was found wandering naked in a hotel corridor brandishing a knife; she set her house in France on fire, and once, also in France, she shot a teenage boy (in the leg, but that may have been poor aim) in a neighbor's backyard for making too much noise—and for answering her complaints with what she understood as racial insults. (A French court psychiatrist concluded that she was incapable of evaluating the consequences of her actions, and she was given a suspended sentence.) In the early eighties, she was prescribed a new medication that helped her to perform when she was willing to take it, and when it didn't incapacitate her in other ways; its long-term effects included erosion of her motor skills and of her voice. Yet the ups of her life could be almost as vertiginous as the downs. In 1988, just a year after she'd been sent to a hospital in a straitjacket, her charmingly upbeat 1959 recording of "My Baby Just Cares for Me" was chosen by Chanel for its international television ad campaign. Rereleased, the record went gold in France and platinum in England. In 1991 she sold out the Olympia, in Paris, for nearly a week.

She toured widely during her final years. In Seattle, in the summer of 2001, she worked a tirade against George W. Bush into "Mississippi Goddam," and encouraged the audience to "go and do something about that man." She was already suffering from breast cancer, but it wasn't the worst illness she had known. She was seen as a relic of the civil rights era, and on occasion she even led the audience in a wistful sing-along of "We Shall Overcome," although she did not believe her country had overcome nearly enough. After she became too sick to perform, she did not return to what she called "the United Snakes of America." She died in France, in April 2003; her ashes were scattered in several African countries. The most indelible image of her near the end is as a stooped old lady reacting to the enthusiastic cheers that greeted her with a raised, close-fisted Black Power salute.

Thirty-four years after Simone released "To Be Young, Gifted and Black," Jay Z adapted the title for a song that describes the fate of many of those gifted children—"Hear all the screams from the ghetto all the teens ducking metal"—in twenty-first-century America. The rap connection with Simone is hardly surprising, since rap is where black anger now openly resides. Simone disliked the rap she knew, however, in part for displacing so much anger onto women—or, as she put it, for "letting people believe that women are second class, and calling them bitches and stuff like that." Back in 1996, Lauryn Hill rapped an anything-you-can-do retort to a male counterpart, "So while you imitatin' Al Capone / I be Nina Simone / And defecatin' on your microphone." Nearly two decades later, Hill performed six passionately committed covers of Simone songs on the tribute album *Nina Revisited* (2015), which also featured performances by Usher and Common. The racial and political climate in recent years has led to a lot of people talking about Simone again, and revisiting her music. There was a minor uproar in 2013 over Kanye West's sampling of phrases from Simone's recording of "Strange Fruit" (with her voice sped up to an unrecognizable tinniness) in "Blood on the Leaves"; despite the emptiness of West's own lyrics, the song had the aura of a social statement. But the wild excitement that greeted Beyoncé's video for "Formation," in February 2016—invoking police brutality, Hurricane Katrina, and black pride ("I like my Negro nose with Jackson 5 nostrils") along with the usual subjects of sex and celebrity—and her performance of the song at the Super Bowl, suggests how desperate we are for someone to take up the challenges issued by Simone.

As for jazz, Simone was largely excluded from the history books for decades. Will Friedwald's seminal *Jazz Singing*, of 1990, mentions her only in passing, as "off-putting and uncommunicative" and as the center of a cult "that only her faithful understand." But Simone's eclecticism has slowly widened the very definition of jazz singing. And ever since presidential candidate Obama listed her version of "Sinnerman" as one of his ten favorite songs of all time, in 2008, the cult has gone mainstream. There's now a burgeoning field of what may be called Simone studies—Ruth Feldstein's *How It Feels to Be Free* and Richard Elliott's *Nina Simone* offer two highly intelligent examples—and Friedwald's even more authoritative volume of 2010, *A Biographical Guide to the Great Jazz and Pop Singers*, includes a lengthy entry on Simone that pronounces her "more important than anyone" in her influence on twenty-first-century jazz singing.

In 2013, two Broadway shows depicted Simone as an inspiration for a couple of unexpected figures: in *A Night with Janis Joplin*, she helped provide her white soul sister with the gift of fire, and, even stranger, in the crude but enthusiastic *Soul Doctor*—revived off-Broadway in 2015—she was the force behind the "rock-and-roll rabbi" Shlomo Carlebach. Nutty as it seemed onstage, Simone's acquaintance with the rabbi appears to have some basis in fact and helps to explain the Hebrew songs she performed at the Village Gate (where he also performed) in the early sixties. While it may be a showbiz exaggeration to suggest that the rabbi and the jazz singer had an affair—the show featured an act 1 curtain clinch that, on the night I saw it, had its largely Orthodox audience literally gasping—the point was the universality of Simone's message about persecution, the search for justice, and the power of music.

The full scale of the Simone renaissance is evident in the release, in 2015, of two full-length documentaries about her life. Garbus's highly polished *What Happened, Miss Simone?*—one can just hear Simone's protest at the absence of the honorific "Doctor"—was a hit of the Sundance Festival, and benefitted from a big Oscar campaign by Netflix. Jeff L. Lieberman's *The Amazing Nina Simone*, released in "selected" theaters months later, is a comparatively underfunded labor of love. Both contain thrilling if also sometimes harrowing archival footage: Simone singing "Mississippi Goddam" at the Selma-to-Montgomery march, Simone looking stunned and fragile at Montreux in 1976, Simone delving deep into a song and bringing up incredible amounts of pain but also, often, joy. Neither film, however, lets the clips run for nearly long enough before various friends and experts interrupt. Nevertheless, when it comes to interviews, Garbus has the dramatic (if, again, sometimes harrowing) advantage. Andrew Stroud, in footage from 2006 (he died six years later) relates without a whit of repentance how he once cut his wife with his ring when he smacked her, and repaired the wound so that it left no scar. Their daughter, Lisa Simone Kelly—who ultimately reconciled with her mother—manages to be both clear-eyed and forgiving, and says wearily of her parents, "I think they were both nuts." Most affecting is Dick Gregory, now a nearly biblical figure with a long white beard, who recalls that, through the years of suffering he watched black people endure, "Not one man would dare say 'Mississippi Goddam . . .' We all wanted to say it. She said it. 'Mississippi Goddam!'" Above all, in both films, there is Simone herself, at her most assuredly articulate: "How can you be an artist and *not* reflect the times?"

Back in 1979, at a concert in Philadelphia, Simone followed a performance of "Four Women" by scolding the black women in the audience about their changes in style: "You used to be talking about being natural and wearing natural hairstyles. Now you're straightening your hair, rouging your cheeks and dressing out of *Vogue*." In 2009, the comedian Chris Rock made a documentary titled *Good Hair* because, he explained, his young daughter had come to him with the question "Daddy, how come I don't have good hair?" For an African American child, nothing had changed since Harry Belafonte's mother's advice, more than half a century earlier. (According to one contented businessman in Rock's film, African Americans—twelve percent of the population—buy eighty percent of the hair products in this country. And although women are the primary consumers, they are not the only ones. Al Sharpton reveals that James Brown first talked him into straightening his hair for a visit they made together, to the White House, to lobby for—oh, the irony—a national holiday for Martin Luther King, Jr.'s birthday. "You get up and comb your exploitation every morning," Sharpton says.) As for skin tone, the cosmetic companies have been expanding their range ever since Iman established a line of darker foundations in 1994, although in March 2014 a former beauty director of *Essence*, Aretha Busby, complained to the *Times*: "The companies tend to stop at Kerry Washington. I'd love to see brands go two or three shades darker."

The question of skin tone and hair and their meaning for African American women exploded on the Internet with the announcement of the casting of Saldana in the Hollywood biopic about Simone. When the idea for such a film was initially floated, in the early nineties, Simone herself gave the nod to being played by Whoopi Goldberg. When, in 2010, the present film was announced in *The Hollywood Reporter*, Mary J. Blige—the reigning Queen of Hip-Hop Soul—was announced for the lead. Once Blige was replaced with Saldana, however, a woman whose skin tone is more than two or three shades lighter than Simone's, the cries for boycotting the film on the basis of misrepresentation—on the basis of insult—were instantaneous. Why not cast Viola Davis? Or Jennifer Hudson? Production photographs showing Saldana on the set with an artificially broadened nose, an Afro wig, and—inevitably, but most unfortunately—dark makeup that is all too easily confoundable with blackface rendered any hope of calm discussion futile. It's been suggested that the filmmakers might as well have cast Tyler Perry in full Madea drag.

Simone's daughter has come out against the film because its story focuses on an invented love affair as much as for the casting of Saldana, although she is quick to point out how much her mother's appearance shaped her life. (Lisa once told an interviewer that her mother would sometimes "traumatize" her because she is light-skinned—"and I'd remind her that she had chosen my father, I didn't.") The fight over the film ultimately extended to a lawsuit filed by the director, Cynthia Mort, against the British production company, Ealing Studios Enterprises, for cutting her out of the final editing process. The suit has been dismissed, however, and the North American rights to the film have been acquired by another company, so *Nina* may yet show up in a theater near you, or at least become available on your home screen. And Saldana may give a compelling performance—may well prove that she can play not only women who are sci-fi blue (as in *Avatar*) or green (as in *Guardians of the Galaxy*) but real-life black. Still, there is no escaping the fact that her casting represents exactly the sort of prejudice that Simone was always up against. "I was never on the cover of *Ebony* or *Jet*," Simone told an interviewer, in 1980. "They want white-looking women like Diana Ross—light and bright." Or, as Marc Lamont Hill writes in *Ebony* today, "There is no greater evidence of how tragic things are for dark-skinned women in Hollywood than the fact that they can't even get hired to play dark-skinned women." Well beyond Hollywood, these outworn habits of taste reverberate down the generations.

Simone's favorite performer in her later years was Michael Jackson. She brought cassettes of his albums with her everywhere, and she recalled having met him on a plane when he was a little boy and telling him, "Don't let them change you. You're black and you're beautiful." She anguished over his evident failure to believe what she'd said: the facial surgeries, the mysterious lightening of his skin, the fatality of believing, instead, what the culture had told him, and wanting to be white. Simone appeared onstage with him just once, amid a huge cast of performers gathered for Nelson Mandela's eightieth birthday, in Johannesburg, in the summer of 1998. She was sixty-five years old, and photographs of the event show her standing between Mandela and Jackson, overweight yet glamorously done up, her hair piled in braids and her strapless white blouse a contrast to the African costumes of the chorus all around. But she was also very frail. In one photograph, Jackson—in his glittering trademark military-style jacket, hat, and shades—holds her left hand in both his hands, in a gesture of affection. But in another shot he has put one steadying arm around her, and she is grasping his hand for support. Few people seem aware of what is happening. The stage remains a swirl of laughter and song, a joyous African celebration. And at its center the two Americans stand with hands clasped tight—one hand notably dark, the other notably fair—as though trying to help each other down a long, hard road.

ACKNOWLEDGMENTS

INDEX

ACKNOWLEDGMENTS

My deep thanks to Jonathan Galassi, the great encourager, and to all the conscientious and creative people at Farrar, Straus and Giroux, especially to Christopher Richards, Jonathan Lippincott, Scott Auerbach, Jo Stewart, and Lottchen Shivers.

None of this book would have been written without the still-astonishing opportunities offered by *The New Yorker*. I am wholly indebted to the contributions of the extraordinary people I have been lucky enough to work with there, above all to David Remnick, Ann Goldstein, Henry Finder, Alice Truax, Dorothy Wickenden, Leo Carey, Neima Jahromi, Mary Norris, and Elizabeth Pearson-Griffiths.

I am also happily indebted to Robert Gottlieb, best of friends and best of readers, and to Robert Cornfield, who eases every trouble.

To Dr. Jeffrey Liebmann, the continuing gratitude of continuing sight.

To Shiva Rouhani, so many thanks for your talents and your charm.

To Robert Pierpont (eternal first, second, and third reader), Julia Pierpont (astonishing writer!), Shirley Roth, Allan Roth, Bob and Mary Pierpont, Doris Garcia, and Diana Garcia: no end of gratitude and love for sustaining me through everything.

INDEX

Page numbers in *italics* refer to illustrations.

ILLUSTRATION CREDITS

ML

11/2018